In Search of Your Image

In Search of Your Image

*A Practical Guide To The
Mental and Spiritual
Aspects of Horsemanship*

Jill Keiser Hassler

*edited by Jessica Jahiel
illustrated by Jeanette Manley and Emily Covington
front cover art by Eleanor McDonald
back cover art by Jeanette Manley*

Published by:
  Goals Unlimited Press
  c/o Hilltop Farm, Inc.
  1089 Nesbitt Road
  Colora, MD 21917

Production by:
  Mountain Press Publishing Company
  P.O. Box 2399
  Missoula, MT 59806

Printed in the United States of America by BookCrafters

The author is grateful to the following publishers and individuals for
their permission to reprint excerpts and share their ideas:

Hastings, Arthur, *With the Tongues of Men and Angels*, Holt, Rinehart and
Winston, Inc., 1991.

Loehr, James E., *Mental Toughness Training for Sports*, The Stephen Greene
Press, 1986.

Lowe, Pamela, "Everyday Angels," *Karmakaze,* issue #9, CA.

McNeil, Craig, "This Season Ski with Goals in Mind," *The Missoulian*,
December 24, 1992.

Nadel, Laurie, *Sixth Sense, The Whole Brain Book of Intuition, Hunches, Gut
Feelings and Their Place in Your Everyday Life*, Prentice Hall Press, 1990.

I dedicate this book, with gratitude, to the following:

The horses, students, and professionals who have provided me with experiential learning, open communications and continual feedback.

The dedicated, hardworking Hilltop staff for the understanding, communication, dedication, and responsibility that provided me with the time and mental freedom to write.

The productive and successful lives of my children, Patti, Chip, and Scott, as well as the many other young people who grew up in our extended family. Their lives have given me the confidence to put my thoughts into words.

The new friends who provided my mountain top for writing, my Montana home: to Sharon Gordon, who searched with dedication until she found the perfect homesite, to Dr. Earl Pruyn, who was willing to sell his unlisted land, and to Ed McHatton, who built the perfect house to capture the nature that so energizes me.

Vonnie Groff who provided the inspiration and hope to pursue spiritual development.

Jessica Jahiel, who called at just the right moment and then shared her editing skills and quick-mindedness!

Jeanette Manley and Emily Covington, for their illustrative ideas and art work.

Jane Mac Elree, owner of Hilltop Farm, who has provided a place for my dreams to make a difference. She has trusted me to manage Hilltop while writing in Montana. Jane's vision, intelligence, dedication, and compassion have made her an inspirational role model to me.

Russell Scoop, who exposed me to a new awareness and has continued his support with endless hours of discussions, reading and editing. Every page has passed before his eyes at least three times!

TABLE OF CONTENTS

Author's Note:

> Look deeply into yourself,
> Look deeply into your horse,
> Evaluate what you find.
> Compare it to what you know.
> Ask questions, especially, "Why?"
> Practice each new thing until it is second nature,
> And, most of all, enjoy your horse and yourself!

Beyond the Mirrors was meant to inspire; *In Search Of Your Image* gives many practical applications to help you:

+ Better understand your horse, yourself and others.

+ Understand the balance of body, mind and spirit.

+ Improve communication skills with horse and man.

+ Learn to create realistic, meaningful goals that build confidence.

+ Learn to develop your "feel."

+ Experience peace, joy, and harmony with your horse.

This positive, full of suggestions, and encouraging book has been written to satisfy the requests of many readers of *Beyond the Mirrors.* It is a step-by-step approach to help animal lovers discover ways to know and accept themselves through their love of and involvement with horses. The more we know ourselves, the more success we will have as horsepersons. I have tried to reduce complex issues to their simplest form. Life is not as easy as I make it seem. However, if we take each issue that seems to overwhelm us and break it down, we may discover that it can be dealt with reasonably. To assist the reader, valuable information about goals, the stages of live, the resources that can help create a successful journey, and how to overcome some of the obstacles frequently encountered are included. Both *In Search Of Your Image* and its Workbook are designed to help you simplify and solve problems. Don't expect yourself to be able to do all the exercises mentioned at one time. Give yourself time with this book. Look through it, decide what is most timely for you and then begin to read. Take one thing at a time, understand it, practice it and evaluate it. If it does not work, try something else.

Be certain to understand the meaning that I have attached to key words such as mind, spirit and soul before you read on. These definitions are listed on page 361. As you are reading, periodically refer to these definitions to insure clarity.

*"**In Search Of Your Image** will help riders acquire a better understanding of themselves, their horse, and the wonderful and unique communication that can exist between them. Inspiring reading for anyone who truly loves horses."*

Phyllis Dawson

Phyllis Dawson, USA Olympic team rider and Three Day Eventing Trainer and Coach.

———————————— ◆ ————————————

*"**In Search Of Your Image** confirms my belief that you must first capture a horse's mind if you expect to capture the rest of his body. Set goals for yourself and your horse but remember, never fight him. If you do your I.Q. becomes lower than that of your horse; and if you pick a fight, you'll lose, because you're fighting out of your weight division."*

Jimmy a Williams

Jimmy Williams is a trainer and instructor of Western, dressage, harness horses and jumpers. He is the winner of the 1960 AHSA Horseman of the Year, 1987 CPHA Horseman of the Year, in 1989 was inducted into the Show Jumping Hall of Fame, was the 1989 recipient of the "Jimmy A. Williams" Lifetime Achievement Award presented by the AHSA and in 1993 was inducted into the Reined Cow Horse Hall of Fame.

———————————— ◆ ————————————

*"Sequel to the well-loved **Beyond the Mirrors**, **In Search Of Your Image** is a well-reasoned, goal oriented, psychologically sound, technically correct, spiritually uplifting approach to horsemanship.*

"An accompanying Workbook offers the serious student self-documentary help in developing better ways of achieving personal goals, particularly at the collegiate and student instructor levels."

Lazelle Knocke

Lazelle Knocke is the founder and current president of the USDF, an international judge, an FEI dressage rider and clinician—as well as a student of dressage, people and horses for sixty years. Now in her seventies, she is still judging, teaching, riding, goal setting and learning!

Preface

Many readers of *Beyond the Mirrors* asked me for a book on how to reach the ideals of inner harmony, spiritual unity and natural beauty that I presented in *Beyond the Mirrors*. Before writing such a book I had to ask myself many questions. How can I write a book on "how to" about something when the answer is based on my own life experiences and the skills I have acquired? Doesn't everyone need to have his own experiences, and don't those personal experiences affect the way he can reach these ideals? And there were other, more searching questions I had to ask myself. When did I become fully aware of the kind of love I have for horses? When and how did I understand the type of love offered by horses? When did the issue of spirituality become important to me? When did I start to understand the meaning of life beyond materialistic goals? What gave me the feeling of "inner harmony?" How do I connect inner harmony with horses and riding? I pondered these questions and meditated on the answers that came to me. These answers make up the content of this book.

Looking back, I realize that my love of horses, my attitude toward them and my relationship with them have not changed since my childhood. My love of horses, and my connection to them, has been the one unvarying part of my life. As I reviewed the stages of my life, I saw that horses had always played a major role that had helped me grow as a person. Because of the circumstances of my life, my constant thirst for knowledge, my open-mindedness and my love of horses, my day-to-day life began to change, and I began to recognize a new meaning to my life. It is such a wonderful feeling that I want to share it. Perhaps my discoveries may help spark ideas that will add fulfillment to your life as well.

My life has always been filled with many challenges. At a young age, my father suffered from heart disease and died. I married young and had step-children to raise. I suffered a life-threatening disease, had three corrective eye operations, experienced a mysterious healing after twenty years, survived a depression that resulted from a tragic death in our immediate family, raised a third generation of children, and became divorced after twenty-seven years of marriage. Despite these circumstances, I grew as a person and became healthier. My love for and involvement with horses was the only common thread woven through all of these experiences. But what was the real importance of horses in my life? On reflection, I discovered that my love and understanding of horses had always helped me to process information and situations by viewing them through the eyes of a horse. The horses had kept me involved in life. They had allowed part of me to remain alive, even when everything else was collapsing. This ember, all that was left in my life, glowed and grew as I sought help from professionals to repair my life and rediscover its meaning. The combination of my deep love of horses and my new knowledge allowed me to become a calmer, less judgemental person and a more compassionate teacher. I found a new, more significant purpose in my life. If my love of horses could do this without my conscious awareness, what could be the results of deliberately using the love of horses?

Beyond the Mirrors is about the image that lies beyond the mirror. This is not the view that one is accustomed to seeing, but the one that has never really been seen: the inner being that lies beyond. When you get the first glimpse of this image, the first view of your inner being, you may experience a shock. What you see may not be what you expected to see; it may not match the person you thought you were. Ultimately you may develop a deep understanding of, relationship with, and appreciation for this image; the real inner you. Through this book, I will try to convey to you how to make this connection and hold on to it, allowing yourself to understand yourself better and better. *In Search of Your Image* is designed to help you use your love of horses to help you find your own self, accept it, and unite with it. I hope that this knowledge and understanding of your inner being will serve you in all your horse and 'real' life challenges. I am sharing the tools from my own journey; perhaps some of them will work for you! This is my hope.

Introduction

To get the most out of your riding or horse time, examine the reasons you are involved with horses. Horse activities require considerable time, money and energy. Part I, Goals, will help you recognize your initial incentive. As your journey progresses, you may discover that your motives were actually quite different from what you originally thought they were.

Once you learn why you are involved with horses, you must begin to understand both horse and man physically, mentally, and spiritually. You may want to reread Part II, Understanding Horse and Man, later on, because it contains the theory that will be important to you at different times in your travels.

Understanding the 'normal' stages of your life and relating them to your goals is an important step in self-awareness. Each stage offers new challenges, and your horse involvement must coincide with the timing of this challenge. Part I, section 3,

Stages of Life, explains the psychological principles of several stages and their connection to your horse activities.

The real content of this book is in Part III, Resources, where I've explained a variety of ways for you to develop the realizations and tools for your journey. In Part IV, Journey, I've explained how to use the tools (resources) to advance you toward your goals; that is, to get the desired results from your horse endeavors. To meet your expectations, the results must be both correct and rewarding. The tools you develop should allow you to enjoy the challenge of your journey, remain determined through the switchbacks and wrong turns, and maintain a positive attitude as you overcome obstacles.

As a result of this process, you will discover the inner you. Part V, Discovery, challenges you to look at what you may have learned. Discovering who you are allows you to be lighter, quicker, freer, calmer, and healthier. But even more importantly, you will become a more feeling, flowing, compassionate and coordinated horseperson. Both you and your horse will be happier!

Philosophical Statement

The underlying assumption of *In Search of Your Image*, and the key concept that you will carry with you on the journey I will invite you to take, is that horse and man share the same mental and spiritual make-up, although man has a more highly developed brain. Man's reasoning ability allows him to reflect on his experiences, assess their meaning, and draw a conclusion. This reasoning ability can both protect him and allow him to improve himself, but it can also interfere, causing pain. This pain comes in many forms, but most pain causes man to distort or hide the truth. If we could simplify our way of thinking and encountering life, the complexities of our life experiences could be reduced. I contend that we can learn the art of simplifling our perceptions by learning to "know" our horses. Once we do

2

this, we can use our brain to give us the information we need, information that is related to the subject rather than to the expectations that we have created in our mind. Being able to view our lives through the eyes of the horse will allow us to achieve a better understanding of ourselves and others.

I believe that both horse and man are created by God, and that we all have the spirit of God within us. The spirit of the horse, unlike the spirit of man, is not discolored by its thoughts, because the brain of the horse is less developed. It is this spirit that we must try to get in tune with. Perhaps you will discover some aspects of your spirit as you read on. I hope so. Look closely at your horse: he will tell you more than you can imagine.

Once you have completed *In Search of Your Image*, you may have developed your own philosophy, agreed with mine, or disagreed totally. But whatever your conclusion, you will have been exposed to a different thinking that will give you 'food for thought'.

Goals

Introduction

Goals give a purpose and direction to your journey through life and with your horses. Many people travel without knowing where they are going. But setting goals is not a mysterious process, it simply requires a little work and forethought. Practice setting goals for your riding, and the habit will carry over into the rest of your life.

Setting goals is the first step of turning dreams into reality. The process involves examining your motivation, understanding the physical, mental and spiritual stage of your life, and then recognizing and accepting the limitations of time, money and energy. Balancing all these considerations will allow you to choose the dream you wish to pursue. Intermediate and short-term goals are the stops on your way to your destination, your long-term goal.

This section of the book is designed to help you take a careful, realistic look at all of the factors that will help you to set realistic and attainable goals.

Motivation +	*Stages* +	*Outside Influences*	= *Choosing*
Love of horses	*child*	*money*	*Goals*
Exercise	*pre-teen*	*time*	
Challenge	*teenager*	*energy*	
Profession	*young adult*		
Recreation	*early adult*		
Social activity	*middle age*		
Mental well-being	*late middle age*		

Motivation

Why do you ride? Look honestly at your motivation, it is important to YOU.

Take the time NOW to answer the question, "Why do I ride?" Since this book is designed for your self-exploration, I suggest you write down the answer on Questionnaire #1 in your Workbook, so that you can review it later. I hope you will discover more about your reasons while reading *In Search of Your Image.* You may learn that you were correct in your original assumptions, that you were confused, or that you have discovered new motivations. Any discovery has its good consequences. If you were correct, you gain confidence in your self-understanding. If you were confused, you have already begun to eliminate the confusion. Or if you discover a new motivation or purpose, you can redefine your goal before you have wasted much time.

Each of you is involved with horses for a reason. Horses themselves, or the physical activities associated with horses, fulfill some role in your life. Why is it important to understand and acknowledge the reason? Understanding your motivation allows you to balance your involvement, to survive the lows and enjoy the highs of your journey with horses. Spending a few minutes defining your incentives may save you time, money, energy and frustration. It may also enhance your energy, heighten the experience, and help you to feel the beauty of every moment of life—something few of us have mastered.

The second question to ask yourself and record on Questionnaire #1 is, "How important are horses in my life?" Why am I involved with horses, rather than with other activities? For you to determine how important horses are to you, you must understand why you are involved with them. Throughout your life, you will find that various aspects of your involvement will change due to your life style, yourself, or your feelings about horses. Horses must be woven into YOUR OTHER NEEDS throughout your life. You must strive continually for balance between your family, community, financial, social and educational needs, and your individual need for horses.

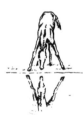

There are no right or wrong motivations for being with horses. The important issue is to identify your reasons for yourself.

My own example may help clarify this idea. I love horses, love to teach and love to ride. What do I love most? When I went to college, I discovered that it was being around horses that was essential to my mental well-being. I discovered that studying in a pasture where I could glance occasionally at the horses, combined with doing some grooming, fulfilled my needs. I did not need to ride or teach. The discovery was confirmed when I married. I was unable to ride competitively because of finances and raising a family, so my love was transferred to sharing the horses with my stepchildren. I had found yet another way to get joy from horses. There is no right or wrong motivation for being with horses. The important factor is to identify your reasons for yourself. Each of us is different. Our differences make life interesting. Examine yourself and your horse-related motives. Later in the book, you will understand how important this step is toward choosing your goals.

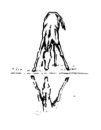

The Seven Basic Factors that draw people into a horse oriented life

- ✦ *Love of horses*
- ✦ *Exercise*
- ✦ *Challenge*
- ✦ *Profession*
- ✦ *Recreation*
- ✦ *Companionship & Social Interaction*
- ✦ *Mental Well-being*

There are seven basic factors that draw people into a horse-oriented life; 1. love of horses, 2. exercise, 3. challenge, 4. profession, 5. recreation, 6. companionship and social interaction and 7. mental well-being. All are equally significant, and you may be involved for a combination of reasons.

1. Love of Horses

This is the most complex of the reasons for your horse involvement. Many of us like horses; few love them. There is no value judgement implied with liking or loving, it is just a reflection on how involved you are. Without a doubt, people would not be involved with horses if they did not like them. But for those who feel that they MUST be around a horse, who feel a certain warmth and connection to the horse, who feel that they have 'horses in their blood', there is a deep, indescribable love for the horse. This attraction often works unconsciously to involve people with horses. I think that a person who likes horses often learns to love them. However, for some, horses meet a deep need. For people with this need, horses offer the unconditional love that all humans seek.

11

When you are around horses do you feel fulfilled, warm, comfortable and energized?

How much do you miss horses when you are away?

2. Exercise

Some people choose riding to get some form of exercise. Exercise is not just a means to get out of a chair and be active. It is a combination of movements that leads to increased strength, improved coordination, greater muscle tone, more suppleness and relaxation. The combination of fresh air, sunshine and exercise is one of the most pleasant aspects of involvement with horses. Riding is not usually a form of aerobic exercise, because, it usually does not significantly elevate the heart rate for fifteen minutes. Nor does riding tone all of the body's muscles. However, after riding, you feel calmer, relaxed, refreshed or fulfilled.

How much time a week do you spend on exercise?

How important is the exercise to you?

How completely does your horse activity meet your exercise needs?

3. Challenge

A fast gallop, racing the barrels against the clock, a bucking bronco, a race over hurdles, or the fine tuning of dressage, hunter or jumper performance all fit into the category of challenge. A successful short, fast, confrontational situation gives you an inner thrill of achievement that energizes your entire life.

How important is challenge in your life?

How much challenging time do you need a week?

4. Professional

I hope that no one becomes a professional horseperson without loving the animal, the physical activity, and being out of doors. If a person does love all of these factors and can accept not becoming financially wealthy, then that person is blessed in his profession. I often say to a student who is having a good lesson that I feel very lucky to be paid to enjoy myself so much! I am thankful that I have been able to survive financially, because I cannot envision myself so happily involved in any other profession. I enjoy it so much that it does not feel like work.

Do you feel lucky to have your profession?

Do you look forward to getting up each day to start work?

5. Recreation

The recreational horseperson uses horses to satisfy his need to have fun. Much of the time per week allowed for entertainment, is devoted to horses.

When you are finished with your time with horses, do you feel refreshed and ready to attack your real life?

Is riding horses a form of recreation to you?

How much time a week do you spend this way?

6. Companionship & Social Activity

Many activities in the horse world bring you into contact with other like-minded people. Horse shows, rodeos, fox hunts, and competitive trail rides are a few examples. Even boarding your horse at a stable instead of keeping it at home provides social interaction. All of us need a sense of community involvement. Perhaps it is the people in the horse community that you enjoy spending time with.

When you have completed your time with horses, do you feel closer to the activity or to the persons involved in the activity? Do you feel that a sense of sharing with people of similar interests is sufficient reward for the time you have spent?

How important are the people in the activity to you?

7. Mental Well Being

This area is related to all the others. Students told me so frequently that they were riding for their mental health that I began to explore this area. Besides one-on-one contact with a warm creature, the horse, the rider often also has one-on-one contact with an instructor. The bond between a trusted instructor, horse and rider can provide wonderfully fulfilling mental ther-

significance of this relationship, I have included many examples of how various horse goals either do or do not 'work' for a particular stage of life. Please use this section to learn about the stage of life you are in now, rather than to evaluate your goals as you now perceive them.

Stages of Life
- *Child (6 - 10)*
- *Pre-teen (10 - 13)*
- *Teenager (14 - 17)*
- *Young Adult (18 - 21)*
- *Early Adult (22 - 42)*
- *Middle Age (43 - 65)*
- *Late Middle Age (Over 65)*

Child (Ages 6 - 10)

At the child stage of life, play, experimentation, fantasy and exploration are most important. Many children ride and some are very competitive; others are not. Most parents are very competitive. The success they dream of for their children is a barometer of their success as parents. Children have no need to set goals, they just want to have fun! Even the competitive child must learn without too much formal training, or the natural requisite of fun will be destroyed.

If we insist that a non-competitive child like Doug practice on his pony to improve his performance, what began as fun may become a chore. The parent will be creating an imbalance in this stage in life by substituting seriousness for fun. How will the parent know this is happening? Often the child will begin to show behavioral changes. Doug withdrew. Once a bubbly and talkative child, Doug gradually became non-communicative and sullen. His parents did not notice the gradual onset of his unhappiness, because they were too focused on Doug's meeting their objectives of successful competition. He was forced to take instruction and practice daily; he was never allowed to ride just for fun. Finally, his parents asked him if he wanted to compete.

He answered, "yes." Most children, afraid to displease or upset the adults they love, give their parents the answers they know the parents want to hear. With a "yes" answer from Doug, how could the parents know they were making a mistake? They could not, unless they had learned to understand the stages of a child's development. Children at this age have a sixth sense; they know what their parents want and expect. It takes a wise, experienced, or lucky parent to recognize this trait in a young child. Most parents learn from trial and error. By the age of twelve, Doug quit riding.

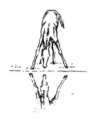

Essential to a child's balanced development are: PLAY, EXPERIMENTATION, FANTASY and EXPLORATION

It is not uncommon for parents to try to live out their lifetime dream through their children. Very few parents will allow the children to 'call the shots'. Billy's family was one of the few who understood the importance of this fun stage of development. Billy's family was competitive. His brothers and sisters showed every week. At nine, Billy began to ask to ride. Finally he was given a pony, but all he wanted to do was play Cowboys and Indians. Billy's parents found it difficult to see their youngest just playing with his pony. But, from their fifteen years of experience raising six other children, they knew the value of fun. They made no effort to inflict instruction on Billy. By the time Billy was twelve he was winning in rodeos. How did he learn? He watched his siblings ride and imitated them; an instinctive learning tool for a child. He had short sessions of instruction that developed his natural feel and balance while he was having fun. The ultimate result was his competitive success and his continued riding career.

Like Johann Pestalozzi, the Swiss educator, I do not believe in serious and formal instruction for children. Pestalozzi refused to let children learn by memory only. He felt they should learn through their total experience, so they would clearly understand and feel what they were learning. A child learning to ride must also learn through observation and experience; the total experience is then absorbed into the child. Children will learn this way naturally if we offer the correct guidance and freedom. It is essential for a child's instructor to understand the character requirements for this stage of development, and to have a gift of teaching with fun in mind. Group lessons employ several valuable learning tools for children: games, observation and playful interaction. One instructor even lets her advanced teenage riders have fun by offering occasional fun days filled with games. What a wonderful balance is maintained for these young people who can still have fun playing games with their horses! More often, I see parents selecting the serious-minded professional whose demands and expectations would be more suitable for adult students. These instructors are creating an imbalance with nature. Children need to have fun. The role of the adult in a child's life is to encourage the child in spontaneous activities, self-evaluation and experimental learning. Any effective method for developing the mental and physical aspects of horsemanship in a child must incorporate freedom and fun.

Pre-Teen (Ages 10 - 13)

During the pre-teen stage, a child begins to develop some finer foundation skills of life. The important mental character traits for this stage are consistency, realistic expectations, responsibility and discipline. This is the time for serious instruction, practice and horse care. Earlier, the child learned the correct balance and seat; now the pre-teen learns to use this seat for more advanced control. Since children look to their parents for authority during this stage, parents must set the rules and regulations that will create a good foundation for physical and mental development. Parents should nurture the inner qualities of discipline and responsibility, which are very easy to bring out in a horse-loving pre-teen. Practice and correct horse care must be CONSISTENTLY ENFORCED. It is the most important time for external stimuli to influence the development of good character in a young person's life.

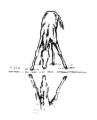

The inner qualities of DISCIPLINE and RESPONSIBILITY must be nurtured by the adults in a pre-teen's life through loving CONSISTENCY.

Ellie's childhood was filled with fun as she went foxhunting with her family. When Ellie reached her pre-teen years she continued to foxhunt, but having fun was no longer enough for her. After the hunt her groom took her horse, and she ran into the house and began to phone her friends and listen to her music. Ellie's life had no enforced discipline, responsibility or commitment. By the time Ellie reached fourteen, she gave up riding and devoted herself to a very involved social life. This might not have been bad, except that Ellie really had "horses in her blood." The failure to develop her horsemanship skills deprived her of something that would have fulfilled the needs of this stage of her life.

Sally, like Ellie, grew up foxhunting with her mother. Since the age of six, she had participated in the local Pony Club. Fun instruction started young, but serious instruction and competition began when she was ten. Sally began to learn about the care and responsibility of her pony, the correct use of her seat and aids and the disciplines involved with eventing, her area of particular interest. By the time Sally was thirteen, she was a Pony Club "C" rider and a good student in school. Sally had a balanced social life for this stage. She had her Pony Club friends and her school friends, but her priorities were her horse activities. Sally graduated from the Pony Club as an "H-A," went to college, and got her degree while teaching riding in the summers to earn spending money. Today, Sally is an avid horsewoman who continues to balance her horse activities with her career and family responsibilities. Sally's journey from childhood to adulthood was smooth, because she was lucky enough to have experiences that balanced her stage of life with her love of horses. Her parents were clever enough to arrange to meet the needs of their horse-loving daughter, thus giving Sally a good foundation for the rest of her life.

During the pre-teen years, children need parental DISCIPLINE, CONSISTENCY and RESPONSIBILITY. Their minds must be challenged to learn. If rules are not initiated and enforced, the children experience a loss of balance that is likely to result in negative teenage behavior. The pre-teen years are easy years for parents and young people. But if the child does not receive the correct basic foundation during this time, both the parents and the young person may suffer the consequences in the future stages of life.

Teenager (Ages 14 - 17)

The teenage years are usually the most difficult years for both teenager and parents. A young person between fourteen and seventeen naturally challenges authority and places major emphasis on peer pressure and social acceptance. This is when he must begin to break his ties with his family and become independent. Meeting challenges successfully helps prepare him to be a successful adult. Peer approval and social interaction replace the role of parents, another step toward the break from the family. For Sally, this challenging period of life was very fulfilling, but unfortunately there are only a few Sallys. How do you direct the energy of a rebellious teenager? This is the six-million dollar question. It is easier if the young person has had a fun-filled childhood and has absorbed the basics of discipline, consistency and responsibility during the pre-teen years. Let me make it clear that it is not only riding that can prepare a child for the future, the same effect can be achieved if the child pursues an interest in music or other forms of art or sports. But the point to remember is this: the process is smoother for the child with a special interest than for a child without one.

Too often I hear parents tell their horsey pre-teen that she will get a horse when she is thirteen if her grades are good. Before you say "wait," please reconsider. If you wait until your child becomes a teenager to start riding it will be a rocky road. Nevertheless, it is better to start riding during the teen years than never to start at all. Let me share the example of Bob. Bob had begged his family for a horse for years. Horses were in his blood. He was given the standard answer: "Do well in school and if your grades are good you can have a horse." Bob graduated from eighth grade with honors. His parents were proud and happy to fulfill their promise. They contacted a local riding instructor, enrolled Bob in lessons and bought him a horse. He was very happy until he discovered that all of his contemporaries rode much better than he did. Bob was a beginner at fourteen. He loved horses, but his natural desire for peer acceptance left him feeling very inadequate and unaccepted. He could not do what the others were doing. They made fun of his beginner status. There was no way he could catch up with them in experience, though his interest and love of horses equalled theirs. They were ready to act and show the results of their skills while Bob was way behind. Bob felt that he was inadequate at the sport he loved, and that because of this he was not accepted by his peers. Fortunately for Bob, his parents provided extra instruction, encouragement, and several horses to ride. His extraordinary interest, combined with the benefits provided by his family, allowed him to develop his skills and within two years he became a successful event rider. By the time he was sixteen, he had received the respect of his fellow riders. If Bob had missed any of the ingredients (love, parental support or being a well-balanced teenager who could honestly discuss his feelings with his family and accept being behind other riders), he could have been as lost as his friend, Kelly.

Kelly's initiation into riding was similar to Bob's. However, when she was faced with being a beginner in a stable of accomplished riding teenagers, Kelly pretended that she was better than she was. She lied to her parents and to herself. She wanted to be the best, but was unable to be the best because of her lack of experience. Unlike Bob's parents, Kelly's parents were unable to afford the extra lessons. What they could and should have done was move her to a less competitive stable. Perhaps this would have saved her. By age fifteen, Kelly stopped riding and devoted herself to her social life, a pattern not uncommon for a teenager. The problem is that too many teenage social scenes are filled with sex, drugs or alcohol. Usually teenagers who are involved in activities in which they feel fulfilled, challenged or accomplished are able to keep their social interaction within a safe margin of time and behavior. Kelly had already started a pattern of self-deceit by covering up her riding inadequacies. It was only natural that she would continue this pattern in her social environment. Sadly, Kelly ended up in a serious depression with suicidal tendencies, for which she needed, and received, extended treatment. Could this pain have been avoided by balancing her social needs and her love of horses in the teenage stage of life? The answer is probably yes.

Let's return to Ellie's life for a moment. When Ellie became a teenager, after her unfulfilled pre-teen years, her imbalance drove her into unhealthy relationships with boys. She ended up with an unwanted pregnancy and an abortion. Now Ellie's life was a mess: she was behind in school, she was emotionally distraught, and she had nothing to fill the void created by her strong love of horses. By the time she was ready to graduate from high school, her grades prevented her from being accepted by a college that matched her intellectual level. For Ellie, a horsey college was a positive solution. She was able to recover, both emotionally and educationally, while in college. When she graduated, she had a 3.5 GPA and was able to move forward to a graduate program to prepare her for the career of her choice. She now has a good job, owns her own horse and is involved in a satisfying relationship.

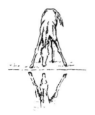

Teenagers who are involved in activities in which they feel fulfilled, challenged or accomplished are able to deal effectively with peer pressures and with their own rebellious nature.

Challenging authority is the most difficult aspect of dealing with the teenage years. Involvement with horses can help even a very rebellious horseloving teenager stay out of trouble. Cindy fought every rule at home and at school. She was suspended from school for a week because she refused to get to class on time. Her parents could do nothing about the school problems because they could not even get her to come home by the designated curfew time. Cindy had taken riding lessons as a child, but her parents did not feel that her interest in horses justified the expense. Therefore, when the pre-teen years arrived, they encouraged her involvement in school sports. Suddenly, because of Cindy's suspension from school, she was not allowed to participate on the hockey team. In desperation, her parents decided to get her reinvolved with horses. They found a supportive stable with other teenagers who were not too advanced. For the first six months, Cindy's parents thought they had made the wrong decision. However, when show season began and Cindy found herself very busy with her horse, she began to be more controllable. Slowly, her behavior began to change and she began to challenge the rules in a more acceptable fashion. Why? When Cindy was in college, I asked her what it was that she felt had changed her during those years. She told me that she had two major memories of that period. One was the enjoyment she got from working with her horses, and the other was that she had been so busy she did not have time to break the rules!

Nature dictates that a teenager strive to become independent. This paves the way for the future adult stages, and to this end a teenager will fight authority and all that it stands for while he seeks the approval of his peers. It takes a strong teenager to rise above the temptations of negative peer pressure. It is tremendously helpful if the teenager can be strong in his horse skills by the time he reaches this stage. If that is not possible, it is essential that parents either provide private support or find a stable where the teenagers are all riding at the same level. Most teenagers require positive and equal peer interaction; it is a normal aspect of that stage of their lives, and a natural part of their personal growth.

Young Adult (Ages 18 - 21)

From the teenage stage we move into the young adult years. Personal and professional uncertainties accentuate the pressures of society's expectations, resulting in insecurity. The young adult has moved away from his family, but has not yet established himself in his life pursuit. He is usually in college or beginning professional job training. This age group is plagued by uncertainty, sometimes accompanied by fear of committing to a profession.

Teenagers whose horse interests were unfulfilled often choose a college with horses. They pursue horses seriously instead of looking for a more suitable profession. Others flounder by stopping their education and working with horses only. Both of these decisions can interfere with personal balance. Often the young adult is unconsciously trying to meet his inner need to express a love of horses. Many of them love horses but should have an enjoyable and fulfilling horse hobby, not a horse-related profession. Their unfulfilled yearning causes them to place horses in the wrong role. Because professional direction is the focus of this stage of their life, it is easy for them to think that their interest in horses should be professional.

I feel that the emphasis placed by our educational system on increasing enrollment has helped create illusions for the horsey young person, who is led to believe that by attending a horsey college he will emerge in four years with his horse skills and his academic skills at a professional level. It is difficult for an educational institution to provide a thorough education in horses and in the academic skills required to become a successful professional of any type. Many programs cater to the young person who has always loved horses but remains a beginner. Although these programs imply otherwise, it is impossible for someone to become a professional horseperson in only four years. It is my opinion that the academically oriented horse lover should have a well-rounded education that will enhance a non-horsey profession if it is ever needed. Parents should guide their teenager toward balancing his horse interests and his academic needs. Enrollment officials of colleges have one thing in mind, increased enrollment. It is up to the parents to help select the right combination of courses and academic competitiveness that their son or daughter actually needs in a college.

Tania is a typical example of a young person who decided to attend a horsey college because she had never fulfilled her love of horses. Her parents had not allowed her to work off her riding at a nearby stable because they were afraid that her school work would suffer. This is seldom true, students involved with horses usually do better in school, but parents usually have no way to know this. Luckily, Tania had survived the teenage years with minimal behavioral problems because she had been so involved with music. Since her grades were good, she received a scholarship. Instead of choosing a school that matched her intellectual level, she chose a college based on her need to ride. Tania graduated from a mediocre college and became an average rider, but found no career skills. Before her college years, Tania had always excelled at what she did. After college, neither her academic nor her riding skills could be considered excellent. She was about to begin her adult life with an imbalance. At this stage in life, all she knew was that she was unhappy, unfulfilled and dissatisfied. She did not know why. Tania's insecurities created a void that led her into a relationship that later ended unhappily. Why did Tania get involved in a serious relationship? She was unhappy. Her peers constantly discussed serious relationships. Young people feel that they need to settle into a serious, life-long partnership during this stage of their life. All these factors added together encouraged Tania to find a partner. Had Tania met the academic challenges that she needed, gotten a challenging job, and then resumed her hobby of riding, she might have avoided the disastrous relationship. If Tania had selected a university at her academic level and ridden for pleasure only, she might have started to meet her love of horses without harm to her future. As it was, she ended her relationship at the age of twenty-eight, still did not have a satisfying job and still could not support a horse. After she recovered from her failed relationship she went back for her master's degree at a more stimulating university. She began her career at the age of thirty. By the time she was thirty-five, she was able to fulfill her love of horses by buying her own horse. She finally had the time and the money to enjoy her love. A few years after that she met a man whom she later married. As of this writing she is a happy wife, a proud parent and the horsewoman of her dreams. You may ask, "what is wrong with Tania's life?" Nothing, except that she lost some valuable years through her floundering between the ages of eighteen and twenty-eight.

Tim took another route. He finished high school and took time out from his education to ride. Tim became a working student for four years. He worked such long hours that his social life, a natural need during this stage of development, suffered. By the time Tim finished his working student program he had no money, no time, and no social life. He did not even know what he wanted in a relationship. Again, the social demand to find a serious partner by age twenty-one prompted Tim to marry a woman who shared his interest in horses. They decided to start their own horse business. However, they had a problem: not enough capital. And neither of them had the education that would allow them to earn enough money to start a business. After years of struggling, Tim abandoned his professional horse goals and took a job that gave him a better income. He was able to support his wife and her riding interests. Tim discovered that he could find pleasure sharing his wife's riding enjoyment.

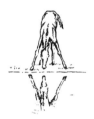

The social pressures to find a life-long partner and a profession are powerful influences in a young adult's life.

Early Adult (Ages 22 - 42)

Joseph Stone and Joseph Church, in *Childhood and Adolescence*, offer a summary of the skills a young person needs to begin his adult life.

"The adult with a capacity for true maturity is one who has grown out of childhood without losing childhood's best traits. He has retained the basic emotional strengths of infancy, the stubborn autonomy of toddlerhood, the capacity of wonder and pleasure and playfulness of the preschool years, the capacity for affiliation and the intellectual curiosity of the school years, the idealism and passion of adolescence. He has incorporated these into a new pattern of devel-

opment dominated by adult stability, wisdom, knowledge, sensitivity to other people, responsibility, strength and purposiveness."

I have attached the ages of twenty-two to forty-two to this stage of life. During these years you develop your career, nurture a partnership and raise a family. How can there be time for horses? Free time is often a serious issue in people's lives during this stage. How can you give up horses now, if you have been involved with them your entire life? If horses are "in your blood", you must acknowledge it. You will need some form of association with them, although not to the same degree as in the prior stages. Let us look at Cary's life. Cary had been able to satisfy her love of horses proportionately through all the stages. She rode throughout her college years, met her future partner while in college, married, and is now busy raising her three children. When Cary's children began to arrive, Cary had to reevaluate her activities. She had been riding and teaching math in high school. Her time was already limited, so she not sure how she could be a responsible parent and continue with the current activities in her life. Since Cary and her husband lived on a small farm and had plenty of space, she decided to breed her mare. So as to have a flexible schedule to meet her children's needs, she retired from her job teaching math and began teaching riding as time permitted. She had satisfied two of her needs: a job with horses and being a caring mother. In time, Cary's children began to ride, and her extra income was used to provide her children with horses. Cary made another discovery: she was able to enjoy her new role with the horses as much as she had enjoyed her riding. Because Cary had a well-rounded horse exposure during the formative years of her life, she felt no need to continue to ride or to compete. She felt fulfilled enjoying the horses with her children. Later, when Cary's last child left home, she took up driving. Cary told me that her involvement in a new horse sport helped her overcome the emotional complications of her husband's serious illness and her son's failure to find his way professionally. Cary is one of those lucky people who have had the blessing of balance throughout life, and whose love of horses has helped them through the crises we all must face.

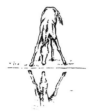

Balancing the nurturing needs of partnership, family and career leaves little time for personal needs during the early adult years of life.

Life was not as balanced for Tina. She, like Cary, had a family, a career, and a husband. The difference was that Tina had never had the opportunity to fulfill her love of horses as a youngster. When one of her children expressed an interest in horses, she immediately started him riding. Tina pushed her child. She wanted him to ride and to win when he was only four. She was also jealous of the opportunity that he had, and that she had missed. Later she enrolled her son in a nearby 4-H Club, where she was unable to control her jealousy of all the other parents who rode or whose children did well. Eventually her jealousy provoked trouble within the club. Anytime another child did well, Tina became nasty. She ultimately caused the 4-H club to divide. Whom did she hurt? She hurt herself, because eventually her son stopped riding. When her son gave up riding, Tina took it up. She remained frustrated, going from one instructor to another, always looking for the miracle learning secret. Unfortunately for Tina, no one was able to break through her barriers of insecurity and jealousy, and so she remains unhappy and frustrated.

The early adult stage is one of the longest stages in life, and carries the most responsibility. If you are balanced and have been prepared with the appropriate tools, this stage can be a journey filled with rewarding challenges. The first twenty-two years of life should have provided you with the skills for success, yet the adult years are often filled with frustration and dissatisfaction. If you missed the ingredients for success during earlier stages, you may experience the void in this stage. If all has come together satisfactorily, you are able to balance partner, children, self, career, social and recreational needs. All are real parts of this stage of life. During this period, I think that horses fit into the recreational category for most people, unless they are professional horsepersons or have no other demanding obligations.

Middle Age (Ages 42 - 65)

Many people are afraid to turn forty, but when I talk to those over forty, most of them admit that it is a great time in life. For some, it really is when life begins! The greatest challenge during this stage is to accept the aging process with dignity; those who achieve this seldom show their age. It is during this stage you can pursue your interest in horses in any way you wish. If you have traveled the traditional road of life, you will have raised your children, developed a successful profession and have a partner, profession, and preferred activities on your list of responsibilities. Most people begin to reflect when they turn forty, so they generally "know themselves" better than during the previous stages of development. If you allow yourself to participate in life's activities, there is freedom at this stage of life. Your only limitation is your body. As you grow older, it takes more careful attention to exercise and diet to maintain health. Coordination may require more patience as you advance in age. However, a greater range of learning techniques can more than make up for physical short-comings. Evaluation can be more realistic when it is based on self-knowledge and experience, giving you more tools to use for successful horsemanship.

Many women experience a difficult time when their children leave home because they have devoted so many years to childrearing and have allowed their own lives to wither. One such mother had given up riding to raise her three children. A year before her youngest was to leave home, Karen began to take riding lessons. She had always wanted to learn dressage, but until her child-bearing years she rode hunters. She decided that this would be an ideal time to fulfill her dream. With three children in college, she could not afford a horse, but Karen and her husband agreed that she could work off her lessons at the local dressage stable. This she did. Karen discovered that she felt no loneliness or pain when her youngest left home. She began saving money, and when she had enough funds, she purchased her own horse. When Karen was young she could do whatever she wanted on her horses. Now she realized that she had a lot more trouble getting the message through to her horse. When she was performing familiar movements, she had only to 'allow' her body to function. But when she started learning new movements, like the half pass, she became frustrated. It took longer for her to achieve the necessary coordination than it had when she was twenty. Mentally, however, she found that riding at forty-five was more challenging and rewarding than it had been at twenty.

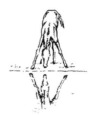

Freedom can begin during middle age because most people have raised their children and developed a successful profession. The only responsibilities left are those of partnership and profession.

Silvia did not have such a smooth experience. Unlike Karen, Silvia had not ridden until she was thirty-eight. She had loved horses all her life, but her life had been filled with constant disappointments. Her parents were divorced when she was young. Her mother could barely support the family, so Silvia had to work. Her interest in acting had provided an outlet for her needs during her pre-teen and teenage years. Silvia continued to work after graduating from high school. She experienced two unsuccessful marriages, and finally at the age of thirty-eight decided to give up on relationships with men and begin with horses. Silvia loved the time she spent on the ground with horses, but found her physical limitations very distracting when she rode. It was difficult for her to be patient with herself. She expected her body to do what her mind wanted. Unfortunately, she floundered for ten frustrating years. Finally, at fifty, she accepted her body and mind as they were and discovered that she could be satisfied with slow progress. That discovery was all she needed. Within one year, she went from barely training level to successful first level. This stage of life can be whatever you want to make of it. The more realistic and patient you are, the more progress you can make.

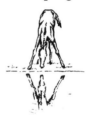

During middle age the physical body becomes more of a challenge, but mental and spiritual development begin to play a more influential role in learning and life.

Late Middle Age (Ages 65 and older)

After age sixty-five, you can enjoy the wisdom, honesty, awareness, and acceptance gained through the previous years of life. You are not old, you are wise. I hope the balance of your being has progressed equally so that you are healthy. The major challenges of this stage are maintaining the body and accepting the idea of death. Those who are lucky have already accepted the idea of death as a natural part of the cyle of life, so it no longer causes fear or concern. However, many people hide from the idea of death until they begin to get closer to the end of their lives. This can work in two ways. On the one hand, it can create the need to fill their lives full of whatever they may want to do. On the other hand, it can also create in them a desire to sit and observe life while waiting for death.

I will always remember one remarkable woman who began her dressage career at the age of sixty-two. Teresa had ridden as a child, and when her own children left home she continued to show jumpers. For a few years she continued to ride, but reduced her show schedule so that she could travel extensively with her husband. Teresa had always had an interest in dressage, but never wanted to take the time to learn the fine tuning because she loved the thrill of jumping. When one of her favorite horses could no longer jump, she decided to make the change. She and her jumper started dressage together. By the time Teresa reached seventy-two, she was competing her ex-jumper at second level. At seventy-four, she was competing at fourth level. Her mind enabled her to be a fantastic student; her challenge was her body. To keep her body in shape, she had massages, did weekly yoga, swam, and walked briskly. Teresa will admit that she had to be very patient and understanding with her body. This was one reason she stopped jumping and riding green horses: she accepted that her bones were more brittle and easier to break.

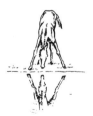

The spiritual and mental wisdom and learning during late middle age allows us greater self-awareness and, thus, higher levels of enjoyment from each of life's experiences.

Ralph, a retired lawyer, took up foxhunting three days a week when he retired from his practice at sixty-five. Until then, he had been able to hunt only on Saturdays. I think that older middle-age people would say that they receive considerable enjoyment from their time with the horses, but wish their bodies were younger.

Summary of Physical Development

Physical development begins with the growth and maturation of our body, from birth to physical maturity. The latter usually occurs between the ages of thirteen and seventeen. As the body experiences growth, the coordination and balance of the rider change. Young people usually adapt to this naturally; only a few struggle with the differences they experience. Between the ages of eight and eighteen the body will respond spontaneously to the mind.

Through the young adult years the body causes us no concern: it is in prime condition. As the years of our early adult stage pass, we gradually experience some changes. We gain weight more easily, and it requires more effort to stay physically fit and to keep our muscles toned. After thirty-five, our body does not respond to our mind quite as rapidly. By late middle age, our bodies have become our biggest challenge. The physical plant that houses our mind and spirit has become more brittle, less flexible, and less coordinated.

Thus, as we make our journey through life, our physical condition peaks between the ages of fifteen and forty, offering us maximum usefulness and requiring a minimum of care. If you are an instructor or parent, you should help your students or children if they experience frustration due to the physical changes of the early years. Those of you in the later years should have developed enough self awareness to help yourselves accept the natural changes of life.

Summary of Mental Development

Our earliest mental development is characterized by having fun, experimenting, exploring and wondering. Adults should understand that this is normal for children, and stand by to patch up the bruises that result. During the pre-teen years, it is vital that children develop the characteristics of responsibility, discipline, and realistic expectations. To secure this foundation, the adults in a child's life must be committed to providing clear expectations and consistent enforcement of rules and responsibilities. Without this substructure, the teenage years can be a horror. Even with the best basics, parents and young people are bound to experience rebellion, resentment, rejection, conflict and misunderstanding during the adolescent stage. Once we emerge as a 'unique' person, we are ready to pass into the adult stages.

The first of the adult stages is most commonly colored by uncertainty. The young adult is preoccupied with the future, both in terms of career and relationships. This turmoil begins to subside as the young person passes into the early adult stage of life. It is during this time that we have the most responsibilities to our partnership, children, career, and society. This time can be most rewarding if we bring to it the attributes from the earlier stages (playfulness from childhood, strength and awareness from the adolescent years, certainty of direction from the young adult years) to create an atmosphere of fulfillment during these years of responsibility. It is also during these years of parenthood that we must oversee the balanced development of our children. It can be a feeling of freedom from years of responsibility when we enter the middle adult years. As we enter this stage, we can add fulfillment to the attributes of our being: fulfillment for surviving the challenges of our responsible years and, perhaps, fulfillment for feeling successful during this challenging time of life. The achievements and accomplishments of our early adult years naturally add to our self-confidence and help orient us to our next stage. What to do with our freedom? For the well-adjusted, these next twenty years can truly be the best years of life: a time when dreams can be fulfilled.

As we pass into late middle age, we have established a pattern of working toward our dream. The knowledge and experiences accumulated during the past sixty years enable us to understand and enjoy the benefits of living life at a deeper level. It is during this time that we have our greatest sense of inner awareness.

It is obvious that, as we travel the path of life, we are growing mentally. Our mental growth allows us to respond to society's pressures with more maturity. We see our relationship to our community in a different light with each stage of our growth. If we are able to keep the good of each stage and let go of the bad, our spiritual growth will parallel our mental growth. If we are not so lucky, we still can catch up at any time. Each year should make life more fulfilling, more rewarding and more satisfying. However, because of the complex nature of the interaction between our conscious and unconscious developement, we may not recognize the rewards of our experiences until later.

Summary of Spiritual Development

Our spiritual growth begins at birth when we are nurtured by our mother. This early nurturing paves the way to the security of the child stage. Nurturing love is the basis for security. As our spirit develops during childhood, we come to understand good and bad and right and wrong. This understanding is strongly influenced by family, friends, and community interaction. By our preteen years, we begin to see our own identity and responsibility related to our lives. We grow into the individual of the teenage years, where the 'I' predominates. While few of us recognize our inner struggle, it is during the teenage years that we are unconsciously trying to balance our spiritual being. Our childhood beliefs are challenged, and we try to understand the idea of God or of a higher power as it relates to us. Few of us resolve the issue during our teenage years, but as we explore and pass into the adult years we are accumulating inner knowledge. We begin our adult years conforming to the standards and beliefs of the community of peers with whom we associate or wish to associate. We begin this process by selecting as our role models people who are socially or financially successful. As we pass from the early adult years to the middle adult years, our own experiences cause us to challenge these beliefs. We have seen, heard and felt things that make us question these external standards and modify the way we relate to them. Gradually, our natural desire to balance our lives helps us to accept ourselves as individuals searching for beliefs that fit into our experience. We begin to see that we are unique individuals, each of us relating to the world differently. By the time we reach our late middle-age, we will have changed our focus because of the the knowledge acquired during our life. During this stage, we feel that life has acquired a new and different meaning. Knowledge accompanied by experience has become wisdom, and most people in this stage want to share their wisdom.

How does this all happen? Most often it just happens. For those who are open-minded, curious, and self-accepting, changes flow naturally and the road is much smoother. For those who are out of balance, the need to change is prompted by specific circumstances or crises. No matter which stage of life you are in, when you hit a bump, you have options. You can ignore the bump, or you can try to find a solution or an answer. The process of searching for answers prompts change and growth.

Our spiritual growth is like our mental growth. The foundation should be laid during our early years as we question the wonders of the universe. However, even if our spiritual growth flounders, the potential for such growth is still in each of us, waiting to be developed. We can begin that development at any time. Little is lost. Life can be rewarding even without spiritual understanding, but what is often missing is the deep feeling associated with each experience. Also missing is the inner knowing, that allows us to be less judgmental, more intuitive, and more at peace with life and our place in life.

We are often apprehensive about the spiritual side of our being because we do not understand it. This is why it is so often kept locked inside ourselves. Life confronts us spiritually time and again. One way is through death. Who wants to think about death? Very few people. Yet, most of us must deal with the death of a relative, friend, or horse by the time we reach our middle adult years, and often even earlier. If we lose a loved one, whether a person or an animal, and we do not allow ourselves to experience the grief or confront the question of death, this blocking of our feelings can also block our spirituality. We are afraid to get in touch with feelings we do not understand. We may need help to get us started.

To progress on our spiritual journey, we must come to understand the greatest love in life and associate ourselves with this love. We must understand our purpose and accept our destiny. All these are benefits of spiritual growth. Unless our lives have been particularly disrupted, we can let the natural growth process occur without our conscious effort. The journey actually becomes a part of our life in our middle years. When and how we pass through the stages of spiritual growth remains a mystery. What is important is acknowledging the role of our spirit and allowing it to develop as we travel through life. In this way, our spiritual development will advance, like our mental development, through the integration of experience in an open, aware being: US.

Outside Influences

TIME, ENERGY AND MONEY

*An honest assessment of
your time, energy and
finances will pave the way
to fulfilling your dreams.*

Horses are expensive. There is no question that they are
major consumers of time, energy, and money. As part of
setting your goals, you must ask yourself how important
horses are in your life. What portion of your time, energy and
money are you willing to allocate to support your horse interests? You must also examine how much time, energy, and
money you have available. The first is a qualitative question—
a matter of priorities. The second is a quantitative question—
a matter of resource management.

In the chapter entitled "Motivation" you decided why you
are involved with horses. Now I am going to ask you how
intensely you want to be involved and how realistically you are
able to be involved. How high do horses rank in your life? If your
involvement is recreational, is it your only recreation, or do you
also enjoy other activities such as golf, tennis, or music? Do you
try to fit as many of your interests as possible into your busy
schedule? Or do you focus on enjoying one interest to the fullest?

If you review the Motivation chapter, you will realize that there is a wide range of expenditures required for the different reasons for riding. The Stages chapter pointed out the various demands that can be created by life itself. Within all of the factors, there are degrees of involvement that can result in a varied expenditure of time, money, and energy. The only constant among all the variables is the fact that a competitor or professional must be prepared to invest more.

Still another way of looking at the quality issue is to ask yourself how near to the limits of your resources you want to operate. Are you willing to be in danger of overdrawing your checkbook every month so you can pay the feed bill? Are you willing to juggle your schedule every day so you can find time to ride? Are you willing to be exhausted every night because you rode and cared for two horses after working eight hours at your job? Are you willing to eliminate other activities from your life so that your horse involvement can be relaxing and enjoyable? If something has to go, will it be horses or something else?

To answer these questions, you must know yourself. There are no categorically right or wrong answers. Your individual needs will dictate what is right or wrong for you. Pleasure, enjoyment and fulfillment come wrapped in different packages for different people. My life pleasures result from fitting as much as possible into every day. No matter what I am involved in, I try to enjoy the beauty of the activity, of nature, and of the moment. Since I am a teacher, I get a great deal of pleasure in life by helping riders attain their riding goals. But no matter how much I love horses or how fulfilling I find my teaching, I need other activities such as theater, travel, management, nature, reading, and learning to fulfill my overall needs. Fitting all this into my life is a challenge that I enjoy. Luckily for me, I have the energy to match the demands on my time. Like everyone else, I must balance my activities. I have chosen to limit my social life. I am a social bore, going to sleep at

9:00 p.m. so that I can get up at 5:00 a.m. to get the most out of every day! I accept that I am different, and hope that others can accept this too. On the other hand, I know people who prefer a much calmer life. They also fully enjoy every moment by being involved in their profession and their hobby. This gives them time to sit and read or sip wine in the evening, interact with other people, and go to bed without being exhausted. Their focus is on doing fewer things, and on doing them in depth and in a relaxed manner. This use of time and energy pleases them. My lifestyle would drive this type of person crazy, and their life style would drive me crazy. We must learn what gives US pleasure and satisfaction, so that we may eliminate as much frustration as possible from our lives, while still meeting the needs of society. However, we must not be critical of other people's balance of time, money, and energy. Just as we expect others to accept our balance of these factors, we must accept theirs.

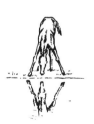

We must accept and respect other people's balance of time, money, and energy. We must assume that they understand and accept our balance. We must not make assumptions or comparisons, or expect others to have the same balancing priorities that we have.

No matter where horses fall in your priorities, and no matter what pace you prefer, you can achieve a more effective use of time, energy and money. Approaching this question from a quantitative standpoint, the amount of time, energy, and money you have to spend will influence the type of riding you do. Competition is more expensive than recreational riding. You may want to compete, but, if your resources are limited, you may not be able to. You may want to be a professional, but find that it is possible only if you also have another source of income. You may like the challenge of training a young horse, but find that you are too tired after working all day to have the patience that the task requires. You may want to seek national or zone awards, but find that your work schedule does not permit the flexibility required to get to the necessary horse shows. Your decision must take into consideration all facets of your life, not just your dreams.

Keeping a horse costs a lot of money. If you begin with the purchase price and then add to that the maintenance fees and the cost of training, equipment, instruction and competition, you substantially increase your financial obligations. Chart #2 in the Workbook will help you evaluate how much money you can realistically allot to your riding. Actually, most of the cost of horses goes into the care of the horse. Fortunately those with limited finances who have the time, energy and suitable attitude may be able to fulfill their wishes through working student or apprenticeship programs. Barter is still possible for the dedicated and commonsense horseperson.

Another element to be considered is energy. Physical energy is required for the long hours of work, and mental energy is necessary to stay fresh. If you are not mentally fresh and energetic, it will be difficult for you to communicate effectively with your horse. Tired people cannot enjoy the experience they are working so hard to achieve. On the other hand, some feel that their time with horses energizes them mentally. It is important for you to determine if horses use up your energy or create more energy. You must also learn to distinguish physical energy from mental energy. Chart #2 is designed to help you evaluate your personal use of energy with horses.

If you do not have enough money to board your horse, you will need considerable time and energy. Horses take a good deal of your time. Their care and training and your training are VERY TIME CONSUMING. You can expect each ride to take one to one and a half hours. Add to that the travel time to your stable. If you want to work off the expense in some way, you must have extra time to barter. Expect to offer an average of five hours of work for every lesson received.

Now take a serious look at your time. Begin now to keep a time chart to learn how much time the various demands on your life require. The time chart, Chart #4 in your Workbook, will help you to get a clear picture of the demands on your time. Chart #5 has been provided for you to customize. Feel free to customize your time chart. I suggest keeping it by the month, but I myself fill it in daily. Time charts became a required part of my daily life when I found I had too much to do. I had no idea where my time went each day. Now I find it impossible to live without my time chart. My time chart is customized for my life. I have discovered that it is a valuable tool for me. One of my students discovered that she had lost two hours every day by not using her time effectively; when she realized this and used those hours for her horses, she was elated.

It is essential that you make honest evaluations of your time, money, and energy before you set your goals.

The busy person must be very clear in setting priorities and then be flexible in adjusting to meet them. I once taught a very busy medical doctor. He loved to foxhunt, but the demands of his profession prevented him from riding more than a few times a month. He would have loved to hunt on those days, but he questioned whether it was fair to his horse and his body. He solved the horse problem by hiring someone to exercise his horse. He decided to challenge his body. Because he was in the prime of his life, he did not feel any serious limitations. As he approached his later middle age, however, he discovered that he had to reschedule his professional hours so he could ride in between hunts. His body began to lose its elasticity and he experienced muscle soreness, but he was unwilling to give up the mental refreshment that he received from his riding. Fortunately, he was able to adjust his office hours so he could ride four times a week to keep his body in shape. This allowed him to meet the goal he clearly wanted to attain.

An accurate time evaluation can prevent you from taking on more than you can handle comfortably. Al came to me for a working student position. He loved horses and wanted to ride competitively. As I discussed his situation with him, we discovered that he had two problems: no money, and limited time. He thought that he had a lot of time because he had a night shift job in a local factory, which gave him the day-light hours free. However, his other responsibilities did not leave him enough time to be a working student. He barely had time to ride his own horse, not to mention taking lessons and working those lessons off. I could not make him see that he did not have enough time and energy to add the necessary hours of work required to be a working student, so I let him try it out. After three months, Al began to get discouraged because he was not making the progress he expected. Why not? He was exhausted, and he could not learn while exhausted. He could not abandon his family or stop his job, but something had to be sacrificed. Al started to keep a time chart, and after three months he saw for himself the demands on his time. Using a time chart before setting his goals might have prevented him from making a costly mistake.

Be honest and realistic in your evaluation of your time, energy, and money. Do not let your wishes about what could be, blind you to what really is possible for you. Be open-minded once you know what your priorities really are and what the demands on your life really cost in terms of time, energy and money. What trade-offs are necessary or possible without sacrificing your health, your family, or your financial stability? Ask questions like these: what would my spouse do or say if I spent X hours a month away from home training with my horse? If we eliminate ABC from our budget to have money for lessons and shows, will we be sorry? In the short run? In the long run? Do I really need the mental and physical challenge of training a young horse now, when I am also starting a new job which is really important to me? Continue with questions of your own to refine your appraisal of how horses can fit into your life. With this enhanced self-knowledge, you are now ready to set your goals.

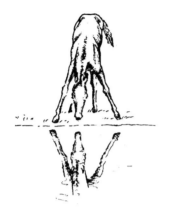

Choosing Goals

*Meeting goals fulfill dreams.
Realistic goals are
determined by knowing
your motivation, assessing
your outside influences
and being aware of your
stage in life.*

Every one of us has dreams, but few of us know how to turn a dream into reality. The key is in goal-setting.

Goals do not have to be scary. Goals are not set in stone. They do not last forever. The evaluation that goes into setting the goal can be as valuable as the goal itself. Goals generate confidence, enhance awareness, expand communication, create energy, and develop responsibility.

The long-term goal comes first. The intermediate and short-term goals are chosen to be the stepping stones toward achieving the long-term goal. The more specific the long-term goal, the easier it will be to choose the right intermediate and short-term goals, which are used to evaluate progression and success. A long-term goal would be something you hope to achieve in one to three years. An intermediate term goal might take three to six months. A short-term goal would be a daily objective. An example of a long-term goal could be to show successfully at third level dressage. If you are a training level rider, the intermediate goals would include learning the movements in each level. In addition, you would want to show one year successfully at first and second level. The short-term goals would include keeping the horse straight, balanced, rhythmical, and round as you learn and confirm these intermediate steps.

Value of Goals

Begin to think about all of your dreams for yourself and your horse. Why is it important to convert these dreams into goals? Setting and revising goals is work; why not be content to just ride and do what you can? Why bother to categorize goals into time periods? Before I give you specific suggestions on how to set your own goals, I want to convince you of the importance of goal-setting. It should not be an academic exercise, but a natural part of your life.

Goals give direction to life. Striving for the goal is more important than meeting it. Each time we attain a goal, we must set a new one. It is this process that improves the quality of our lives. To make the best use of goal-setting, we should practice this approach in all areas of life: physical well-being, relationships, career, social involvement, finances, spiritual development, and problem solving. Although I am focusing on your horse interest, please remember that the same system applies to all areas of life. Your self-confidence, awareness, communication, energy, and responsibility can all be developed or enhanced by your use of goal-setting.

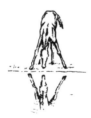

Goals give direction to life. Striving for the goal is more important than meeting it.

Developing self-confidence is one of the challenges we all face in life. Confidence comes from knowing that we can do what we want to do. It results from experience, the experience of meeting goals successfully. We must have some way to evaluate an experience, some way to know whether it was good or bad. This is where goal-setting comes in. The goals contain standards for the evaluation.

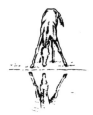

Confidence comes from knowing that we can do what we want to do. It results from experience.

Let's look at an example of an intermediate goal of performing a correct leg-yield consistently. You give the aids for leg-yield and, when your horse responds, you know you were correct. After you repeat this several times, you become confident that you are doing it right. Sue came for a lesson frustrated because her horse would not leg-yield. Although she thought she understood the correct aids, Thunder's unwillingness to yield had undermined her confidence. Sue's previous trainer insisted that it was her fault that Thunder would not perform what he was asked. This may have been true, but the more Sue heard it, the less she was able to use her aids correctly. Together we analyzed the aids and the response. Then I rode Thunder to make certain that he did know what to do. Finally Sue got back on him. In these few minutes, we made certain that Thunder understood, and that Sue knew the correct aids for a leg-yield and would recognize the correct response. I advised Sue to become slightly more definite in her aids. Thunder responded. We repeated this several times, until Sue was certain she could reproduce the feel. Having a goal to do the leg-yield, pursuing it, and finally achieving it, gave Sue the confidence to set another goal. It also gave her confidence in her ability to get Thunder to execute the movement that he knew. This was a valuable building block for Sue.

One of the most exciting advantages of goal-setting is the extended, colorful enhancement of life through our greater awareness. Achieving the successful completion of a goal requires that we be aware of what both we and our horses are doing. Let us return to the example of Thunder and Sue. The short-term goal that I helped her achieve was the execution of a proper leg-yield. To help her communicate with Thunder, I told her to close her eyes. She was able to feel Thunder respond by crossing his legs under himself. Because of her dedication to her goal, she became aware of another dimension of the leg-yield movement.

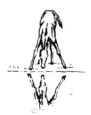

One of the most exciting advantages of goal setting is the extended, colorful enhancement of life through our greater awareness.

It is obvious that Sue needed to communicate effectively with Thunder to get him to do the leg-yield. Her lack of confidence kept her from communicating decisively enough. Her need to reach her goal ultimately encouraged her to seek help to communicate with him in a fashion that he could understand and accept. Communication with a horse is not only what you execute with your aids, but how and when you do it. As Sue evaluated Thunder's performance to decide whether or not she had achieved her goal, she gradually became more precise and timely with her aids.

Sue was elated when she finally felt the leg-yield. This thrill renewed her energy. She could not have experienced this elation if she had not met her goal. Meeting a goal reassures us, and we experience a feeling of renewed energy when we achieve something we set out to do.

When we are tempted to become lazy and non-directed, the responsibility we feel to meet the goal inspires us to persevere. Repeated failures to do the leg-yield made Sue feel frustrated and tempted to quit. But she did not want to quit without reaching her goal; she felt an obligation to herself and to Thunder to continue.

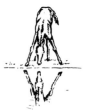

Meeting a goal reassures us, and we experience a feeling of renewed energy when we achieve something we set out to do.

Setting The Goals

While I was preparing the manuscript for this book, I read an article on the front page of the December 24th *Missoulian*, by Craig McNeil, who writes a column for the *Rocky Mountain News* in Denver.

"Setting goals in skiing, such as committing yourself to the number of times you will ski this season, is important because it gives you something to focus on. Most people do not set goals because they are afraid of what will happen if they fail to meet the goals.

Having a goal is simply a matter of saying to yourself, "This is what I want to accomplish." Deciding what you want is the first step on the path to success in skiing. To support the process of setting goals, it is important to set an intention each time you ski. Having an intention empowers you to be the kind of skier you want to be.

It could be a simple as saying, "I want to have fun and relax," or "I want to be a great skier." The more specific your intention, the more focused you will be in the process. The key to the idea of goal-setting is to have something firmly in mind, something to work toward. . . ."

To set your goals, begin by writing down all of your dreams about your involvement with horses. Take several days to let your mind flow over the possibilities. Do not worry if your dreams overlap or if they seem unrealistic. Include everything, no matter how long it might take you. Questionnaire #3 in your Workbook will help you record your horse dreams. You may wish to repeat this exercise when you learn to use your mountain top [Mountain Top chapter in Resources section].

The editorial process begins with selecting those dreams that seem long-term: those that would take you one to three years to meet, or perhaps even longer. Then combine those that overlap and write each at the top of a piece of paper. Use what you learned about yourself in the chapters on Motivation, Stages of Life, and Outside Influences to choose those goal possibilities that are realistic for you. Set aside any that seem crazy, and concentrate on the two or three that seem to fit you. Questionnaire #4 in your Workbook will allow you to review what you have learned about yourself.

Give special attention to whether your motivation was primarily pleasure, competition, or professional. To a large extent, these broad categories measure the importance of horses in your life. Horses must have a higher priority for the professional than for the pleasure rider. If you are still unsure about yourself, allow your goals to reflect taking pleasure in your horse. It is easy to move up the ladder to competition or profession if pleasure does not offer enough challenge. It is harder to accept moving down if you overextend yourself.

After you have chosen the long-term goals, go back to your original list and pick up any intermediate and short-term goals that will help you move toward your long-term goals. Write them on the appropriate pieces of paper. Be sure that the intermediate and short-term goals are in order. Goals must be achieved in the proper sequence for training to be effective. Keep brainstorming until you have a clear idea of how you will proceed toward your long-term goal. Reflect these ideas on Questionnaire #4.

The last step is to edit the language of your goals. The more long-term the goal is, the broader it should be. Even a long-term goal must contain standards by which you may measure its completion. The benefit of the goal-setting is as much from realizing that you have met your goal as it is from knowing where you are going.

Steps in Choice of Each Goal
- ◆ *1. Brain storm dreams*
- ◆ *2. Consider motivation, your stage in life, and outside influences*
- ◆ *3. Choose realistic long-term (dream) goal*
- ◆ *4. List steps to attain long-term goal, intermediate goal*
- ◆ *5. Make day to day plan to meet first intermediate goal*
- ◆ *6. Set new day to day plan as you achieve each day's goal*
- ◆ *7. Go to second intermediate goal after you meet first*

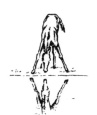

Goals In Action

Joan is in her early thirties. She has two small children, a job as a teacher, loves horses and owns her own horse, Willy, whom she keeps at home. Joan almost failed in her long-term goal-setting because of the turmoil created by her instructor. He told her that Willy could not go beyond low hunter, and yet Joan's dream was to show amateur/owner. Her instructor pushed her to sell Willy and buy a more talented horse. Willy was young and of average ability; both his mother and his father had been good athletes. His mother had run successfully over timber, while his quarter horse sire had shown both Western and English. Joan had raised Willy and could not bear the thought of giving him up, so she procrastinated. Joan attended clinics whenever she could, and fortunately found an instructor who liked Willy. This instructor explained that Willy needed some basic suppling work, but should be able to fulfill Joan's dream if she was patient. This was all the encouragement that

Joan needed. She had her long-term goal, showing Willy ama-
teur/owner. The second step was to have an intermediate goal,
so Joan evaluated her time, her teaching, her family responsibilities, and her money. She decided that she should move up
one level a year: low hunter, first year green, second year green
and then amateur/owner. If all went well, Willy would be
twelve when she met her goal. Her short term goals included
learning to supple him, doing basic ground work, strengthening
his body, and fine-tuning her communication with him. She had
three days a week to ride, and her showing budget allowed her
to enter eight shows a year. The clinician was from far away,
so Joan's first task was to find a knowledgeable local instructor
who shared her positive attitude and would work with her.
Joan's cooperative husband was willing to take care of the
children so that Joan could drive the hour to her instructor.
Everything was now in place to begin the program. Willy
progressed with his suppling: each day he was more willing to
work with a relaxed body, requiring less effort for Joan. Then
suddenly, one Monday, he came out stiff and unwilling to work.
Because Joan's program was based on her goals, she planned
every day's work according to the progress made during the
previous workout. She immediately noted a difference. She
could not do what she had planned, but she could simplify his
exercises for the level at which he was comfortable. Had she not
had her day-to-day goals, she would not have recognized the
need to change the riding plan for that day. Later, she remembered that her previous ride had been in deep footing from the
rain. She had learned that, in the future, deep footing would
dictate a shorter training session. Joan's daily training program
progressed like this until it was November and time for her six-
month evaluation. How close was she to being ready for the
low hunter division in April? She would have to jump a course
at 2'6" to 2'9"; she was doing grids and suppling work; it was
November. If she overfaced Willy and he lost confidence, she
would lose time trying to fix the problem. After consulting

with her instructor and the clinician, Joan decided to give Willy more time. She realized that her responsibilities as mother, wife, and teacher prevented her from dedicating her full energy to her horse, therefore this seemed like a fair compromise and a safe decision. By the time the second six month evaluation time came around, Joan was pregnant. Now what? Joan decided that she would try to remain on schedule with her goals. She asked her instructor to ride Willy while she took a three month leave of absence. This worked well. By fall, Willy and Joan were able to get back to work together; by the following spring, they began showing low hunter. They were successful. Today, Joan is showing the fifteen-year-old Willy in amateur/owner and her children are showing him in the junior divisions. He is truly a family horse who is giving pleasure to everyone.

To give you an even broader picture of goal-setting in action, I will share with you the role goals played in my life during the various stages. I did not recognize until my thirties that I automatically set and used goals, and that I had been setting them even as a child. I have two overriding and life-long motivational requirements, my love of horses and my need for challenge.

Until I was eleven, pony rides were my only association with horses. For as long as I can remember, my poor parents had to listen to constant begging: both my sister and I wanted a horse. Finally they sold their house in town and bought an old farm house with land, and buildings that could become a stable. As I look back, I realize that this must have been a sacrifice for them because my father had to drive further to work and my mother had to deal with a house that was not as good as the one we had lived in. My childhood was consumed with the fantasy of having a horse. My parents answered an ad in the paper and we bought our first horses. I had to take care of my horse myself. There was no question of discipline or responsibility, it was strictly expected and enforced. My sister and I enjoyed our horses for fun, we went on trail rides and explored.

Our formal training came from our father, who read books and then taught us. We had already begun to attend the local horse shows when our parents decided to investigate a Pony Club. This must have been another major effort for our parents, because the Pony Club we joined was an hour away from our home. The Pony Club had instruction twice a week, once mounted and once unmounted. Before my parents selected a Pony Club, they visited the various local clubs to decide which one would best meet our needs. Despite the distance, the quality of the instruction was so good that it was a perfect choice—and a good lesson in investigating before committing! During my years in Pony Club, I learned from some expert horsepersons and developed lasting friendships.

By the time I was fourteen and able to use my mind for more than fun, I decided that I wanted to ride in the Pennsylvania National Horse Show in Harrisburg. It was the first show of the winter indoor series. I also wanted to become an 'A' rated Pony Clubber. This was my first long-term goal put into action. My parents did not have much money, so I had to do local farm work to earn entry fee money. Luckily my instruction was free, and I had time to go to Pony Club twice a week. My intermediate goal was to get successful horse show mileage that would prepare me for my long-term goal. I worked very hard to learn the skills: I watched older Pony Clubbers, I watched the horse show riders who always won, I listened intently, and I read constantly. Meanwhile, I kept my grades high in school because I knew this would please my parents. My socialization was limited to my time in school and at the Pony Club. During my early teenage years, I did not get involved in school social activities. As my teen years progressed, I advanced in my Pony Club ratings and won at many horse shows. My level of self-confidence was higher than that of the other kids in my class. I did not like being labeled 'different', so I made another goal: To become involved socially at school. To this end I joined the yearbook staff, served on committees, and had limited social interaction with other students. I was never tempted by the teenage experiments with sex and alcohol, because I did not want to risk my riding goals. Those goals were clearly a motivation to me. During these adolescent years I had no money, and only limited time, but lots of energy. I loved horses and competing more than life itself. In 1960 I reached my first long-term goal, I rode and placed at the Pennsylvania National Horse Show. The ribbons I had won until that point had built my confidence and kept me faithful to my goal, but they had not given me the indescribable feeling of elation I felt from winning at Harrisburg. To this day, I can reexperience the ecstacy of the ride and the win! My adolescent years seemed to end with all that I could want: Success with my horses, graduation (third in my class!) and acceptance into a good college.

As I entered the young adult stage in life, I was clearly a 'horsey' person. My parents expected me to get my college degree. My time with horses had been well-rounded, but now it was time to gain the skills to support myself and use my mind. My heart broke when I sold my horse, but, with my usual positive attitude, I went off to college completely uncertain about the future. It was my first time in eight years without a horse.

Once in college, it took me less than a week to discover that my mental health would deteriorate if I did not somehow get near a horse. I thought I needed to ride, but that was not possible. Luckily a local farm allowed me to groom their horses. This experience taught me that all I needed was to be around horses: I did not need to ride or to compete. Horses provided me with something I missed when I was without them. At this stage in life, I neither knew nor cared what that ingredient was. My focus was what was I going to do with my future. Early in my college days, I set another series of goals: Get through college with the best possible grades, socialize to become better adjusted with people and go at least twice a week to the farm to groom the horses. I did not meet the long-term goal of graduating, but I did meet the goal of spending at least two days a week with horses.

My young adult stage of life came to an abrupt halt. At nineteen I jumped prematurely into the early adult stage. My limited social development from my adolescent years, combined with fate, caused me to think I was 'in love.' Even when I was eighteen, I had to complete things. Although I did not graduate, I did finish the year with good grades. In June after my freshman year, I married into an already-made family and found myself with a husband, two young children and three horses! This was the end of my educational goals, and the beginning of my responsibility to partnership and family. I had no career other than mother and wife. The children liked horses, so my 'horsey' side was automatically satisfied. Since my husband had known me as a competitive rider, he encouraged me to compete. However, I had no need to compete because I had attained my competition goals as an adolescent. Challenge was still a major drive in my life, so I channelled my horse energy into founding a Pony Club and teaching. This met several of my needs: fulfilling social obligations, making some money, and being around horses. I was clearly involved for pleasure, I foxhunted three days a week, taught for fun, and challenged myself by educating people about Pony Club in an area of the country where western riding predominated. My long-term goals included founding a Pony Club that would improve horse care in the local area and teach progressive riding to youth and motivated teenagers, teaching privately to earn money, improving my horse knowledge by watching successful riders and trainers at major competitions and by reading, and preparing students for competitions so that they could improve their self-confidence through competitive success. Notice that, as in my teenage years, I did not set a time limit on my goals. My main priorities during this early adult stage were partnership, family, and pleasure. Each time a Pony Clubber was successfully up-rated, a team attended a competition, parents became more actively involved, or a student won a well deserved competitive award, I had met one of my intermediate goals. Each time I did this, I gained confidence and expanded my experiential learning. Attaining these intermediate goals also met my need for pleasure. Meanwhile, I also had specific goals with my husband and my children. When I had to balance my interests, I always honored my goals in the following order: to husband, to children, and then to pleasure. In each of life's activities, I used this system of goals and priorities. This was a long stage for me; it consumed twenty-seven years. My family responsibilities included raising three generations of children.

By the time my second generation of children grew out of their infancy, my goals focused on what horses could do for human development. New goals were essential because I had attained my long term goal. My Pony Clubbers were becoming "A" and "B" members, and many of my riding students were experiencing competitive success. The Pony Club parents were taking an active role in the club, the membership was expanding, and I had taught several people to teach the lower levels. I had met my long-term goals in ten years.

I proceeded to set a new long-term goal; making a difference in the lives of handicapped and exceptional children by using horses. By now I was aware of my goal-setting tool, so I established the necessary intermediate and short-term goals toward this end. During the next fifteen years, my goal gave me the strength to overcome all the obstacles of the most challenging task I had yet undertaken. I was rewarded during these years by seeing many young people solve their problems and become productive citizens. Horses, the animals I so dearly love, had a primary role in this rehabilitation.

By now I was reaching the middle age stage of my life. My journey had taught me a lot. My thirst for knowledge and need to become a better teacher had remained with me during all these years. Being an effective teacher was probably the real, ultimate goal that spanned all the stages of my life. As a teenage Pony Clubber, I began teaching as a way to earn money to pay my horse bills. I continued to teach and coach students through my young adult years. Besides teaching students, I taught instructors how to teach correctly. By middle age, I had realized that I wanted to change more than just the rider's performance. I had learned that there were many more dimensions to riding successfully. I wanted to share these additional skills to make a difference in American training and riding.

During the middle age years our spiritual development focuses on finding a meaning for our life. Over the years, I had become convinced that one purpose of my life was to teach the value of balance. Goals were essential not only to success with horses, but, more importantly, to becoming a balanced person. What was success? My definition included knowing what you wanted, accepting who you were, working to balance yourself, and then putting that into effect on the horse. If you know yourself, you can have a fairer relationship with a horse. If you really know yourself and your horse, you will be able to enlist the cooperation of the whole horse and produce results that make you equal with anyone at your level in the world.

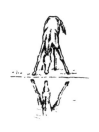

My definition of success includes
KNOWING what I wanted,
ACCEPTING who I was,
WORKING TO BALANCE myself,
and then putting this
into effect on the horse.
If I could not do it off the horse,
how could I do it on the horse?

Throughout my life I had limited funds, so I feared it would be impossible to make a significant difference with what I had come to believe. I settled on an ultimate goal of teaching and exposing those horsepeople I came in contact with to the best possible basics related to balanced learning. I frequently witnessed instructors and trainers inflating their egos and misusing their positions to fill riders with illusions. In my own small way, I was dedicated to producing a core learning program that would enable America's dressage riders to achieve honest, world class performances. My goal was not based on the result, but on the journey the person had to take to become a truly effective horseperson. My intense love of horses, my stage of life, and my self-imposed responsibility to the horse world set my current goal into action.

At this time, I am in the late middle age stage. As astonishing as it seems, I have met two of my long-term goals. I have written a book that was successfully received, and Hilltop Farm has come into being. Hilltop is a complete Sport Horse Center dedicated to the proper training of horse and rider. It has been developed around my philosophy, which is shared by the owner, my son and the staff. Thoughts are turning into reality.

Now what? I need to establish another set of goals. I still love horses, I still love to teach, and now there is a facility and staff at Hilltop in a position to help those ready to learn. At this time I must use my organizational skills, my understanding gained by experience of human nature, and my dedication to the Hilltop philosophy to oversee the development of Hilltop and support the staff. This will enable the staff to use their energy and knowledge with the students and horses, creating a comfortable learning environment for horse and man. My goal is to help the owner keep Hilltop running smoothly so that it can meet its goal to provide the horse community with an ideal learning environment. In addition, I want to document the valuable knowledge that I have gained through my experiential learning to help other lives become as full of joy and reward as mine. To that end, I am writing this book.

I have fulfilled many long term goals that started as dreams:

Winning at the Pennsylvania National
Founding two branches of the United States Pony Club

Raising happy, well-rounded, productive children
Helping young people grow into productive, successful adults
Writing two books
Helping riders attain National awards
Helping riders enjoy and communicate with their horses
Sharing in the development of a Complete Sport Horse Center

My love of horses and challenge have remained constant throughout my life. They were inescapable parts of my being and I am lucky that I recognized them. The way that they interacted with the other requirements of my life changed with each stage, as my degree of involvement with horses adapted realistically to conditions in my 'real life'. My goals changed; most were met, a few were not. My evaluations learned when to change, when to forget and when to persevere.

No matter where you are starting, I hope that you can discover the confidence, energy, and awareness created by using goals to enhance your life experience, whether with horses or any other aspect of your life.

Understanding
Horse & Man

Introduction

From the level of the smallest cell to that of the universe, nature dictates a constant search for balance. Balance affects the outcome of all endeavors, whether equestrian or life experiences. The more balanced your horse is, the easier it is for him to do his designated task. The more balanced we are, the easier it will be for us to smooth out the bumps as we seek to attain our goals. Both horse and man have three areas to balance within themselves: body, mind and spirit. In a partnership the two beings, man and horse, come together and create a new balance together. If not interfered with, nature strives to reach a balance within each creature. Horses are closer to natural balance than people are, because their lives have fewer interferences than ours. It is my theory that horses can provide the horse enthusiast with a vital understanding of the essence of balance. This improved understanding can help simplify the idea of our own balance, which can lead us toward greater inner equilibrium; this, in turn, will enhance our balance with our horse. Studies have shown that inner stability will enable us to have a happier, healthier life.

Do not think the pursuit of balance is easy. Problems or issues that upset us are often ignored, not even thought about or locked away. Why? Because we do not recognize the 'real' cause of an issue, or because we are afraid to deal with it.

Eventually these problems build up and create damaging blocks. However, if we undertake the pursuit of understanding and learning, the end result will offer us more success and harmony in our endeavors. It is a pursuit that will last a life-time. As we journey through life trying to attain greater understanding, we can experience both highs and lows. As we allow ourselves to enjoy the highs and get out of the lows, we will discover an improved equilibrium. I am trying to make a difficult subject more understandable; be patient with yourself. It is a worthwhile, challenging, and difficult journey that must be taken a step at a time. We cannot make balance happen, we must allow it to happen!

By definition, balance is a harmonious or satisfying arrangement of proportion of parts or elements. More specifically, for the purposes of this book, balance is a fine-tuned state of existence in which the physical, mental and spiritual elements of man and horse are in harmony with each other.

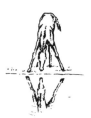

Become aware, and understand what you are aware of. Consider change, make room for change, review the effects of the results, decide if you want the change to remain a part of your life, and enjoy the results.

The following chapters are designed to help you understand my theory of the physical, mental and spiritual characteristics that make up horse and man. Understanding my theory will help make the Resources section more useful. There are many theories. I am sharing the hypothesis that works for me, and it certainly does not need to be the same as yours. You may have your own theory, you may agree with mine, or you may develop another theory while reading this book. What is important is to develop an understanding while maintaining an open mind. Theory is the underlying basis for confidence and security. From time to time, as you pass through the stages in life, you will discover that your life philosophy will undergo changes. Don't be afraid of change, and don't change without following a carefully thought-out procedure. Basic understanding is the first step.

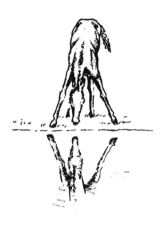

Horse-Physical

The more correct a horse's conformation is, the more easily he can balance himself.

You assess a horse's physical balance by evaluating its conformation. There is a small variation which corresponds to differences in breed types, but correct structure is very basic. Here is a quick summary of standard, sound conformation: a well-proportioned horse will have a balanced body, with about one third each in forehand, middle and hindquarter. It will have a smooth topline, straight legs with a 45 degree angle in front, and a 30 degree angle for pasterns and shoulders. There are many books that will give you specific details for each breed. The more correct the conformation, the more naturally correct will be the horse's physical balance. Correct balance has a direct relationship to the ease with which a horse can be trained.

Another aspect of physical balance is the horse's center of gravity. This changes with use and training. You determine the center of gravity by drawing an imaginary line through the horse's chest, parallel to the ground, and another line through its withers, perpendicular to the ground. The point of intersec-

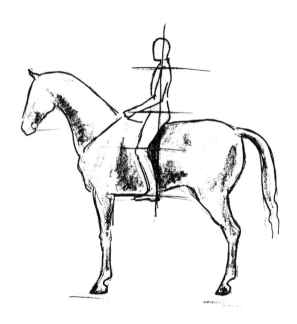

tion of these lines is the horse's center of gravity. The location of this point has considerable influence on how you sit when you ride.

Closely related to the horse's physical build and center of gravity is its gait and way of moving. Almost all horse lovers have observed a horse moving unobstructed through a field. You may have noticed the beauty of the free, flowing movement created by the animal. When he changes direction or comes to a screeching halt, the flow of movement is uninterrupted. This picture is created because the horse is naturally rebalancing himself according to what he is doing: moving, stopping, or turning. His legs are always working as shock absorbers. A "loadline" drawn constantly from his center of gravity always falls inside the rectangle formed by his four feet. The moment this line falls outside this figure, his balance is impaired and he may fall. When the horse is moving unobstructed, his center of gravity is constantly changing, up and down, right and left, or a combination of the two. Man balances himself naturally this way. Now picture a horse with a rider on his back. Even before the horse is backed, the saddle already shifts the horse's center of gravity. The rider further changes the horse's natural balance just by sitting on his back! Any movement of the rider affects the horse's balance. He does not want to fall, so he unconsciously moves his own body to remain in balance with his rider. This enables him to stay on his feet. He does this naturally for his safety. Both horse and rider require extensive training to allow the horse to move freely and correctly with a rider. To make it as easy as possible for the horse to carry the rider, the rider must follow the center of gravity of the horse. To create a beautiful or winning performance, the rider must learn to be flexible, supple, and stay in balance with the horse.

Training and riding a perfectly-built and perfectly-moving horse would be a wonderful experience, but there are few perfect horses in the world. More frequently, we find ourselves dealing with a variety of imperfections. Sometimes the imperfections go to the point where they cause soundness problems, more often they affect only the balance. The more imperfections, the more time training will take. You must consider and take into account the imperfections when you are determining the use of a horse.

Usually an imperfection will not be a problem unless it affects your goals. The first action that you must take is to learn all you can about the specific flaw from a few experts. Once you know the facts, relate them to your goal with your horse. An example: Star Fish had been working very well for Mary as a preliminary jumper. Gradually he started to refuse oxers. Mary eliminated a "rider caused problem" first, because she knew that she had neither changed her riding style nor lost her confidence. This was very strange behavior for Star Fish, so Mary called her vet in to examine him. The veterinary exam showed that Star Fish had degenerative hock problems, making the extra push for the wide oxers painful. The refusals were the result of pain. Mary discussed the vet's diagnosis with her trainer. Together they considered several options. Mary could change her goal from jumper to hunter, or even to lower-level dressage horse, she could sell Star Fish, or she could medicate him and continue. Mary had a difficult time, because she had to make a choice between her love of Star Fish, whom she had owned for twelve years, and her goal of being Grand Prix jumper rider. Mary asked herself, "Can I change my goals and continue with Star Fish, or should I sell Star Fish and continue to pursue my goal?" After many agonizing days of deliberation, Mary decided that she would redirect her goal so she could continue with her beloved friend. Star Fish was fourteen years old, with only about six more years of regular work in him, therefore Mary decided to learn lower-level dressage with him. She did not give up her goal, she just postponed it, and simultaneously she improved her dressage. Mary made her decision out of her love for Star Fish. Her decision gave her a way to continue to ride her friend without hurting him, and it also gave her time to save her money for her next jumper. While Mary postponed her original goal, she was happily looking forward to learning new skills with Star Fish and to being better prepared for her jumper career.

Physical stiffness in a horse can affect its balance. Stiffness can be the result of unsoundness, old age, poor training or heredity. It is essential to know where and why your horse is stiff. You may need the assistance of an experienced veterinarian or trainer to do this. Once you know the problem, you may be able to use exercises while riding or massage while unmounted to help supple the horse. In training, it is important to remember that the balance of a stiff horse will not be the same as that of a supple horse.

Stable management is a physical aspect of horse care that has a close relationship with both the physical and mental well-being of the horse. Some important considerations are regularity of schedule, careful individualized feeding program, regular veterinary, dental and farrier care, well-monitored freedom (pasture), and appropriate cleanliness of body and stall. The absence of proper care will have obvious physical effects; it will also affect the inner tranquility of the horse. Let me take an example from one of the most controversial areas; freedom. Sand Dollar was a flashy mare with superb gaits. Because her owner was afraid that she would hurt herself in the field, Sand Dollar was forced to live in her stall twenty-four hours a day. Each day, Sue, her owner, tried to work her in the ring. Each day there was a constant battle with shying. Six months later, Sue became so frustrated that she sold Sand Dollar. The new owner, who believed in freedom for the horse, took the risk and turned the mare out in pasture. Within two months, Sand Dollar was winning all her classes at the shows. There was no more shying. Freedom in the field had allowed her to release the energy that had been built up from constant confinement. Her mind was more relaxed because she was not constantly on edge every minute of every day. Thus her body felt more in control for her new owner. Sand Dollar's physical situation controlled her mental attitude.

Understanding the physical body and the care necessary for your horse enables you to create a situation that can lead to success. Failure to recognize these needs will put blocks in the way of your progress, ultimately causing both you and your horse discomfort and frustration.

Evaluate the conformation and the balance of your horse. Write it down. Use Questionnaire #1 in your Workbook. Relate it to the riding goal that you have. If you do not know the answers, take the time to learn them.

Evaluate the care received by your horse. This is included in Questionnaire #1 in the Workbook. Write down the important care that he receives and what he is missing. If something needs to be changed, change it. Again, if you do not know the answers, take the time to learn them.

Man-Physical

*We must learn to
accept and love our
physical structure as it is.*

W hile there are few physically perfect horses, we have a choice of what imperfections we are willing to accept. We cannot do this with our own physical structure. We must accept our imperfections and care for our bodies as they are. To prepare ourselves for our journey with horses, we must learn the ideal structure for a rider, recognize our own body's relationship to the ideal, and then take the responsibility of adapting our structure to make it functional. This acceptance and understanding will help us enter a fair partnership with our horse.

The ideally-proportioned human body that enhances balance and control is a slender figure with a medium build. The hip, the base of support, should be low and narrow, allowing the center of gravity to be low. Buttocks should not be too fleshy. According to Suenig " the surplus of flesh that sticks out behind interferes greatly with the pushing forward of the buttocks." [Page 45]. The thigh should be long and flat on the inner surface. The shoulders should sit naturally, not too high, to help the rider maintain a low center of gravity. Arms should be a length that allows them to fall naturally at the side, with the elbow meeting the point of the hip. The arms and upper body should not be too muscular, or they will interfere with the fine tuning that is necessary for the hands. Heavily-muscled arms and upper body also make the rider 'top-heavy'. The spine should be of suitable length. Too long a back will make the center of gravity too high; too short a back will limit the flexibility of the neck and the small of the back, the points of flexibility most necessary for riding. The spine should have a normal curvature. In addition to this basic structure, it is essential that the rider maintain elastic muscles, so that they can stretch and contract easily for communication with the horse.

Go to a mirror and compare your body ratio, weight and height with this model. List what is different in your body from this ideal. See Questionnaire #2 in your Workbook for specific questions. Your riding instructor also should have noted these differences. Once they are identified, your instructor should take these factors into consideration and help you to compensate for them.

Each discipline of riding has an ideal position that corresponds to the task to be performed. This position is designed to promote comfort for the horse and efficiency for the rider. See the AHSA Rulebook for the basic positions of equitation. The basic position is the starting point, and the Rulebook also offers specific adjustments for the various uses of the position within the sport itself. Depending upon your conformation, your position may need to vary slightly from the ideal. A quotation from the master Suenig;

"I should like to quote from an old proverb: 'There is more than one way to run.' Just as classic races are won by thoroughbreds whose configuration is anything but perfect, there are and have been riders who do not meet the canons set forth above in many respects but still have managed to achieve an enviable degree of skill and great success because of fanatical zeal, energy

and passion. On the other hand, I know riders with the figures of an ephebe who barely achieve mediocrity as riders. For they lack the spirit that conquers stubborn matter and makes it serve its purpose!" [Page 47]

Looking at your body's balance and its relationship to the ideal body allows you to set reasonable expectations for your own physical performance on a horse. It is essential to accept your body and its balance. One of the first uses of this book may be to learn to accept and love your body. Too often, people wish that they had a different body. "Change what you can change, accept what you cannot change"—this is the first step that enables you to care for your body properly. Questionnaire #2 asks you questions that will help you to identify what you do not like about your body. You should review this later, after you have read the book, and see what you have learned to accept about your body.

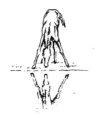

Change what you can change and accept what you cannot change.

Once we love our body as it is, we can accept the responsibility of caring for it. The way we care for our body can influence the image we project to the world. Accepting our structure is necessary, but accepting an inappropriate weight is not necessary or correct. We constantly monitor our horse's weight, but fail to monitor our own. Many riders are insensitive to the weight they make their horses carry.

Weight control is our responsibility, both to our horse and to ourselves. If our weight is too great, it will be very hard for us to carry ourselves with lightness and grace. It is even more difficult for the horse to carry our weight with ease and comfort. If you are overweight, you should look for a weight control program that matches your life style. But being too heavy or large is just one kind of weight problem that can interfere with your riding and with your horse's movement. It is equally incorrect for a rider to be too light and weak. If your muscle development and protection is inadequate, you will be exposing your skeletal structure to unnecessary risk in the case of a fall. Some aspects of horse sports are not particularly inviting to an underweight body because of the increased risk of a fall: polo, roping, foxhunting, driving and eventing are examples. You must have the muscular strength to allow your body to remain balanced on the horse. Properly toned muscles are also necessary for effective communication: muscle tone is the strength referred to by the riding masters.

If you have the proper weight and strength, the next form of responsible body care involves understanding physical stiffness. As years pass, our bodies endure wear and tear, stress, past injuries and unequal joint and muscle use. This can provoke some stiffness. Learn where your stiffnesses are, and do everything possible to reduce them. I suggest massage followed by a carefully-designed exercise program. The massage and exercise program should be planned by a knowledgeable, experienced professional. You need a program that will satisfy your muscular and skeletal deficiencies, but this program must be balanced with the limitations of your time and money. If you spend much of your free time doing exercises or going to professional body workers, you may not have enough time to ride. I will always remember Mary. Mary's leisure time was spent showing her hunter. Mary had a very stressful job, and often felt as though she were tied up in knots. Her instructor told her that this muscle tightness in her back was causing her lovely mare to stop. They decided that Mary should begin massage so that she would interfere less with her mare, and so that they could perform better as a team. A greedy professional therapist told her that she needed his services three times a week. Mary's life only allowed her to ride five times a week, so with the additional driving time and time spent with the professional, Mary could ride only two days a week. Her physical stiffness was replaced by frustration, because she was losing her practice time. New problems developed. Bill, on the other hand, went to a therapist recommended by his trainer. They had a few intense initial sessions, after which the therapist planned a maintainance program that matched Bill's limited time schedule. You must balance your physical needs against the limits of your time and money. To determine this balance, you must know your needs, your goals and yourself! Read on to learn more about you . . .

There are some riders who cannot eliminate their stiffnesses for one reason or another. This does not mean that they cannot learn to ride. It is essential to discover and understand the boundary of your physical limitations. Do not accept the opinion of one person only, but ask several qualified individuals. Evaluate the various opinions, and draw your own conclusions based on what feels right to you. If your physical limitations interfere with your goal, you can change your goal. There are many ways to enjoy horses. However, there are only a few physical problems that truly require a change of goals. More often, the permanently stiff individual can perform in the sport of his choice—if he can accept the fact that he may not be able to reach the highest level of the discipline.

The tools that are expressed in Resources will help you to learn about yourself and accept your limitations. The lists recommended in your Workbook will be beneficial to the balancing work you will do as you read this book.

Horse-Mental

Horses react and respond,
they do not analyze
and calculate.

The mental simplicity of a horse is refreshing. Horses react and respond, they do not analyze and calculate. Their sensory area of the brain occupies more space than a man's, while a man's cortex occupies the larger percentage of space. Therefore a horse's mind receives its primary stimulus from the senses, while man's mind receives stimulus through the senses and then processes them through his highly refined brain. So as to help you better understand a horse, I would like to take a deeper look at the following mental characteristics: leadership, control, routine, social interaction, sensory perception, emotions, intelligence, patience and expectations.

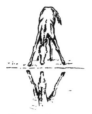

A horse's mind receives its primary stimulus from his senses, while man's mind processes the stimulus. This is why horses are more truly in the 'now'.

Leadership

Most horses willingly submit to man's domination. The horse needs to be cared for, and he needs leadership. History reveals that horses have survived in herds, with the most dominant individual in charge of the entire herd. The leader decided where and when the entire herd ate and drank. Survival is directly related to the horse's willingness to follow his herd leader. For the domesticated horse, man has taken the place of the herd leader.

With domestication, the horse began to look to man for direction and security. If he is provided a safe, clean shelter with food and a regular schedule, the horse will view man with submission and trust. Unfortunately, man tends to forget the difference between his needs and the needs of the horse. Man often wants to inflict his pleasures, ideals and will on a horse, forgetting that a horse's needs are simple and very different from man's. The horse is not ambitious or adventurous; he is satisfied by kind, consistent and routine care that maintains his comfort.

Control

Horses have their own need to control. If you have ever watched horses in a field, there is a pecking order from the leader to the meekest. It is often the meekest who will try to be aggressive with humans. However, if the human offers consistent, kind discipline, even the meekest horse will respond.

Man frequently wants to exhibit his power by using strong, physical control on the horse. Even the strongest, largest of horses is willing to submit and cooperate without force. Control can be enforced with much more ease than most men understand. A perfect example is often the perceived difficulty of handling stallions. People feel they must dominate this animal, but the same principles apply to a stallion as to any other horse. This highly sensitive creature must be handled with consistent discipline, but must not be jerked around. A good example is Timberlane. He was owned by a man who dominated him with aggression. You would see Timberlane being led with constant jerks of the chain over his nose, a loud aggressive voice and tough/rough attitude. The stallion was always nervous and uneasy. Finally Timberlane was sold to a small woman who weighed no more than 120 lbs. With her kind, consistent discipline and her love of horses, she was soon shipping him with mares, showing him and handling him for breeding. Instead of exhibiting a controlling nature, man should accept his leadership role by demonstrating kind, compassionate, definite control.

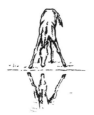

Instead of exhibiting a controlling nature, man should accept his leadership role by demonstrating kind, compassionate, definite control.

Routine

The security of a horse is directly related to his needs for regimentation, regularity and consistency. Years ago I raised horses in my back yard. The pasture was occupied by a thoroughbred stallion, Count, and three mares, Duchess, Proxi, and Loppy. Count bred the mares and supervised them during pregnancy. When foaling time arrived, he separated the foaling mare and walked a circle around her until the foal was born. The other mares respected this. Once all the mares had foaled, Count took the foals on an excursion to another part of the pasture, allowing the mares freedom. The mares made no effort to protect the foals from Count. This procedure was followed every day at the same time. To me, this was a powerful demonstration of the importance of routine in a horse's life. If the horse can trust these factors in his care-taker and rider, he will be more receptive to and retentive of your training.

The security of a horse is directly related to his needs for regimentation, regularity and consistency.

Social Interaction

Most horses do not look to man for social interaction. They look first to other horses, but will adapt to other animals such as cat, goat, donkey or dog. A healthy horse needs a companion. Horses are so adaptable that I have seen them accept the sole company of humans, but they seldom show the same spark and vitality that is exhibited by a horse with horse companionship. Buster is a perfect example of the herd socialization instinct that exists in horses. Buster, twenty-two, has been retired from the show ring where he successfully showed for many years. Once an injury forced him to live out in the field for some time. We turned him out with three mares. When his injury healed and we brought him back into the stable, this twenty-two-year-old's screaming gave everyone a headache. He was trying to communicate with his mares. In only two weeks, he had become the leader of the herd of mares in that field. In all the other years of turnout with the other school horse geldings, he had been just one of the group, not the leader. The power of his role in the social interaction was evident.

Sensory Perception

The horse's mental equilibrium is greatly affected by his sensory perception, while human's is not. A horses's brain has a smaller cortex and a larger sensory area; thus his senses (smell, taste, sight, hearing and touch) are more highly developed than those same senses in man.

Smell/Taste

Almost every horse owner has experienced, at one time or another, a horse not eating his wormer. Most of us have put a wormer powder in the horse's morning feed, and come back in the evening only to discover that the feed has disappeared—but that the wormer powder is still there. The horse's keen sense of smell and taste enables him to detect the foreign matter in his feed. When he detects the foreign substance, he has three choices: eat it, separate it or not eat at all. His choice will be influenced by the degree of hunger at the time he was fed, but also by the traits of his character. The horse who will not eat his wormer is often very selective about all food intake. A selective eater who is not hungry, will seldom eat any food harmful to himself. On the other hand, a horse who is not selective may eat poor-quality feed, poisonous weeds, or foreign objects. This sort of horse must be protected from harming himself, and thus places a greater burden on his care-taker. The horse's highly developed sense of smell also warns him of danger from predators and fire. His sense of smell helps him locate food and water. What he smells in his environment, combined with his character, can affect his actions and reactions under saddle.

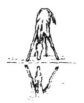

The horse's mental equilibrium is greatly affected by his sensory perception, while man's is not.

Sight

Horses' eyes see things very differently than humans'. Their sight, like their sense of smell, has evolved over the years to promote their survival. While grazing, a horse can see almost an entire circle around him; however, it is very difficult for him to focus on a single object. In contrast, man cannot see around himself in this way, but finds it very easy to focus on a single object. Objects often appear quite different to a horse than to man, because the horse's brain does not register visual stimuli in the same way as man's does. Keep in mind, also, that your horse may not see everything perfectly accurately even according to horse standards. We tend to assume that a horse can see perfectly, unless we see visible scarring in the eye, or unless we know or have been told that an individual horse is blind. But consider how many humans have less-than-perfect eyesight, and must wear glasses or contact lenses to correct or compensate for it. Not all horses have perfect eyesight either, but it is difficult to diagnose specific imperfections in a horse's vision, because a horse cannot undergo a human-style eye examination. While we cannot see things as our horse sees them, we need to be aware of the way in which a horse sees. If we understand how a horse sees, we can understand the fears created by what he sees.

When a horse acts fearful, it is important to reassure him even if you do not know the cause of the fear. Remember, the horse looks to man for leadership. Your calm, certain leadership can help him overcome his fear. Sometimes fear is caused by a previous experience that was so intense that it may take a very long time for the rider or handler to reassure the horse. If you also become tense or fearful, you will reinforce his fear. It is up to you to learn what frightens the horse. This observation will often tell you how he sees. Your training techniques can employ methods to reassure a horse that is nervous because of his poor vision. A young woman once came for a lesson in second level dressage. After the lesson she told me that her horse was totally blind. I was astounded; I would never have guessed. This horse had developed periodic ophthalmia and had gradually lost his sight. But the young woman loved her horse, and because of their sensitive mutual communication, she was able to continue with him. She not only rode him on the trail, she also shipped him to shows and lessons. I think that this horse and rider are a perfect example of the trust that can be developed between horse and man with patience and understanding. This was a happy, well-adjusted horse! Unfortunately, I have more frequently seen the opposite. More typically, I see a shying horse, who most obviously has a hearing or sight problem, whose rider is CERTAIN the horse is deliberately disobeying him. Even when I get on and reassure the rider by showing him that his horse does not need to shy, the rider still believes that the shying is a deliberate disobedience, and so continues to use inappropriate, abusive punishment on the poor animal.

Hearing

A horse's hearing is highly tuned, more like a dog's than a man's. A horse, like a dog, is able to hear higher frequencies than we can. This highly developed hearing originally helped to protect the horse from predators, but it now often causes a horse to become nervous. Loud music and yelling in the stable is very unsettling to a horse, especially if it is not a regularly-heard sound. As in most other areas of a horse's make-up, he can become conditioned to noise. Once conditioned, he will have less negative reaction to the noise. A perfect example was our move to our new farm, "Hilltop." Construction was in progress: large equipment, electric saws, hammers, and eighteen-wheelers constantly caused much noise. When the horses first arrived, they were very worried and restless. We had more riders on the ground from bucking than ever before. However, after one month of exposure, they began to accept the noise and were no longer bothered by it. Now, imagine that you are going to a competition next to a construction site, and that this is the first time your horse has been exposed to this type of noise. Can you expect a change in his behavior? And what if you must travel on a busy highway loaded with tractor-trailers? The tone of voice used in the horse's zone also affects his behavior:

your tone of voice can create energy, or it can soothe a nervous horse. When you go to a competition, one factor that affects your horse is the loudspeaker. Its echo, frequency and static are upsetting sounds to the horse. This is one reason why many horses need "mileage" before they can be expected to perform as reliably and calmly at a show as they do at home.

Tactile Sense

Perhaps the greatest of all differences between horse and man is the horse's tactile sense. Yet this is the sense most conducive to the development of communication between the two. For a horse's protection and survival, the sense of touch through his frog permits the horse to feel vibrations in the ground from far away. The sense of feel through the skin enables him to rid himself of pesky flies and mosquitos by vibrating his highly-sensitive and refined surface muscles. Before these muscles twitch away the unfriendly invader, the horse can feel even the slightest tickle on his skin. This sensitivity must be foremost in the mind of the rider and handler. Is the sensitive horse experiencing reward or punishment from your actions? Often I have witnessed a trainer give a horse a powerful slap on the neck as a supposed reward. I always ask myself, who is getting the reward, the horse or the man? Too often, it is man seeking the applause of his audience. Of course, the horse can become conditioned to accept this powerful slap, but it is definitely not a reward. It is painful to a sense of touch so delicate it can twitch away a fly from his skin.

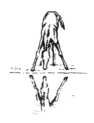

Most actions and reactions of a horse are based on the stimuli given him by his senses. These are directly related to his survival and comfort. It is essential to understand the horse's sensory perception to understand the horse.

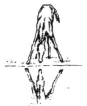 *The horse's mind registers primarily in the 'now' time period. Most information is not processed or stored.*

In contrast to the highly developed sensitivity of the horse's sight, hearing, smell, taste, and touch, the horse's other mental characteristics are simple and uncomplicated. The horse's mind registers primarily the "now" time period. Most information is not processed or stored. This enables the horse to forgive and forget with ease. He can react to the rider's stimuli of the moment, not remembering the details of the past, even such a very recent past as five minutes before. However, if he has had an experience of extreme fear or pain, he can react again to the fear induced by repetition of the previous stimuli. When the animal has any powerful experience, negative or positive, all the senses register a response in the unconscious. When any of these stimuli recur, the pain or excitement associated with the experience may be activated. The same result can be created by repeated abusive or poor training. Although the detail causing the original fear is no longer present, an unconscious mechanism starts to offer protection to the horse. Sam had a horse named Seaweed who trembled violently when he was on the trailer, and scrambled up the walls once the trailer was moving. Sam knew that Seaweed had an experience that went beyond the limits of his pain and fear threshold. Nothing that Sam tried enabled Seaweed to forget his fear, because there is no way to reason with Seaweed. The fearful trailer experience is permanently a part of Seaweed's life experiences. Since the trailer stimulates the fear, his behavior will show the effects. So as to safely trailer Seaweed and maintain his mental equilibrium for competition, Sam had experimented with ways to transport Seaweed. Ultimately he discovered that a double stall would keep the horse comfortable. In handling and training horses, you must use your ability to think. Always analyze and understand, so as to avoid at all costs a situation that may impair your horse's mind.

Emotions

The basic emotions of fear, anger, joy, and surprise are the same for most animals, including man. However, man's emotions are far more complex than a horse's. Emotions are an intense experience that communicates feelings to other beings. Emotions are automatic and involuntary — these characteristics are what distinguishes emotions from thinking and reasoning.

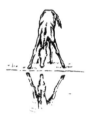

The basic emotions of fear, anger, joy, and surprise are the same for most animals, including man.

Unlike man, horses are free of the deep emotional conflicts that can generate negative behavior. In all my years of horse care-taking, the closest thing to emotional conflict I have witnessed was between Beau and Proxi. It is a strange tale of two elderly horses in our school horse program. Proxi, a thirty-year-old mare, and Beau, an eighteen-year-old gelding, lived with all the other school horses. There were six geldings and one mare, Proxi. Proxi definitely belonged to Beau, as far as Beau was concerned. However, Proxi was a flirt and constantly sought male attention. Thus she hurt Beau's feelings. When they came into the stable each morning to eat, she would sneak into the stallion section and sniff the stallions, who would immediately begin to whinny in response to her. Beau's reaction was to give a quiet whinny, after which he would stand in his stall with his head hanging in the corner. However, once his food appeared he forgot his feelings of rejection. When Proxi returned to her stall next to his, they reunited with pleasure and it appeared that he held no jealousy from her morning flirtation. The morning flirtation seems quietly dismissed, with no resentment or lingering worries! What would happen in a human relationship with such behavior?

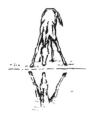

Horses are educated to different levels, thus they must be able to gain knowledge. There are varied levels of intelligence in horses, but the highest level for a horse is well below normal for humans.

Intelligence

Intelligence is difficult to define in man; it is almost impossible to define in a horse. David Wechsler, a psychologist who developed the WAIS-R and WISC-R Intelligence Tests, defines intelligence as the ability to understand the world and cope with the challenge of environment. Horses could not meet those criteria. The American Heritage Dictionary defines intelligence as the capacity to find and apply knowledge. Can a horse acquire knowledge? According to the dictionary, knowledge is "understanding gained through experience or study." Clearly a horse cannot study as we comprehend study, but he can gain understanding through experience. We all know that there are horses educated to different levels, thus they must be able to gain knowledge. There are varied levels of intelligence in horses, but the highest level for a horse is well below normal for a human. Mental activity stops in a horse when the experience stops. One Arabian-Thoroughbred cross learned to open his stall door by trial and error (he had to stay in stall for nine months due to an injury). He experimented with his sliding door until he learned that the door would open if he turned the nuts on the upper rollers. I thought it was an accident, but it was not, because he never forgot how to do it. I had to change the type of door! Another argument for some level of intelligence is a stallion who could untie a slip knot in seconds. While I cleaned his stall he was able to untie himself as fast as I could remove one shovel full of manure. Despite my attempts to fool him with changes in the knot, he was able to release it. I am certain no one taught this show jumping stallion a trick; he must have learned it himself.

A life experience can be good or bad. If it is really bad in a horse it remains bad, while man can process a bad experience, often turning it into valuable knowledge. Man has the ability to view a situation or experience from a variety of perspectives using his highly developed mind. A horse's simple mind can only process what is involved in the experience itself. Thus it is important to provide the horse with as many positive experiences as possible. The way in which the horse internalizes his encounters is very important: he relates his experiences to his comfort and his survival needs. There is no ability to analyze or evaluate, so a horse's knowledge relates directly to what he encounters. The information retained is a result of the intermingling of his nature, the experience itself, and the amount of repetition.

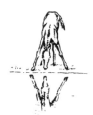

Man can process information and use it any way he wishes. Horses, lacking the ability to process information, must remain with the circumstances of the experience.

In the mind of a horse, positive reinforcement through repetition is essential in accumulating knowledge. You should never end a training session after a bad experience. If your training session has been a disaster from the beginning, you must still find a way to end it on a positive note. You must be sure that the last thing the horse does before the session ends is something that he does well, even if this means simply halting square and then standing quietly on a loose rein. Consistent repetition with positive reinforcement leads to positive learning. Consistent repetition or harsh, painful experiences can lead to negative learning. This basic conditioning applies to both horse and man. When a rider falls, unless he is seriously hurt, he must immediately remount the horse. This prevents the frightening part of the experience from remaining in his unconscious. Trainers and handlers do not want a bad experience to be trained into a horse, so the repetition must be positive. The number of repetitions necessary for learning is different for each horse. Once accepted and understood for a period of time, the information becomes "knowledge." It is up to the trainer to 'know' each horse so that the repetitions are sufficient to produce learning without boredom and subsequent loss of willingness. Not enough repetitions may cause the rider to have inappropriate expectations from a confused horse.

Patience

Standing on the cross ties for an hour while the owner carefully cleans the straw from his tail, polishes his feet and rubs his body, is a clear demonstration of the infinite patience of most horses. If a horse had a choice he would prefer to spend most of his time free or cleaning himself naturally, which is rolling and making himself dirty by our standards.

One example of patience impressed me so much that it still sticks out in my mind ten years later. I was visiting a stable, teaching. I entered the ring at 9:00 a.m to teach a lesson, and saw a young woman warming up her thoroughbred gelding. This very attractive, lightly-built gelding was carrying an overweight rider of two hundred pounds. Forty-five minutes later, I finished my first lesson and began my second lesson. By now the overweight owner and the willing thoroughbred were doing flying changes. I finished my second lesson and began teaching my third lesson. The overweight rider and her thoroughbred were still in the arena, and by this time she had been riding him for at least one and a half hours. By the time my third lesson was over, the two were still doing flying changes. He was lathered; she was all smiles. I had to leave the ring because I could not stand to see any more of this. More than two hours had passed, and the horse was still being worked hard. My private reaction was, "She should be glad I am not her horse, I would be ...." Later, at lunch, I asked the stable owner about the pair and was told that this was the way the woman typically rode her horse. She would ride him five days a week, usually for three or four hours each day! The stable owner went on to say that she had approached the rider about this, and that the rider had agreed to limit her riding time. But it never happened; apparently she had no awareness of time. This patient horse willingly works day after day for this owner. Patience and good will allow the horse to cooperate, but I feel certain that his body will not last as long as his mind. Clearly, this is a case where the quality of patience allowed the horse to be abused. On the other hand, this quality of patience is what allows us to make mistakes, recognize our mistakes, and try something else. The patience of a horse must not be abused. We are alerted if we continue to make the same errors because the horse will not give us the expected results. Instead of repeating the aids, we must ask ourselves if we are causing confusion by an incorrect position, or by using confusing or clashing aids. After a quick review, we must try something else. We can continue to try various changes until we get the desired answer. If after various unsuccessful corrections we do not get the desired result, we should seek some help. While the horse's patient and tolerant nature allows us to use repetition as a teaching tool, we have an obligation to use it fairly and wisely.

Expectations

Does your horse shy in the corner and expect you to kick him with your inside leg, or expect you to get upset? Of course not, unless you have taught him to do this by constant repetition. What does he expect? When he hears the feed door open at feeding time, he expects to be fed. When he walks into the ring, he expects to work. For those who like to pick up the reins and trot immediately, he will soon trot or jig each time the reins are shortened. His expectations are related to a pattern in life that we have helped him to become accustomed to by providing him with repetition. His expectations are specific, and reflect what he has learned through repetition and association. One equine foxhunter, who loved to hunt, would get diarrhea when he was braided for the day's hunt. His nervous system was stimulated by his expectations about the running and jumping to come. It took him two months of running and jumping twice weekly in the hunt field to develop this reflex. Interestingly, his diarrhea returned on the opening meet of the fall season, although he had not been braided or taken in the trailer for six months. This is an example of a conditioned reflex. The horse's expectations depends upon his temperament, the activity and the experience itself.

We cannot expect our horse to understand our expectations, but we must learn to understand his. Observe your horse's reactions during one day. What causes him to show emotions? His ears, eyes, tail, and general behavior express his feelings. What causes his ears to be more alert, pawing, banging on his door, balkiness, or nervousness? These behaviors will tell you about your horse's character and his expectations. A key point to remember is that most horses are not at all manipulative; their behavior simply shows the results of previous conditioning. One of the few things that upsets a horse is interference with his feeding schedule. Many behavior problems and illnesses are associated with changes in the intricate balance of his digestive system, which is affected by his expectations related to food. Remain alert, observe, and learn what your horses's expectations are: you will be better able to help him become a happy and relaxed horse.

We cannot expect our horse to understand our expectations, but we must learn to understand his.

Horses, like people, can develop behaviors that are connected to imbalances that go undetected. Vices usually develop from boredom or nervousness that is caused by an unobservant owner or caretaker. For horses, just as for people, there is a fine balance between the character and environmental conditions. If the care-taker does not know and understand the needs of the individual horse, or if he allows the horse to be in contact with a horse who has a vice, a horse can develop what will ultimately be an irreversible vice such as weaving, cribbing, wind-sucking or stall-walking.

We have a highly refined brain, while a horse has highly refined senses. Our mind allows us to use various learning methods to process more information and move toward gaining knowledge, while a horse is limited to learning by repetition, association, and trial and error. Because the horse lives in the moment, he is usually more patient than man. Both horse and man seem to share a varied level of leadership and socialization depending upon their individual needs. When we compare these mental factors, it seems reasonable to think that we could learn from our horse how to use more of our senses. We use our mind automatically, but if we could simplify our mental perceptions and use more of our natural senses, perhaps we could find them more effective. Our mind can enable us to be more or less understanding depending upon our development. I feel that horse lovers should look toward a horse for ideas and examples of how to regain the simple basic qualities of life. This balance may reduce our life complications to more manageable situations. A horse only expects the basics, anything beyond the basics is a gift. Man tends to create expectations that cause him hardship.

It is a good idea to list the characteristics of your horse. Go to Questionnaire #3 in your Workbook, which will help you to evaluate your horse's character.

Man-Mental

Horsemen have the responsibility to strive for mental equilibrium.

There are many theories and fields of study that offer explanations for man's complex mental make-up. Psychologists, neurologists, philosophers, biologists, sociologists—each expert in each discipline can provide you with a different hypothesis. I have formulated my own view, based on my reading, my experiences, and my observations of interactions between man and horse.

Man is considered a superior creature because of his brain that houses the mind, the mental operating system. Our mind is far more capable of solving complex problems, reflecting and sorting facts than the mind of any other animal. Our mental ability allows us to create and process thoughts. We can direct our thought process through our conscious mind, or we can let our mind wander freely. We also can direct our mind to experience the 'now'. Most people find it easier to control thoughts than to let themselves freely experience the moment, like a horse. Our mind can be a fascinating and useful instrument in all of our endeavors; whether past, present (the 'now') or future. The better we understand it, develop it, discipline it, learn to give it freedom and learn to use it, the more our body and spirit can be included in creating better total balance. Our mind is the control center of all of our life functions, physical, mental and spiritual.

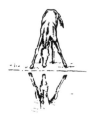

The better we understand our mind, develop it, discipline it, learn to give it freedom, and learn to use it, the more our body and spirit can be included in creating better total balance.

The Layers Of Our Mind

Our conscious mind simplifies and selects the information we receive. Our consciousness frequently oversees and guides our actions and thoughts. While consciousness, the first layer of our mind, is on the surface of the mind, the mind has other layers of awareness that we should learn how to access. Each plays a valuable part in our balance.

The second layer of our mind is the subconscious awareness. Walking is an example of the subconscious in action. While we are walking, we are automatically aware of what is under our feet, although we are not thinking about where we are putting our feet. Successful riding must be trained into our SUB-CONSCIOUS level of awareness so that the rider can act without thought. Mounting a horse becomes a subconscious act shortly after you learn to mount. The Knowledge chapter in Resources explains this in more detail.

The third level of our mind's mental awareness is the preconscious memories. This is the area of stored knowledge that allows us to perform the tasks we know. For example, a dressage rider must learn 'how to' do a shoulder-in. The aids are learned through the cognitive domain of the conscious mind and then stored in the preconscious mind, to be used when we wish, even years later. Some years ago I saw a wonderful illustration of this phenomenon during a jumping lesson. A woman who had not jumped for fifteen years came to me to get reinvolved correctly with her riding. Her children were grown and she wanted to foxhunt again. She was amazed that after fifteen years off, her timing was still perfect—even over the very first jump!

The fourth level of our mind is the nonconscious processes. This involves our basic body functions such as breathing and the beating of our heart. If there is a problem, the nonconscious mind and the conscious mind automatically interact, bringing the information to the conscious mind so that we can take action. While this has little to do with riding, it is the information that calls our attention to our body needs.

Last but not least is our unconscious. According to Sigmund Freud, this is where we normally hide our difficult and unresolved situations in life. Although we are unaware of these stored thoughts and feelings, our conscious mind relaxes its control while we sleep, permitting our dreams to reflect the thoughts that are stored in our unconscious. Studies have shown that meditation can allow stored thoughts and experiences to be revealed. Robert Ornstein, in *Psychology, The Study of Human Experience* gives an explanation appropriate to the subject of this book,

> "Freud also compared personality to a horse and rider. The horse is like the unconscious: it has a 'mind of its own,' but seemingly submits to the direction of the rider, the conscious. But sometimes the horse takes the bit between his teeth and goes off in the direction it pleases. The rider may try to control the horse, but if unable to, he or she may try to rationalize the event, for example, by saying 'I really meant to go that way in the first place.' Alternatively, the rider may unconsciously alter his or her understanding of what happened."

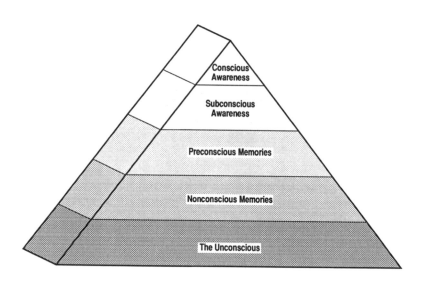

It is our conscious mind that we normally use. This part of our mind is what we tap for all our thinking, our learning and some of our reactions. Our unconscious mind houses the perceptions that accompany an experience through sight, hearing, smell, touch, and taste. During a dream or meditation you may smell, taste, hear, see or feel something totally unpredictable. Whatever this may be, it is likely to be associated with the stored experience. It is the intricate interaction of these two parts of our mind that enables us to function as individuals. Seeking to understand and develop our mind will provide us with a framework to balance our mind and spirit. Since our mind is the nucleus of our being, we can learn to use this instrument to help align our body and spirit. We can learn to access the different levels of our mind to become a more balanced person, and to enable ourselves to use more of our mind to help us attain our goals.

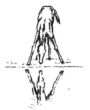

We use our conscious mind to think,
to learn and for some of our reactions. Our
unconscious mind houses
our perceptions, which include all
of our other senses.

Horse and man perceive things very differently. A horse's perception is simpler than ours. The signals that contribute to our perception come together in our brain and are sorted and evaluated in terms of our environment, our culture, our knowledge, our experiences, our genes, our chemical balance and the tuning of each set of receptors. A horse shares these but does not have the complex mental perceptions and memory that makes humans unique. If we can simplify our mental functions to the level of a horse and then add our human fine-tuning, we can have the best of both worlds. The horse's mental interpretations are for survival and social concerns; ours must also take into account consider social, economic, psychological, philosophical and religious influences. Let us review the arrival at a show through the perceptions of Tina and Flying High, both seasoned competitors. Flying High is alert and aware of the new sounds from the loudspeaker and the voices of all the people at the show. He feels the changes in vibrations of the ground, smells the fumes from the nearby highway, and sees all the activity of horses, trailers and people. After a short time on the show grounds, he munches his hay and continues to observe with more alertness than he had at home. Tina, on the other hand, had been up late the night before and had left without her normal hours of preparation. She felt anxious because she might not have everything as clean and sparkling as usual. As she drove onto the grounds, she was surprised to see all the large, expensive, matching vans and trailers. Tina thought that this might mean that there could be too much competition for her at this show, and the thought made her feel anxious. As she took Flying High off the trailer she noted that he had gotten his bandages all dirty, and she worried about what the neighboring competitors might think about her dirty equipment. When she saw the rings, she wondered what effect the hard, dry footing was going to have on her performance. Nothing seemed to be what she had hoped for, nothing about the show was what she had expected. As her concern rose she began to have flashbacks to the argument she had had with her family about missing church and the family picnic in the afternoon. Was it all worth it? These worries, plus many more mental interferences, can influence each of us during any ride. It would have helped Tina if she had taken a few minutes to watch her horse, and see how quickly Flying High had adjusted to the new conditions. Why did he? How did he? What benefit could Tina derive from all of her worried thoughts? She could have learned a lot from her horse, whose mind was only on the conditions of the show at that moment. I contend that we can all learn to master the art of the 'now'.

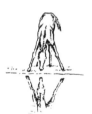 *If we can simplify our mental functions to the level of a horse and then add our human fine-tuning, we can have the best of both worlds and even learn to enjoy the NOW.*

One mental problem that man inflicts upon himself is the desire for power. Man is power hungry. When life situations put us in the position of leadership, we must learn to control with kindness, compassion and humility. Most people have a need to control something or someone. This is not a problem in itself; the world needs controllers. But some people are addicted to control. And it is all too easy to use our controlling nature on the horse. A good equestrian will practice passive control, not aggressive control. This is very important because a horse is a very submissive creature, and harsh, rough control is painful and frightening to a horse. As we seek to balance ourselves, we must always be careful to restrain our controlling nature and practice quiet, loving control.

People need companionship just as horses do, but companionship is often difficult to find. One reason that people have pets or companion animals, which can include a horse, is loneliness. Loneliness is one of the most common problems that people encounter. While a horse can often find companionship in another creature, society demands that humans should be compatible with other humans. This is often a difficult task because of miscommunications, misinterpretations and misunderstandings that do not plague the animal world. These are often a result of interactions that have ended negatively or have been misperceived. If a negative feeling, impression or experience is not dealt with, it can fester into a mental sore that can influence any part of our life. The experience itself may be over, but the protective forces are locked into our unconscious, ready and able to haunt us when triggered by any of the associated stimuli. The complications created by our mind and individuality make true human compatibility a rare and wonderful luxury. Whether they admit it or not, many people retreat to horses, dogs or cats to fill the social void in their lives. It is interesting to note, however, that social interaction in some form is necessary for both creatures, horse and man!

The reward and punishment system of reinforcement is a method of learning common to both horse and man. There are two kinds of reinforcement; positive and negative. Positive reinforcement, a pleasant response from the asker for the answer given by the receiver, is likely to produce an action that will be repeated. Negative reinforcement occurs when an action results in an unpleasant consequence. Punishment or negative reinforcement decreases the likelihood that the action will be repeated.

We learn, just as animals do, through reward and punishment. The difference is that a simple pat will reward a horse, while a human can take a simple pat and turn it around in the mind to make it into a complicated issue. This is done by denying either the punishment or the reward. Let me use the example of Bea. Bea had a difficult time accepting compliments. It was so difficult for her to believe that she was good that she could not even respond while on her horse. If I told her that she made a good correction in her position, she would frown in disbelief. Finally, in total frustration, I began to compliment her horse instead, telling Bea that her horse had responded well to her action. This pleased her, and eventually she was able to pat the horse — but what she really needed was to be able to pat herself! Bea's background was such that her mind would not allow her to accept praise. If she could have let herself think like her horse, she would have believed that my compliment was genuine. Punishment for humans can also be misinterpreted. Often the speaker's tone of voice can act as a punishment, because people turn even the best intended criticism into a punishment far more severe than intended. Since criticism is considered a mild form of punishment, meaning lack of reward, it must be taken constructively. Read on for more information about this in the Resources section, under Knowledge.

Our actions are not as controlled by our senses as the horse's actions are. During evolution, our brain developed to expand our cognitive and reasoning ability's role and reduce the role of our other senses, unlike the rest of the animal kingdom. Man no longer uses his senses to survive. The role of our senses has truly been reduced, perhaps because of our highly-civilized lifestyle, or perhaps just because of our infrequent use of our sensory perception. But each of us can expand the use of our senses on an individual basis. Every day, we have the opportunity to observe and learn how to rejuvenate our senses by observing the behavior, actions, and responses of our horses. How often do you remember an experience by what you saw, heard, smelled, or felt? I was forty-four before I had such an experience. It is a vivid memory. A close friend courageously told me that I spent so much time in the future that I was missing the 'now'. I was in the process of learning relaxation, a form of meditation. We went to a park, and I went into relaxation. While I was in the state of emptiness, he began to describe the beauty of the blossoming trees that surrounded us, the fragrant sweet smell that accompanied the freshly opened blossoms, the quiet wind that made the leaves offer a soft hum, and the feeling of nature's total calm on that day. I began to become one with this tranquil setting. That experience sparked in me the idea to begin to observe the horses more closely. Observing their response to their environment took me one step further in my sensory development and awareness. Now, each time I recognize that I am being controlled by my workaholic state, I stop myself and enjoy the beauty of the moment with more than my cognitive mind. Being in the 'now' has allowed my love for what I do to become more highly developed. For instance, when I am teaching I experience much more than just the satisfaction of seeing a movement performed correctly; I can become enchanted by the beauty of the performance of a horse and rider. Enjoying the 'now' has also given me more tools to help my students get quicker and more lasting results. All my senses are more involved. I will always be thankful for my friend's confrontation, and for the lesson on how to enjoy the 'now'. It is difficult for human beings to absorb the 'now,' because we have so many interferences in our lives. However, observing the horse gives us a daily reminder of the value of allowing some time to be in the 'now'. For the horse, it is part of natural daily existence; for us, tapping our senses allows us to absorb the beauty that surrounds us.

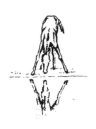

Observing the horse gives us a
daily reminder of the value of allowing some
time to be in the 'now.' For the horse, it is
part of natural daily existence; for us,
tapping our senses allows us
to absorb more aspects of the beauty
or experiences of life.

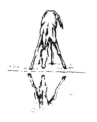

A troublesome thought can be deconstructed, evaluated and examined, and then reconstructed. This will give you a clearer view of the problem.

For centuries, equestrians have recognized the importance of the role of their own mental equilibrium to their ability to relate effectively with horses. "Mental equilibrium" suggests the act of balancing our emotions, reactions, and thoughts. How do we balance them? Once we accept our complexity we can break it down, or deconstruct it, into a more simple form. My broadest breakdown is into body, mind and spirit. My second breakdown is the specific areas within each of these sections. The physical section includes body structure and care of the physical plant. The mental section includes leadership, control, routine, social interaction, intelligence, patience, and expectations. The spiritual section includes love, energy, and attitude. Once we deconstruct, we can determine which areas are those we understand least, and we can then set out to learn as much as possible about those areas. We need not stop and study, we must just open our mind with an investigative curiosity. This will help us to become more observant and relate what we read, experience, and feel to what we are trying to understand. After this deconstruction comes reconstruction. When you have a few moments for reflection, combine what you are learning through the life experience itself with what you already think. This process of analyzing information is called reconstruction, and is unique to humans. Reconstruction provides us with new information about ourselves. This process will help to balance our mental equilibrium and allow us to experience more effective riding and communication. The more we "know" and understand ourselves, the more we understand what is needed for effective communication with our horse.

As we balance our mind, we will eliminate the 'road blocks' that can slow down our feeling and reaction time. The tools in the Resources section will help you in dissecting your complexities. To examine your thoughts, go to Questionnaire #4 in your Workbook. It will give you practice with deconstruction, examination, and reconstruction.

We are like horses in that our emotions influence our actions. Unlike horse emotions, however, human emotions can be very complex. Some people control their emotions; others have little emotional control; still others have their emotions all mixed up. To understand your emotions, you must analyze your actions and uncover the reasons for them. Once you do this inner searching, you will be better able to evaluate the appropriateness of your emotional reaction. The evaluation always takes place after the fact, because emotions are spontaneous. They immediately communicate our feelings through our reactions. Unlike a horse, we can hide our emotions or have mixed-up emotions. If a teenager laughs when her horse dies, it requires a serious look at her emotions and reactions. If another woman does not cry at all when her horse dies, she too must examine her reactions. Or, if a horse is sold and the young owner cries and does not eat for two weeks, there is also a problem requiring examination. These are extreme examples. If an emotion is not appropriate, the resulting feelings may be out of balance and the conscious mind should start a process to understand why. Emotions must be in balance because they arouse us, help us organize an experience, direct and sustain our actions, and ultimately express our actions.

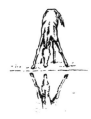

Emotions must be in balance because they arouse us, help us organize an experience, direct and sustain our actions, and ultimately express our actions.

Our emotions have a major effect on our mood. If we get on our horse when we are angry, the horse will feel our mood. When we are angry, we are likely to take his actions incorrectly and assume he is angry. We could find ourselves being unfair and harsh. We must be able to recognize our mood and control it. If we do not recognize it, or if we do recognize it but fail to control it, we allow it to control us. However, by using deconstruction, examination and reconstruction we can usually control or alter our mood.

Other attributes we share with the horse are intelligence, patience and expectations, but, again, these attributes are more complex in humans. Let us review each of these areas.

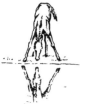

*Whether or not we strive to improve
our underdeveloped mental areas,
we must begin by accepting our level
of intelligence.*

Intelligence

To date the most popular definition of intelligence is David Wechlsler's: the ability to understand the world and to cope with the challenges of the environment. Years of studies have proven that culture, genetics, environment, and childhood stimulation have an affect on man's intelligence. In addition to these external stimuli, the brain itself can be more highly developed in one area or another. We hear the phrases that we are more left-brained than right-brained, or that we may have more mental abilities in the linguistic, musical, logical, spatial, bodily, or personal areas. No one has been able to prove if we are limited to the specific factors that influence our intelligence as we perceive it. Instead, we continually hear that we use only a small portion of our brain. We do know that we are all different, and whether or not we strive to improve our underdeveloped mental areas, we must begin by accepting our level of intelligence and our more finely tuned mental areas.

Both man and horse learn through repetition. Depending upon the intelligence, age, fund of knowledge, and past experience, man should need less repetition. However, man often requires more repetitions than a horse when faced with learning new physical skills. It should be the reverse. It would be reversed if the human were properly balanced, but the horse is usually more balanced than the human. While humans may, and often do, understand the theory, they cannot get their body to cooperate with their mind. There are many factors that influence this situation. Sometimes there is a simple cause such as a physical stiffness or a physical or mental fear, but more often it is a complex combination of factors that prevent the rider from 'feeling' what the horse is doing. Each rider and trainer must learn the amount of repetition that is needed by the rider and the horse. It is important to separate the two, because it affects both the rate and the quality of learning; never lose sight of the differences. A horse's mind is simple, and there is little interference in his attention to the 'now' of learning. Man's mind is more complex—it must first sort all the information and focus on the subject, and only then send the message to the body to practice the new skill. This is not an easy process for man.

Patience

Horses are more patient than most people. This is possible because they are not affected by the stress of holding a job, earning money, maintaining a relationship, raising a family, fitting everything into a day, staying healthy, and being involved in the community. They have no professional, ethical, or religious concerns. It is our enslavement to these demands that tests our patience. However, patience is essential if we are to perform successfully in partnership with a horse. As you learn who you are, you should learn to evaluate your level of patience. It is possible for someone to be too patient, but it is much more common for someone to be too impatient. Much less harm is caused by the former, whether with your horse or with yourself. The more you understand your horse, yourself, and your goals, and the better you are at living in the 'now', the more quickly you will be able to decide how much patience is necessary. You will know when to reward and punish yourself or your horse. Your level of patience will be consistent, and the horse will not become confused. You will be better able to avoid provoking a crisis.

Expectations

Man's mind is complex, and people have complex expectations, whether those expectations are appropriate or not. Horses' expectations are more simple and are based on their experiences and on their instincts. A person's expectations are based on what that person thinks he should do, what he wants to do, or what someone else or society expects him to do. Consequently, it is very difficult to sort out which expectations are realistic and personally appropriate. I have noticed that inappropriate expectations are tremendously detrimental to a student's progress. Our mental attributes have a strong influence in creating our expectations. Realistic expectations are essential to proper training, and we must learn the role of realistic expectations if we are to make progress with a horse. Examine your horse's expectations and your own. You may use the Workbook Questionnaire #5 to guide you.

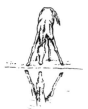

A person's expectations are frequently based on what he THINKS he should do, what he WANTS to do, or what SOMEONE ELSE or SOCIETY expects him to do.

I have repeatedly seen gifted horsemen performing their task, whether it is training, floating teeth or healing a horse. These horsemen are able to use their gift because of their mental equilibrium and their ability to combine their love of horses with their profession. Only a few persons reach adulthood with sufficient mental equilibrium. Most people must work to attain the balance that will allow them to do what they want to do with the horse. The first step in this process is reaching the point at which you are willing to examine yourself truthfully. Horses accept themselves. Since they seldom have emotional or intellectual complications, they readily exhibit what they have learned. You, on the other hand, must first learn to understand your mind. You must understand how you learn, what influences your emotional makeup, how you think, and how you react. You need to know what affects your ability to feel, and what affects your feelings. You need to know what the horse as a creature means to you, and you must be aware of how you are affected by criticism, other people, and the environment. Answering Questionnaire #6 in your Workbook will help you look at what affects you mentally. These factors have an effect on who you are and on how you think and learn. Our minds have capabilities that go beyond our wildest expectations. If we can learn to understand our mind and harness its attributes to our benefit, we are among the lucky few. You can do this. Remember that you can do anything you want with your conscious mind, and that you can learn to understand your unconscious mind and emotions. As you begin to understand yourself, your new mental equilibrium will help you achieve fulfilling horse-related goals. No, you do not need to stop riding while learning. You can work on all these aspects one at a time, some off and some on a horse. The challenge itself can be fun; meeting the challenge can be deeply rewarding. If you follow my suggestions and record your progress in each area, you will gradually recognize that you are finding a fulfilling reward. The advantage is that you will experience success; the drawback is that you will never be able to prove how you did it. The scientist in you will be upset, the philosopher in you will be satisfied!

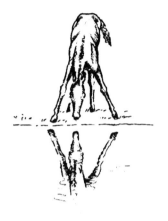

Horse-Spiritual

Horses naturally exhibit the spiritual traits of compassion, calmness, acceptance and inner peace.

"I think that a horse has a spirit." It took hours of reading, days of questioning experts, hours of discussions and extensive meditation for me to gain the confidence to make this statement. As long as I can remember, I have felt a special connection with horses that I took for granted. When I reached the questioning stage in my life, I began to look more seriously at this special feeling. I discovered that my feeling was related to the innermost part of myself, the part of myself that I have come to understand as my spirit. Strength, power, simplicity, purity, inner calmness, and inner stability are some qualities that I feel in horses. Love, energy, and attitude are three characteristics that I have labeled as spiritual. Many people spend a lifetime striving for compassion, calmness, acceptance, and inner peace, while a horse naturally exhibits these traits. Once I made the association of "spirit" and these traits, I discovered that horses have a lot to teach me about life.

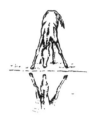

Horses naturally exhibit the traits of compassion, calmness, acceptance, and inner peace. This is seen in their strength, power, simplicity, purity, inner calmness and inner stability.

If we review the definition of "spirit", it is the vital principle or animating force within living beings. Theosophy defines spirit as the unit of consciousness, a spark of the Supreme Fire. St.Hildegard, a German mystic and prophetess, states that "the soul is in the body the way the sap is in a tree." Spirit is our life. I believe that energy, love and attitude are three characteristics that originate or radiate from our spirit. Because this is a debatable subject, I am going to try to explain my theory and the background of my hypothesis.

From as early as I can remember, I was drawn to horses. I never understood it beyond the saying that "horses must be in my blood." I have come to discover that one magnetic factor is the unconditional love I feel with a horse. My father had his first heart attack when I was fourteen. I was terrified, I wanted to cry, but was afraid to exhibit my feelings. When the ambulance arrived, I retreated to the stable and began to sob hysterically with my arms wrapped around my horse. For hours I sat there thinking about the scary situation and crying. What did my mare do? She allowed me to let the tears flow freely while she munched her hay, sniffed me and occasionally laid her head on my shoulder. Without understanding it, I had instinctively sought the stable and my horse's acceptance and compassionate love during my first remembered 'life crisis'.

My horse's compassionate, unconditional love was part of the bond between horses and myself. Love is a word we frequently use and hear used, but usually it is romantic love that we first think of. Unconditional love is nothing like romantic love. It is accepting, trusting, and awe-inspiring. Horses emit and express this love freely and simply. That love is freely available to anyone who is willing to accept and experience it; there are no strings attached. In addition to accepting love from horses, I believe we can learn how to acquire and nurture the same unconditional love that a horse naturally shares with us.

A horse shows this love by accepting, trusting, and responding. When I retreated to my mare in my time of crisis, I felt safe because she would neither lecture nor react, nor was she embarrassed. She did not hurry me, she was just THERE with her soft, accepting eyes. She very simply accepted me in her zone for as long as I needed to be there. Very few people are lucky enough to be with a person who is as accepting as a horse. In my life, I have found more horses than people who allow me to safely express my emotions, with no strings attached, offering only love, warmth, and acceptance.

Why was a horse a better refuge than the woods, the stream, or my room? Unlike an object, a horse has an active animating force that can be felt in the form of action and comfort. I believe that all living creatures share a 'life force' or energy that connects us to God or to the Universe, depending upon one's belief. Many theories consider energy to be the main ingredient in our spiritual make up. Most agree that living creatures are made up of mass (solid particles) and energy (waves). Many centuries ago, energy was considered the main life force, while today mass is considered by many as the predominant life force. Now in the 1980s and 90s, man is beginning to reconsider the importance of the balance of the two components, mass and energy. Throughout the centuries, man has been trying to understand energy. From *In Search of Healing Energy* by Mary Coddington:

> "Hippocrates referred to a healing energy that flowed through all living things as the vis medicatrix naturae. It was called the archaeus by Paracelsus and animal magnetism by Anton Mesmer. It was the odic force of Baron Karl von Reichenbach

and the vital force of Samuel Hahnemann. Wilhelm Reich named it orgone energy and D.D. Palmer, the Innate. It is the ki of the Japanese, the prana of the Hindus, the mana of the Polynesians, and the orenda of the American Indians. However, in spite of its many names, this elusive yet universal force always exhibits the same properties:

1. It can heal.
2. It penetrates everything.
3. It accompanies solar rays.
4. It has properties similar to other types of energy but is a distinct force unto itself.
5. It possesses polarity and can be reflected in mirrors.
6. It emanates from the human body and has been especially detectable at the fingertips and eyes.
7. It can be conducted by such media as metal wires and silk threads.
8. It can be stored inside inanimate materials such as water, wood and stone.
9. It can fluctuate with weather conditions.
10. It can be controlled by the mind.
11. It can cause things to happen at a distance, and enters into the dynamics of many paranormal phenomena.
12. It can be used for good or evil.

This energy that we have is not only within our bodies, but extends to surround our bodies as well. The size of our aura, or energy field, is dependent upon our balance. Horses have the same energy field.

It is this energy field surrounding the horse that allows the horse to react to people even before the horse is touched. Have you ever noticed how horses will react differently to each different individual? Our horse dentist, farrier, and veterinarian

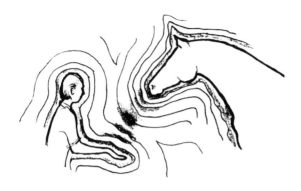

have a calm, compassionate energy that encourages trust. Our horses will calmly and trustingly allow these men to take care of them. I have never seen these professionals inflict their will on a horse with any force; it must be the effect of their energy fields. A similar but less obvious example of this involves a mounted rider. At a FEI dressage clinic, a world-class professional rode several horses. Each horse performed with grace and harmony after only a few minutes with this trainer, although they had not been performing for their riders. He even used the whip frequently. Why did the horses perform for him with happy eyes and attentive ears? When their riders remounted, why did they show resentment and confusion, swishing their tails, pinning their ears or showing the whites of their eyes? The trainer's energy synchronized with each horse's inner energy. The trainer was able to share energy with each horse, the horse felt this bond and offered a partnership that was rewarded with a beautiful performance. If the energies clash, the horse does not receive the communications given by the rider as the rider intends them. Dennis Reis refers to controlling your energy ("turn up your energy") in relationship to controlling your horse. How do we control something that is so difficult to understand? As you read this book, and especially the chapter in Resources about energy, perhaps you will gain deeper insight into this part of the horse's being. Studying some suggested readings about energy fields and your aura may help you to understand the theory, but getting to 'know' yourself is the most vital part of this study!

We can experience a more tangible characteristic of energy by feeling the attitude of the horse, our own attitude, and the attitudes or those around us. Our mood is a common reflection of our attitude. Our spiritual makeup and history play a vital role in our attitude. Most horses exhibit a cooperative, positive attitude once they understand what is expected of them. Few horses display a feeling of negativity, but all express enthusiasm for the simple life requirements of food and water. When asked to work by the trainer, a horse usually has a cooperative attitude despite the innate laziness of a horse's nature.

Horses and humans both arrive in this world with a positive attitude that exhibits the individual's character traits inherited from his biological parents. Raising horses has given me the opportunity to see many foals born and witness the natural curiosity, aggression, and shyness expressed by the different individuals. How the foal is handled in the first twenty-four hours of life and in the subsequent developmental months has a major impact on that foal's future attitude toward work and training. The security gained in the handling and care can create a trusting, cooperative attitude—or a resentful, defensive one. Early experiences will affect an individual's outlook, but if he is handled with love and consistency he will maintain a healthy, positive attitude throughout life. This innate good frame of mind can be reestablished in a confused or abused horse more easily than in a human. I was recently asked to consult an owner who had taken on a seriously abused horse. This horse reflected a kind attitude in his eye, but he was full of fear. He was so terrified that the slightest stimulus would make him jump, kick or strike if ANYTHING touched him. My opinion was that his fear was so great that he was dangerous. The owner, a kind, loving, experienced equestrian, had time to put into this poor creature. He spent time gaining the horse's trust and then took him to a reining trainer who used the "round pen" techniques for a week. The owner, who already had a good feeling 'energy', spent the week observing and being involved. The lucky horse came home having gained so much trust that he could now be ridden! I thought it was a miracle, but the horse had simply learned trust through careful, kind handling by confident trainers with a calm, soothing ENERGY. However, like the energy theory explained earlier, I cannot prove it!

The spirit of a horse is the link that can create the rewarding high of successes even in difficult situations. Understanding and allowing ourselves to feel the horse's energy can help us produce results, but it can also identify part of ourselves. Observe your horse and try to define what constitutes "horses in your blood."

Man-Spiritual

*Accepting our mysterious
spirit opens many doors
that can lead us toward
inner peace.*

Incomprehension, mystery, nonsense, confusion: these are some words that described my view of spirituality when I was forty-two. Today, spiritual development is one of the most important pursuits in my life. At first I was afraid to share my feelings, because most people I knew seemed so confident in their specific religious beliefs. What was my problem? Why did I have feelings and thoughts so incompatible those of many people I knew? WERE my feelings really incompatible? What DID others believe? During my years of confusion, there was no one with whom I could share my thoughts, so they remained my secrets. I am still learning, but I now believe that we do have a soul that houses our spirit. And I finally understand the difference between religion and spirituality: religion is a part of spirituality. I am still searching, still expanding what 'feels' right for me both logically and emotionally, but I am free from the worry, confusion, rejection, uncertainty, and skepticism that previously consumed me.

Few people share the same beliefs, because spirituality is a broad, mysterious and uncertain subject. There are many who are inquisitive and share my thirst for information. Yet they feel alone in their quest because it is embarrassing for them to admit that they do not possess the strong beliefs expressed by so many of those around them. What we do know is that no one really knows the answer. Spirituality is a very personal subject that everyone must come to terms with individually. Now, I am finally comfortable enough to share my point of view. You already have your own views, opinions, and beliefs that may differ from mine, but read on with an open mind. Feel free to compare your beliefs to mine, feel free to prefer your beliefs to mine—yours are just as valuable. What is important is that you "know yourself." Your spirit is a part of yourself that you must get to know.

A short account of my spiritual background might be helpful. I was raised in a church-attending Protestant family. I went to Sunday School and church regularly until I was fourteen, when horse competitions began to interfere. I even earned perfect attendance pins for twelve years!. Despite the number of times I repeated the scripture, Lord's Prayer and Apostles' Creed, they remained words without meaning to me. Occasionally I remember thinking: "Why do people go through this? GOD is all knowing; He knows what I think, feel, and do, so why pretend?" I was only pretending to understand and believe most of what I heard in church. That GOD is ALL KNOWING, LOVING, KIND, POWERFUL, were the only impressions that seemed real and lasting, and I had no idea of how these ideas related to my life or anyone else's.

When I moved out of childhood and became a teenager, my feelings remained the same, but I began to question even more. Again, I noticed a discrepancy between the words of people on Sunday and their actions during the week. I watched many kids I knew cheat in school, smoke in the bathroom, and sneak out to drinking parties. I heard them talk about their families in negative ways, yet I saw these apparently compatible, happy families in church week after week. But I was just a teenager, so what did I know? This puzzle remained within me and contributed to my confusion for years.

When I grew into a young adult, I continued to attend church regularly with my new family. Now that I was an adult, the problems that I saw as a teenager were compounded. Many of those in the church-attending community were regularly swapping wives and husbands and drinking themselves into oblivion, Saturday after Saturday. If you are a Christian, I wondered, how can you continue to repeat the same sinful behavior? While the confusion was mounting, I continued to attend church with my family, secretly searching for answers. I looked for someone whose life would exemplify what I was hearing in church. Fortunately, the woman who came into our house to clean filled that role. She was the only person I knew who lived her professed religion. Despite all of my confusion and only one role model, I continued to believe that religion was the most important part of life. I just could not figure out why or how!

My logic and my religious training told me that the only real rules of life were found in the Ten Commandments. They were meant to be followed. Even within my family, they were broken at will. If all were equally valid as rules for life, how could we justify using Sunday to attend horse competitions? Weren't we making our own rules, and breaking the rules of the Ten Commandments?

After years of questions and confusion, I still had no idea of what the spirit or soul really were; they simply were meaningless words that I recited week after week. I had heard these words thousands of times, yet I could not understand them. Despite my religious confusion, my inner self told me that there was something bigger, higher, and greater than my life. In hindsight, I have been able to identify several experiences that have alleviated my confusion and helped me to develop my current belief system. I now believe that spirit is a part of religion, or should be, but that spirit is, primarily, the part of us that is our relationship to God.

Spirit is the part of us that is our relationship to God.

When I was eight or nine years old and my family was on its annual holiday at the beach, my parents gave me permission to walk a mile, alone, to a local store to buy candy. I took my allowance of twenty-five cents, walked to the store, and bought twenty cents worth of candy. When I had finished my candy and was on my way back, I discovered that I had ten cents left rather than five cents. I can vividly remember having a small discussion with myself. My first thought was, "Who would know if I kept the extra five cents?" As the minutes wore on, I began to feel worse and worse. Finally, I decided to return the five cents, and I turned around and walked the mile back to the store. After I returned the money, my feet hurt and I was tired but I felt much better. At the time I did not understand why I felt better, but now I think that it was God communicating with me through my conscience. That experience has helped me to remain honest with myself and helped me to recognize my conscience.

Years later, when I was married, Vonnie came into my life to be a housekeeper. She was nineteen and I was twenty-seven. Vonnie had a remarkable presence, but only much later did I realize that the "presence" existed because Vonnie lived her beliefs. Vonnie's actions matched her belief system, demonstrating true spiritual balance. She was the only person I knew who exhibited such balance and corresponding peace. While I did not understand this until my spiritual confusion began to clear up, Vonnie was an important role model for me. She was the first person with whom I could discuss God, religion, and life's mysteries. While I could not grasp her beliefs, we could talk and the inner-peace and harmony that radiated from Vonnie made her life a lesson for me. Without her example, the crises confronting me over the years might have driven me away from religion, and my spiritual search might have ended. Every day, I am still thankful for the friendship and example of Vonnie and her life.

There was a third experience that fueled my search to understand life at its deepest level: my healing. For twenty years, I had suffered from a debilitating condition that caused weakness, extreme fatigue, and worsening eye sight. In 1985, my symptoms began to disappear. Today I am on no medication, my eyes have returned to normal, and I am FULL of ENERGY. This happened although I had no anticipation of being healed, no conscious effort to become well, and no awareness that I was being healed. The medical profession denied that it could have happened at all. This prompted a profound search for why and how I was healed. I read about, questioned, and explored every theory that could possibly explain such an unexpected experience. I discovered that I had been healed by someone who did not even know he was a healer. Russell had been given the gift of healing from God. After our exploration and discovery of his healing tools, we are now using this information to help riders. Healing could only come from a higher power; this power must be God or however you may wish to name this spiritual energy. Here was sufficient proof of spiritual power to satisfy me. Nothing else could explain what had happened. I began to see my spiritual belief as separate from any formal religious belief.

These three experiences helped me to formulate my belief that we are all connected to God through our spiritual being. Each of us must explore our own connections to God and learn to recognize the way He speaks to us (intuition and conscience) and the way we speak to him (meditation and prayer). By getting to know ourselves, we also get to know God. This is the beginning of a spiritual quest: we must get to know our inner, spiritual self.

We are all connected to God through our spiritual being.

This was just the beginning. I continue to struggle with many questions. Where does life originate? How can healing happen? What is the source of life? What happens after death? What is the connection between different religions? What is good and evil? I may never know the answers, but I continue to search with an open mind while I live life to its fullest. I am not going to worry, because I feel confident that the information we store in our preconscious memory will become meaningful knowledge when we are ready. What is important is that I never close my mind, that I finally have some understanding of spirit and soul, and that I can honestly say that I comprehend a higher force of life, or God. Many people are not aware of the value of this part of their being. Yet we must all understand something about spirit, because it is a part of our inner balance. You may be like Vonnie, already believing and accepting, or you may need to go through a struggle, as I did. In either case, it is always possible to deepen one's understanding of life.

Now that I have shared the critical spiritual events of my life, let us look at the characteristics of spirit. We share with horses the spiritual characteristics of love, energy, and attitude. In addition, we have the spiritual characteristics of empathy and humility.

Our first thoughts of love are romantic ones. Radio, newspapers, books, and TV try to convince us that romantic love is one of the most important aspects of life. But it is unconditional love, not romantic love, that is of spiritual value. Unconditional love is given without demanding or expecting anything in return. It is a feeling of unity with another being. Associated with unconditional love are feelings of familiarity, peace, understanding, exuberance, or well-being. Unconditional love is important for our life with horses. We have already heard the saying 'horses must be in your blood'. What this really means is that horses are or must become part of our inner being or love. This unconditional love provides a bond and an understanding that carries us over the rough roads and leads us to joy. With this love we can accept and understand the horse for what he is, not for what we want him to be.

Refer to the Objectives section of this book to see how high your love for the horse is on your priority list. I cannot live a balanced life without some connection and interaction with horses. One of my best friends enjoys riding a couple of days a week. Her fulfillment would be my frustration, and my fulfillment would be too much for her. We differ in the depths of our love of the horse. Her love for the horse is lower on her motivational scale than it is on mine. The depth of your love affects your expectations, so it is important to recognize its significance for yourself.

Energy is another spiritual characteristic that is a vital part of my vocabulary. By 'energy', I mean the life force energy, or God, that is in each of us.

Energy is required for our body and brain to function. Where is the source of this energy? What is this energy? Without this energy, could life exist? Refer to the explanation of energy in the Horse-Spiritual section of this book. Just these few questions, when answered, offer the clearest possible conclusion that a life energy force exists. This energy is the driving mechanism that enables our brain and body to function. Spiritual energy plays two major roles, physical and mental. Let us look at them more closely.

Our body is a complex group of organs, systems and cells that are designed to work in close harmony. Our body function control panel is housed in our finely-tuned brain as a nonconscious function. For our body to operate correctly, our blood must flow freely, fueling and cleaning our entire system. Energy animates us, allowing us to walk, run, talk, and ride. Our heart is the pumping station that keeps the blood flowing. What makes the heart pump? Why is the heart the organ associated with love? Is this not a definite indication of spiritual connection? Because our heart is the organ most connected with universal love and energy emitted from God, it is the vital organ of life. This energy force is a gift of God that generates life in our body and mind.

Mental energy is a more difficult idea to grasp. Mental energy stimulates the patience, creativity, perseverance, and will that are closely connected in the balance needed by an equestrian. Mental energy generates the intelligence that is so closely connected to many other of our personal characteristics. Like physical energy, mental energy must flow freely to allow the corresponding areas of the brain to function. Referring back to my healing, Russell used a meditative therapy that he developed as part of my physical therapy treatment. I believe that this therapy allowed me to go into a state of meditation that created a freer spiritual flow. This allowed my mental and spiritual functions to be cleansed. During this relaxed state, the more free-flowing of my body fluids helps recharge my body, while the relaxed mental state helps to release the blocks of my unconscious. Any release of the stored unconscious will help close the gap between my conscious and unconscious mind, thus allowing these two parts of my mind to work in closer harmony. It was part of this process that I have come to recognize that I was 'awakened'. This 'awakening' of my spiritual self helped to unleash the creative, healing, and intellectual energies that have helped me to become healthier, happier, more energetic, more creative, and a better teacher.

Energy flowing freely has much to do with horsemastership. We have the ability to cleanse our spirit, thus reducing our unconscious mental blocks and allowing ourselves to feel our horse's energy more clearly. Feeling the energy makes communication quicker, softer, and more accurate. Energy also allows our body and mind to spend the extra time and perform the extra work required to keep horses. We need energy to accomplish the spiritual search of getting to know ourselves. An image I commonly use with my students once they learn their basic position is: "Picture your horse's FORWARD FLOWING energy. It starts in his hind legs, travels upwards through his hip, through his back, under your SOFT seat, through his shoulder and neck ending in your hand, which you feel through forward, soft, steady, elastic contact with the reins."

The third spiritual characteristic that we share with horses is attitude. While love and energy are powerful spiritual gifts, human attitude is passive and easily influenced. Others see our inner being in the form of our attitude. Our attitude colors not only how others see us, but also how we see the outside world. It is like a light filter on a camera, controlling the amount of blues or yellows allowed to reach the film. The wrong filter (attitude) can spoil the quality of the picture (our functioning). In our lives, negative attitudes or feelings will distort our perceptions and projections of ourselves.

Let me share an example from a horse show. One of my students had trouble in the dressage ring with his sensitive thoroughbred. After several attempts to coach him, I offered to show the horse myself. At our first show, I spent my warmup time thinking about the craziness of what I was doing. I had not shown for fifteen years. I was intimidated by the seasoned competitors. I entered the ring continuing to allow the wrong type of thoughts onto my film. I did a terrible job. As I left the ring reviewing what I had done, I felt foolish. I could ride this horse with the greatest success at home, so why should I be so stupid at a show? For the next class, I remained connected to the horse's energy. I did not let the external interferences through my filter, and consequently I rode a winning test. Within one hour, I had performed two totally different tests by simply changing my attitude.

Here is another example of this same phenomenon, but in a more recent, non-horsey situation. The IRS sent me a letter: I was being audited! Although I had all my records, they were stored in paper bags in my basement. Receiving the IRS notice prompted me to panic, because I knew that there was no way for me to get those records in order, even if I spent an entire month sorting them. For several days, I fought to change my attitude from one of hate, resentment, and irritation, to one of submission and acceptance. The IRS auditor was not my enemy, he was not persecuting me, he was just doing his job, and actually he would suffer because of my messy record keeping. So what was the point of having a negative attitude toward him? The day that he arrived for the audit, I greeted him with a very positive attitude. I explained my situation and waited to see his response. Most auditors are accustomed to being disliked, and as a result are naturally on the defensive. This auditor was no different. I could feel his negative energy all around. Luckily for both of us, my positive attitude persisted, and within half an hour we were working together to solve the problem. He began to trust my attitude, because he could feel my honest inner positiveness: this feeling was more powerful than the spoken word. The audit ended, we had had a good week together, and he left thanking me for my positive attitude! This is an example of the power of positive mental energy, which I believe is spiritually connected.

It may sound strange to equate spirit with a dressage warmup or an IRS auditor, but our spirit is part of our daily lives. We live with our spirit every second of every day. It most definitely is important and to our benefit to learn to understand our attitude. To understand it, we can learn to listen to our conscience, our intuition, and to the answers to our prayers.

Empathy is spiritual awareness of ourselves, others and our horses. When we interpret the energy that we feel emanating from another, we empathize with that other. I have learned to 'feel', the movement, attitudes, and actions of the horses and riders when I teach. I can get myself into their shoes. I usually limit my attempts to empathize with the riders, so as to respect the privacy of their mental and spiritual beings. Only when a student has given me permission do I allow my connection to go deeper. My style and the words I use are appropriate to what I 'feel' from each rider. The horse is another story. I automatically unite with the horse, primarily empathizing with his spirit through his energy. I teach from the horse's point of view. I believe that the most important part of riding, after position, is 'feel'. I encourage all students to understand the horse, but I do not limit my teaching to this area alone. There are many who love horses and who want to ride, but who want to remain superficial. People who choose not to empathize with a horse must learn to have riding goals that match the level of empathy they wish to attain or practice.

Empathy is one of the most important spiritual elements of a successful life. Understanding others at all levels allows us to have a clearer view of each person, animal, or situation.

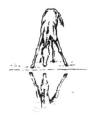

Empathy is one of the most important spiritual elements of a successful life. Understanding others at all levels allows us to have a clearer view of each person, animal or situation.

Humility is the ability to have a modest view of one's own self-importance. We all begin life humble, because at birth we are totally dependent upon adults for survival. As we grow up, we aspire toward independence and some of us become obsessed with self-importance. We may have an independent life style, but we all dependent upon the life-force within us. This knowledge should keep us humble, but frequently it does not, because we take life for granted.

A 1987 visit to the Mayan Ruins in Mexico, the remains of a civilization over twelve hundred years old, is one of my many humbling experiences. The wisdom and knowledge of people from this time period gave me a new view of my relationship with the universe. We think that our technology is superior and yet the Mayans built their main village at one of the only three openings in a 165 mile coral reef. Their artwork is still etched in stone for us to view today. What will remain of our civilization twelve hundred years from now? Stepping into history was a humbling experience for me. There are other humbling experiences all around us, if we will just allow ourselves to see and accept them. We are part of the universe, but the universe will go on without us.

Life with horses is the same. We can direct a horse's energy, but the horse's energy is more powerful than ours. The sooner we take our humility seriously, the sooner we will be able to capture our horse's majesty.

Religion and society both affect our spiritual life. They may complement or contradict our inner being, but we cannot be free from their influence. My perception of my spirit was confused by my specific religion and by the religious practices and hypocrisy of my community. I still seek to comprehend a universal God. Anything short of this causes me to feel incomplete, and thus out of balance.

Our social environment and culture dominates our lives and seeks to define our spiritual values. Society is important; we must learn to live within the structure it provides without causing harm to ourselves or to others. We also must develop our own identity and sense of values. Questionnaire #7 in your Workbook will help you define the role of spirit in your own life and in your horse's life.

Resources

Introduction

Just as a physical journey of any length requires food and supplies, a journey through life requires physical, mental and spiritual resources. Some of these resources, like love and energy, are GIFTS from God. Others, like humility, attitude, empathy, and forgiveness, are attributes of nature that we must nurture. Still others, like concentration, knowledge, relaxation, mountain top, on hold, discipline, commitment, patience, praise, and imagery, are TOOLS that we learn to use to help us on our journey. We can certainly survive without the use of many of these resources, but our lives can be made richer and more rewarding by using them. The effective use of our resources not only makes us feel better, but also improves our ability to have successful experiences and relationships with people and horses.

As you study these chapters, remember to try to make active use of all parts of your being: your body, mind, and spirit. This too will help you have a more fulfilling journey.

GIFTS	ATTRIBUTES TO NURTURE	TOOLS
Love-Horse & Man	*Attitude-Horse & Man*	*Knowledge-Horse & Man*
Energy-Horse & Man	*Humility-Horse & Man*	*Relaxation-Horse & Man*
	Empathy-Man	*Concentration-Man*
	Forgiveness-Horse & Man	*On Hold-Man*
		Discipline-Man
		Commitment-Man
		Patience-Man
		Praise-Man
		Imagery-Man

Love

Love is a feeling that motivates us to appreciate life with delight, awe, and wonder, to be aware, appreciative, open-minded and accepting of what is less than perfect, and willing to change what can be changed.

Each one of us was born with the capacity to love ourselves, others, and life. Love is inherent to our being; it is a God-given gift. Unfortunately it is often buried deep beneath the surface, suppressed in much the same way that we suppress our ability to understand our spirituality. I believe that learning to love ourself, others, and life is a function of our soul. We can think we love but, more importantly, we should be able to feel love and we must act in a loving way. Understanding love will help us to understand our spiritual self.

Romantic love, the type we hear the most about, is not the type of love I am referring to. I am referring to love as an energy that motivates us to appreciate life with delight, awe, and wonder, to be aware, to be open-minded and accepting of what is less than perfect, and to be willing to change. This type of love functions for us in relation to ourselves, those around us (including our horses), the universe, and all of life. It is a gift that allows us to strive to improve ourselves, so that we, in return, can give what we have. Giving what we have in return for God's gift of love to us is essential to our inner well-being and balance.

Later in this chapter, I am going to ask you to explore how you feel about yourself physically, mentally, and spiritually. To help you understand why these questions are pertinent, I will begin by describing some characteristics of love in both horses and humans. Notice how closely related the characteristics of love are. When you realize how important love is to all aspects of your life, you will understand why I spend so much time questioning your ability to love.

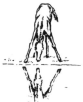

Each of us was born with the capacity to love life, love others, and love ourselves.

One characteristic of love in both horses and humans is a simple delight in life's experiences. Horses express this daily. They show love through their gratitude for and appreciation of the food we give them. Almost all horses enthusiastically accept their food. When a horse hears the feed room door open, he pricks up his ears, often nickers or whinnies, and sometimes even bangs on the door. Once he is fed, his eagerness is replaced by the cheerful munching of his grain. His ears are relaxed, his eyes are soft, and he is totally involved in the joy of eating. How often do you show appreciation for your food to the purchaser, the preparer, and the person cleaning up? Not as often, nor as completely, as your horse does! Even if you are the provider and preparer of food, how often do you enjoy the preparation and the meal itself? More often you take it for granted, or worse yet, rush through it just for the sake of eating? Yet, at least two hours a day are spent nourishing your body, so wouldn't it be nice to enjoy the sight, smell, and taste of this important part of your daily life? Wouldn't it be nice to appreciate the time and effort involved in preparing and eating your meal, even if you prepared it yourself? Have you ever cleaned a stall and freshly bedded it only to have the horse immediately lie down and roll, oblivious to your presence, completely absorbed in the scratching of his body in the fresh, crisp bedding? Most of us have seen this. What is he doing? He is completely immersed in his joy of the moment, taking full advantage of the clean, fresh stall. How often do you enjoy the smell of your fresh air-dried sheets, and take a moment to feel the cleanliness and softness of your bed? Do you really enjoy the total sensation of how your body feels in your bed before you go to sleep? Not often. We are too busy getting into bed to watch TV, read a book, or go to sleep. It took your horse less than two minutes to enjoy the sensation of his stall. Taking several minutes a day to enjoy the total sensation of your bedroom, your living room, your garden, and yourself could be a great learning tool for appreciating more aspects of your being. Successful riding requires awareness, and awareness is enhanced when we learn to know and love ourselves.

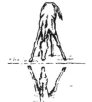

Love of life experienced through ALL of our senses adds to the fullness of life.

These are just two of the many examples of the ways in which a horse expresses and demonstrates his love of life. Love of life should be simple. We can awaken our senses by allowing ourselves to experience the joy and beauty of these small, everyday occurrences. The demands and influences of our western civilization have pushed most of our instinctual awareness into a dormant part of our consciousness. The more parts of our being that we can use to experience life in the 'now', the more tools we can use to help us learn and grow. Most horsepersons are quick to notice and enjoy their horse's pleasures. Why not notice and enjoy their own? Love of life experienced through ALL of our senses adds to the fullness of life.

Once our spirituality has been awakened, we can go beyond delight in the present moment. Wonder at the gloriousness of the universe, or awe in the face of its complexity are to our spirit what delight is to our senses—a form of acute awareness. We experience this spiritual love when we marvel at the birth of a foal or feel chills when we watch a beautiful performance. When we acknowledge our wonder or awe, we admit that we are witnessing something over which we have no control. When we recognize and accept our position as a part of the universe, but not its controller, then we also accept our role with our horse, as his partner, not his master. Our capacity for spiritual love molds the form of our relationship with our horse.

Unconditional acceptance of yourself and others is another manifestation of love. Our horse accepts us as we are. He does not say that we are too tall, too loud, too heavy, or too thin. He tries his best to do what we ask. Remember the horse in the chapter Understanding Horse-Mental, whose overweight rider continued to practice flying changes for hours? This horse continued to try to do what she asked, despite the confusing repetition and discomfort on his back. People would have rebelled; I would have dumped her. Obviously, I have not mastered acceptance as well as most horses have. Our critical mind usually directs us to avoid the abuse this horse endured. We say, "That person is not worth associating with." It is a necessary form of self protection. Yet acknowledging who we are and accepting our vulnerability are early steps in learning to love ourselves. Love, and only love, can be totally accepting.

Once we accept who we are, we can dare to become open-minded and examine an issue from the other person's point of view before we react. We are no longer threatened by the differences between us. We can better evaluate what should be accepted, rejected, or changed. A horse does not have the mental capacity to look at a problem from our point of view. It is up to us to do this for both.

Your horse's nature allows him to love and accept himself and you, free of judgement. But humans tend to judge themselves and one another. They find it hard to be objective. So we evaluate ourselves based on norms established by our parents or by society, rather than on any standards based on reality. We neither accept reality, nor are we open-minded about deviations from our pre-determined notions of what is acceptable. In other words, we humans must struggle constantly to emulate our horses in their ability to accept their conditions without judgement. We can learn from them how to love unconditionally.

The final characteristic of love I wish to mention is the energy to change ourselves for the better. Throughout this book, I will encourage you to change what needs to be changed. The prospect of change may be scary, the process may be difficult, but self-love and honesty will require it. The questions can help you decide where change is needed, and the examples can help reassure you that others have faced similar issues, have changed, and have survived. But you are the one who must summon the courage and energy to change yourself.

If you would like an evaluation of your ability to love yourself, go to your Workbook and fill our Questionnaire #1. This will ask you to evaluate what you like and what you do not like. Once you have completed this evaluation, it will be time to change what you can change and accept what you cannot change. Being overweight is the most common physical condition that can be changed, but is too often accepted. There is no reason to accept it and make your horse accept it. It is not easy, but you can find a way to be the proper weight.

There are many conditions that you cannot change, and these conditions you MUST learn to ACCEPT. This is a far more difficult task. Question #5 in Questionnaire #1 will ask you to give as many reasons as you can for your dislike of each characteristic you listed. Once you have given this considerable thought, you will be asked to answer another important question, "What effect does this physical fault have on my life?" Answering the last question, #7, should present the solution: "What can I do to accept what I cannot change?" This Questionnaire, answered honestly, can add to your self-knowledge and have a powerful impact on your future.

Cindy's case is an excellent example of accepting what cannot be changed. Cindy's arms were disproportionately short for the rest of her body. No matter what she tried, she was continually criticized for her hands being too high or her reins too long. There was no way she could create the classical straight line of elbow to bit with her short arms. Cindy was uncomfortable with her body even when she was not on a horse. When Cindy made her list, she realized she did not like her arms because her clothes did not fit correctly and because of her riding short-comings. Sixteen-year-old Cindy had been riding in Hunt Seat Equitation, and her goal was to qualify for the 'Medal' or 'Maclay' classes. When Cindy asked herself, "What can I do to accept what I cannot change?", she discovered that she had two concrete solutions. The first was to spend a little extra money and have the sleeves of her blouses and coats shortened so they were not too long. The second solution was to change her goals, stop working in Equitation and change to Junior Hunter. She knew that she had to put on a good performance to be certain that the judges would overlook her arm position. Who knows what worked, the change she made in her feelings about herself or the change of her goals? What we do know is that something did work. She began to feel better about her life and her riding. She began to get compliments about her performance, yet she had not changed her body structure!

Now let us look at mental aptitudes. The Workbook's Questionnaire #2 parallels Questionnaire #1, but asks you to consider your mind rather than your body. This may not be a subject you have thought about often, so let me give you some questions to get you started. Can you learn easily? Do you have good communication skills? Are you a quick thinker? Do you have appropriate reactions? After you have listed your strengths and weaknesses, you must decide what weaknesses you can change. This is even more difficult to determine, because many of us do not use our mental facilities to the fullest. We are capable of more improvement than we realize.

If you know that you have a specific problem, let us say a learning disability, you must accept it. You cannot change it. Larry was a very good example. Larry began riding as an adult. Since his friends competed in horse trials, he too was interested in horse trials. Once he had developed his basic seat and understood the use of his aids, he wanted to compete. He struggled to learn the training level tests. His first event was a major discouragement because he went off course in dressage, cross country, and in show jumping: it was simply impossible for him to remember those patterns. Larry was very self-conscious about his learning disability, so he did not share this problem with anyone. He was most embarrassed when he could not remember the courses. Since he had not accepted his learning disability, his inability to remain on course made him feel stupid. Luckily for Larry, he had an intuitive instructor who delicately helped him accept the problem. After two years of careful, supportive instruction, Larry was able to share his problem with his friends. He continued to go with them to events, but without his horse. He went as a spectator, and was able to enjoy the atmosphere and the social interaction. Later, he met his competitive needs through dressage. At dressage shows he was able to have a reader, so he did not need to remember the test. One of the discoveries that he made in this process was that sharing his problem did not change his relationship with his friends.

Our spiritual love includes our ability to witness and enjoy the wonders of the universe. This indescribable sense of awe is experienced each time we see a seed develop into a plant, a dependent child grow into an independent adult, a bird glide by totally carried by the wind, a horse running free, or the birth of a foal. We experience awe, wonder, and respect when we experience the mega-force winds of a hurricane, the blinding snow of a blizzard, the shaking, crumbling ground of an earthquake or the black cloud drifting in our direction from a volcano, hundreds of miles away. Spiritual love is felt as an overwhelming sense of wonder and awe.

My studies have given me the confidence to say that LOVE is the most important common denominator in life. A few of the questions that I have explored include: What or who created these natural wonders? What or who created life itself? What causes bad and good?

It takes much time to answer these questions, and even after extended study, the most outstanding revelation is that there are many different answers. My only certainty is that there must be a higher power that controls all of life. My studies give me the sense that this power is love—love of God that is in all of us, every living creature in the Universe, including both horse and man. Since I believe we were all born with love within us, the next question that presents itself is: Are we capable of discovering the love that we are born with, that lies deep within our being? I think the answer is yes. The search for this love will enable us to know our spiritual self much better. It is a never-ending search that we are each responsible for.

Once we accept that spiritual love exists, we must find a way to bring it out of hiding and incorporate it into the way we live our lives. Questionnaire #3 asks you many difficult questions about your spirituality. Answer them honestly, and if you do not know what you think, say so. The importance of these questions is to create an awareness. Later in life, you will discover that you will be able to answer them with less effort. However, the answers will change as you pass through life. Your spiritual growth should be documented every six months, so you should fill out your second copy six months after you have completed your first copy. Do not look at the earlier questionnaire before completing the second. It is important to see how you feel compared to how you felt.

Once you are able to accept your weaknesses and love yourself, even with those weaknesses, you will be better able to love others in spite of their weaknesses and habits you do not like. You will become able to evaluate adverse situations from all perspectives before you react. You will discover that you are more able to release your own point of view and adopt another's, whether in horse or man. Let us use the example of Todd and his young horse Water's Edge. Todd had bought Water's Edge six months before. As an ex-timber horse, he seemed a good event prospect. Water's Edge could jump well, but he was stiff and found dressage work frustrating. Todd knew that he first had to supple his horse, but Water's Edge did not respond consistently. Over the first four months, the horse got more and more supple. Todd spent two months confirming the new softness until it was consistent. When he encountered major resistance after two months of submission, Todd was upset. Todd put himself in his horse's shoes and realized that he had recently introduced cavalletti into his suppling program, and that the cavalletti reminded Water's Edge of his racing days so much that he became excited. Todd remained understanding, gave Water's Edge extra time, and ultimately got him quiet while jumping as well as in dressage. If Todd had not understood his horse, he could have ruined his chances of creating a top event horse!

CHANGE is essential to solving most problems. Our capacity to change is a major part of our uniqueness.

Notice that change is essential to solving all of the problems described in this chapter. The capacity to change is a major part of our uniqueness. Each experience, each personal encounter, and everything we see and hear in our environment changes us. We must not only accept change, but constantly review to see if change could spark an improvement in life. People are often afraid of change, because change represents the unknown. We have been conditioned to believe that we are safe with our present belief system, and it is hard for us to see the possible betterment that could result from a change. Only if we are willing to accept change can we improve and grow. We acknowledge that working with horses successfully requires adaptability, but we find it more difficult to apply the same standards to ourselves. Being able to change is part of loving ourselves. Almost all of us must change to fulfill our responsibility to develop our gift of love. As we encounter life experiences we should examine them and ask ourselves, how does the experience affect our love of ourselves and others? The answer to this question will allow you to examine the development and quality of your love. This can give you the information to change toward betterment if you wish. Horse lovers have the added advantage of learning from the horses that we so dearly love.

Energy

*Your energy is personal,
get in touch with it, allow
it to flow freely and enjoy
the results.*

Think of energy by comparing it to a fire. Our energy is the heat from the flame. The logs are our body, the oxygen our mind, and the draft our spirit. All three are necessary to keep the fire blazing. If the fuel is spent, the oxygen missing, or the draft blocked, the fire subsides or dies, and there is no heat. Likewise, if we lose our health, block our mind with negative emotions, or smother our spirit through inattention, our energy vanishes. We feel tired, frustrated, confused, depressed, angry, impatient, or indecisive.

Energy is frequently misunderstood because it is invisible, like heat. I can describe energy, but I cannot define it well. Just as I know the fire is hot because I am warm or because I see it cooking the food, I know my energy because I can feel and use it.

Physical Energy

Energy empowers our life. Physical energy in the form of movement is the easiest to understand, but even here our vocabulary often leads to confusion. Let's look at how the horse expresses energy—he runs, he jumps, he is impulsive. His movement is supported by stamina, which is created through careful conditioning. But when we try to define the energy in his actions, our terminology frequently misleads us. We mistake the appearance of energy for the actual energy. A horse with quick, short steps appear to be fast, but the horse with long, reaching strides actually wins the race. Dressage riders often equate speed with impulsion. They see a horse with much nervous, up-and-down action, and say he has impulsion. Also in dressage, the phrase "moving forward" is frequently misunderstood. Actually, the horse that is going fast is not moving forward energetically. He is losing energy.

What is forward energy? Energy that is moving through the horse and that is smooth, powerful and flowing. I compare the motion of good energy to that of the ocean waves moving toward the shore. As the water approaches the coast line it wells up higher and higher until it spills over in a burst of energy as a wave that breaks on the shore. A dressage horse has a very similar energy flow. The energy begins in the hind legs, travels up through the legs, over the back, under the elastic rider, through the shoulder and neck to the rider's hands. The rider feels the energy flow through to his hands with power and elasticity that can be directed into any movement with a minimum of effort. On the other hand, the physical energy generated in the horse's hind legs can be blocked by a rider who is stiff, or it can be ignored and allowed to escape by a rider who allows the horse to "run through" his hands.

Mental Energy

Our mental energy functions in the form of our thought process. How our mind works (uses its energy) dictates our interaction with humans or horses. To a large extent, we can choose how we will use our mind. We can be aggressive or passive, patient or impatient, understanding or intolerant, thoughtful or thoughtless, analytical or reactive. To interact effectively, however, our mental energy cannot be blocked by negative emotions or attitudes.

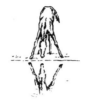

*Live each experience fully by
expressing the feelings involved.
Do not block or hide.*

A common cause of blocked mental energy is an unresolved, hidden, or unpleasant emotion that was not dealt with appropriately or in a timely fashion. Take the example of Julie. Julie's father died unexpectedly when she was eleven. The shock put the entire family into an emotional shut-down. In order to function, Julie blocked out the pain of the loss, never allowing herself to feel the grief. While she blocked the pain, she also suppressed some of her ability to remember and to feel. A good student and a successful rider before the tragedy, Julie slowly became dysfunctional. She began to do poorly in school, had violent temper tantrums and aggressive behavior. Her mother bought her several horses during those years, and each one became a nervous wreck. Finally, when Julie was suspended from school, her mother took her to a psychologist. Her mental energy block had grown for six years, so it had done considerable scarring. Although it was the psychologist who diagnosed her problem, Julie claims that her horses actually rehabilitated her. She learned to see life more wholly through her horses' lives. Although she is functioning satisfactorily now, some scars remain. The mental block has changed the course of her life.

We all have blocks. But we can learn how to prevent further blocks of our mental energy, and how to repair those we do have before they cause irreparable damage. Our mental energy can be available for us to make rational, cognitive decisions. One of the most important steps is to live ALL the

EMOTIONS of each experience, good and bad. Express your feelings through smiles, tears, yelling or laughter. Do not deny your emotions or thoughts freedom. Allow yourself to experience joy, sadness, and anger completely. It is easier to experience a happy emotion than a sad or bad one. Frequently, unhappy or bad experiences cause us to withdraw, but it is through the expression or communication of our feelings that we gain control over them. If you do not have a loved one to share with, go to your horse. If your horse does not offer enough relief, go to a professional. Emotional blocks are the biggest detriment to effective mental energy. The longer the blocks remain in effect, the more damage is done. Deal with emotional pain as quickly as possible, and do not deny yourself the opportunity to experience it.

 Energy blocks can be caused by fear, anger, confusion, jealousy, misunderstood communication, or withheld emotions.

If you continue to feel short-tempered, depressed, irritated, or impatient, your self-treatment may not be working. You may need the help of a professional therapist to retrieve the information stored in your unconscious. We generally use the unconscious to store information that is not resolved, or that is too painful for us to face. There are many techniques to help you retrieve, evaluate and let go of the block. Most important is the choice of a counsellor and a technique that will not present you with information you are not ready to receive.

To evaluate your mental blocks, please fill in Questionnaire #4 in your Workbook, a diary of mental energy blocks.

Preventing mental energy blocks requires being able to express your emotions, but often the expression or communication is a problem in itself. If any communication with a person or horse leaves you unhappy, hurt, confused or angry, you must pursue the communication until you can release the negative emotions, whether now or later. It is usually a good idea to give yourself a few minutes to evaluate the discomfort from all sides. Then, being as positive, objective and open-minded as possible, confront the situation. Continue the communication until there is a positive outcome, not necessarily the one you wanted, but the one that solves the problem. If the difference can be resolved, resolve it. If not, accept it and move on. If the issue seems too complex, too threatening, or too time consuming to resolve, put it 'on hold' until you have the resources to deal with it. Put all the negative emotions, as well at the communications and thoughts 'on hold.' Deal with them as soon as you feel ready. Otherwise it may block your mental energy. Questionnaire #5, your communication blocks diary in your Workbook, can help you discover communication blocks.

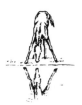

*Fully experience ALL EMOTIONS,
both good and bad.*

How we use our mind is closely related to our attitude. We can learn to generate positive thoughts. Positive thoughts can bring about positive actions. I am a firm believer in the value of positive thinking. Each time a negative thought comes into my mind, I examine the thought. Why do I have it? What has caused it? Could I be looking at it incorrectly? I have a conversation with myself to determine the cause and come up with a positive version of the thought.

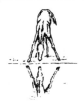

*If a difference can be resolved,
resolve it. If not, accept it,
and move on, learning from it.*

In summary, our mental energy is not just the process of our thoughts, but also the feelings that lie behind them (our emotions) and the use to which they are put, positive or negative. We measure and evaluate the energy, not by examining the process, but by identifying the emotions and determining the nature of the actions we are taking.

Positive thoughts can cause positive actions.

Spiritual Energy

Our spiritual energy is closely related to our mental energy, just as the oxygen and draft are closely related in a fire. No matter how invisible it may be, we all have a spiritual component that affects us. The energy from our spiritual side is manifest through prayer, conscience, dreams, ideas, or intuition. It takes the form of feeling or revelation, although in the process of recognizing it we often confuse it with thinking.

For years I felt a conflict between my thought process and my intuition. I had inner feelings or thoughts that I denied because I did not understand them. I now know it was my intuition. I wish that I had learned the value of my intuition years ago, so that I could have listened to it more closely. If I had respected my intuition when I was a Pony Clubber, I would have avoided damaging my horse from azoturia. The Regional Rally was coming up and I had to make a decision. I had won a scholarship to train with Fred Marsman the week before the Rally. After what I thought was careful consideration, I trusted a friend to keep my mare fit. I did not feel comfortable with the decision, but repressed the feeling. When I shared my gut feeling with someone else, she shrugged off my fear as being unfounded. It turned out to be a well-founded feeling. I came home, met my horse at the Rally and did a fine dressage test.

Cross-country day came, and Demi, my horse, did not feel right. However, again, I did not listen to my inner voice but continued on course. She was not going freely forward, but again my logic overrode my intuition, and I pushed her. She ended up being out of work for three months. I felt horrible. When I investigated the situation, I discovered that my friend had not worked her for three days before the Rally, but had neither told me that nor reduced the mare's feed. Demi had been very fit before I left, and if my friend had followed the program, my mare would have been fine. As I look back, I realize that from the very beginning my inner voice, my intuition, was warning me not to let someone else ride Demi.

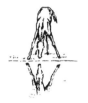 *It is important for you to recognize the energy blocks, determine their origins, and find a cure. To keep your energy fire blazing, you must keep the fuel, oxygen, and draft in balance through your awareness and care.*

Spiritual energy is the easiest of the three to ignore. Therefore, I am going to devote the rest of the chapter to describing techniques to help you recognize, trust, and use your spiritual voice. These techniques helped me to become more aware and accepting of this voice.

Looking back, I can give countless examples of my logical thoughts overriding my intuition. This started to change in 1985 when my curiosity prompted me to try a 'channelling'. My channelling experiment opened an additional window to learning. Why did this far-out experience have such a profound affect on such a practical, logical, rational thinker? The channeling presented information to me that no one else could possibly know. It acknowledged feelings that I had, that I had never listened to or admitted to myself or to anyone else. This overwhelming experience seemed trustworthy, but I still had to research, experiment, and prove it to be true and valuable.

Channeling is "receiving information from some source outside the ordinary mind" (from Arthur Hasting's book *With the Tongues of Men and Angels,* a study of channeling). A channeler is "a person who claims to communicate messages that come to him or her from supernatural beings, spirits, or other nonphysical intelligences." Quoting Hasting Further,

"Some basic characteristics of this kind of channeling are as follows:

*1. **The message must be coherent and intelligible.** The transmission is "information" in the sense that it has meaning; it is not random words or phrases. It is not speaking in unknown languages or writings in unknown and unrecognizable script. One of my friends spoke with a woman who said that she channeled the spirits of the dolphins. "What do they say," he asked. "We don't know," she said, "They just go boop, boop, beep, queep, toot." She was apparently serious in her belief, but such a message would not meet this standard for channeling.*

*2. **The source must be perceived as coming from out-side the conscious self.** This may occur n several ways. Some messages just appear in the mind as fully formed thoughts in words, but without having been constructed or processed by the individual and without the identifying feel of it being one's own. It is as though one is listening to a mental telephone.*

The message may come through automatic writing or drawing, with the person's hand moving "by itself"; the person is not consciously controlling it. Sometimes the "writer" as differentiated from the "author" can be talking with a friend, drinking coffee, or even reading something else while this is happening. Whole books, stories, drawings and poems have been written through this form of channeling.

The channeler may also feel some other "person" physically influencing or controlling the body and speech from the inside. Usually, the channeler "steps back" to let the other take over.

In extreme cases, the other personality completely controls the body, and the individual is in a trance state. The channeler's memories of the experience are vague or nonexistent. The common point is that the person experiences the messages or actions as being alien, different from his or her own self-identity.

3. **The origin of the message is perceived or identified as a definite source that is, it has an existence of its own.** The origin may be from God or a celestial being. It may be a strong personality with a name, with writing or speaking mannerisms, emotions, and other personality characteristics. There may be minimal nuances, with only a feeling on the part of the human being that the message come from an "entity." Sometimes the source may seem to be a principle such as "creativity" or "limitless love and light," or the planetary logos. The person may speak under the inspiration of the Holy Spirit. If the person senses another presence communicating, this would fit within our definition.

This third characteristic excludes "open channeling" in which people receive inner information without an identifiable source. It is more specific than William Kautz's description of channeling as "a means of access to intuition" (Kautz and Branon, 1987). Poets such as A. E. Housman and Rainer Maria Rilke (1939) reported that verses simply appeared in their minds, fully written. Mozart and other composers heard inner music playing spontaneously as they composed. These, along with intuitions and creativity, are not channelling according to this criterion. Studies in philosophy and psychology have illuminated many characteristics of intuition and creativity. It is not clear that the process of spontaneous creativity or intuitive thinking is the same process as one in which there appears to be an outside personality or entity. This book will focus primarily on the "definite source" type of channeling. The three characteristics described above define classic channeling. There are some further aspects that are essential components of channeling in human affairs.

*5. **Trust** it. Become aware of how you respond to your intuition. Do you 'undermine' yourself? Do you suffer from intuition anxiety? Do you judge your intuition as weird? Create a place of inner safety, a personal sanctuary. Learn how to shift your point of focus so that you experience feeling safe and secure.*

*6. **Nurture** it. Deep breathing, yoga, and relaxation exercises are especially valuable. Learn how to defocus your attention from tense, stressful situations so that you can be receptive to input from your intuition. Make a mind map and a treasure map to stimulate free-form, creative ideas.*

*7. **Value** it. Respect your intuitive intelligence as another mental ability. Affirm that you deserve to make full use of your whole brain, including your intuition. If your voice of reason opposes this intention, engage in a dialogue with it. You may want to refer to the voice of reason in chapter 12. Understand how intuition functions as part of your whole-brain intelligence network and affirm for yourself that you will recognize and support the information it sends you.*

*8. **Release** it. Then wait for it to guide you. Ask for advice or direction and learn how to identify the response. It may be a voice, a flash of insight, an emotional impression or gut feeling, or simply a sense of knowing where to go and what to do.*

*9. **Validate** it. How did information from your intuition serve you? Was it accurate? Did it work? Was it timely? Helpful? Use your rational intelligence to assess it.*

*10. **Thank** it. At first, the idea of saying or thinking "thank you" to a part of your own mind may seem strange. But it's important. Don't you work better when someone thanks you for a job well done? As you become more familiar with this step, you will find that you naturally feel appreciative when your intuition transmits helpful signals. Thanking it is a part of learning to appreciate yourself and reinforces the intuitive process."*

For other practical exercises for getting in touch with your intuition, please see Questionnaire #6 and Exercise #1 in your Workbook.

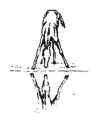

A qualified channeller, astrologer, or psychologist will help you get in touch with your own inner resources and develop your trust in your sixth sense.

Spiritual energy is our creative energy, the energy that allows us to grow and to change. I believe that our spiritual energy does not get blocked as our mental energy does, but that it often remains an unknown asset. We all have spiritual energy, and it affects our everyday lives even when we are not aware of it. Our spiritual energy gives us our dreams and ideas. This untapped resource can be enhanced if we learn to use its power. All of us have creative ability, but most of us unknowingly keep it hidden. Meditation is the only tool that I know that will release your spiritual energy. There are many forms of meditation. Biofeedback, Martial Arts, The Relaxation Response, Prayer, Russell Scoop's Relaxation Therapy(RSRT), TM and Yoga are a few that I describe in the Relaxation chapter. Regular meditation is essential. To help you plot the value of meditation, please see Chart #1 in your Workbook.

To feel the warmth of our energy, we must tend the flame. For our physical energy, we must eat well and exercise regularly. Allowing ourselves emotional expression and communicating honestly and completely will keep our mental energy from becoming blocked. Regular meditation will release our spiritual energy, and trust in our intuition will allow us to make use of it.

The beauty of all of this is that our total being is energized when these forces are fed. The highest level of success with a horse requires unimpeded physical, mental, and spiritual energy. A good ride on our horse heightens our energy level for use in our day-to-day life. One moves the other.

Which comes first? The first step is to recognize and to release all of your energies. You may notice an instant change with your horse, but it is much more likely that the improvement will be slow and gradual. You will begin to have better rides, and after the rides you will start to feel more energetic. Slowly, you will discover that each ride becomes more invigorating and enjoyable for both you and your horse. Unfortunately you will not know exactly what has caused the change, as it will be a result of all the pieces coming together.

Remaining energized is a constant challenge. Day-to-day obstacles, both on and off the horse, frequently threaten your energy level. However, once you establish sound habits you will discover that the difficulties do not stop you, they simply require some immediate attention. Your new tools will enable you to make a quick diagnosis of the source of the problem, and then to take the appropriate action.

Please see Chart #2 to help you diagnose the source of any threats to your energy. The threat may be physical, mental, or spiritual. Each of these three has its own characteristics, and each affects the others. Like the link between physical illness and the mind, your physical energy is frequently affected by your mental or spiritual condition. Physical activity frequently frees us mentally. Mental awareness can free us physically. It is important to recognize the energy blocks, determine their origins, and find a cure. To keep your energy fire blazing, you must keep the fuel, oxygen, and draft in balance through your awareness and care.

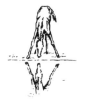

Once you decide that you need to develop your energy, use whatever tools you can to help you release the energy blocks. Relaxation and empathy are two of the most helpful tools at your disposal.

Attitude

Your attitude is your inner-most point of view toward yourself, your horse and the world. Having a positive attitude about life is the first step toward a successful journey. We can all learn to have a positive attitude.

In *Zen in the Martial Arts,* Joe Hyams stated:

> *The mind is like a fertile garden. . . . It will grow anything you wish to plant - beautiful flowers or weeds. And so it is with successful, healthy thoughts or negative ones that will, like weeds, strangle and crowd the others. Do not allow negative thoughts to enter your mind for they are the weeds that strangle confidence.*

Samuel Cypert, director of communications at Masco Corp., a Fortune 500 Manufacturer and author of *Believe and Achieve,* was interviewed for <u>Bottom Line</u>, Volume 13, Number 6, March 30, 1992;

> *"**Positive Mental Attitude(PMA)**. If you expect success, you will succeed. If you expect failure, you'll fail. It's as simple as that.*

Negative thinking is a learned habit. We can condition our minds to think positively by replacing negative thought with positive ones—hour by hour, day by day.

We can't control all of the circumstances of our lives, but we can control our attitude toward them. PMA means having the appropriate attitude under the circumstances.

This is not the Pollyanna-ish approach that says, If I just look on the bright side, everything will be perfect. It requires analyzing your circumstances, minimizing the risk and maximizing the advantages...then approaching the situation with the belief that you will succeed."

The outcome of our actions is influenced by our attitude. The more positive we are when we begin, the more likely it is that we will see and produce favorable results. Our attitude strongly influences our perception of events and conversations. It can also affect the actual outcome of an event. A positive attitude increases our energy, patience, and commitment, all of which contribute to the quality of our performance. Attitude is self-perpetuating. If we begin with a positive attitude, the chances of a positive outcome are greater and the affirmative outcome will improve our self-confidence. The opposite can happen with a negative attitude.

What exactly is attitude? I think that attitude is the reflection of our mental and spiritual makeup. It is defined by the dictionary as "manner of acting, feeling or thinking that shows in ones disposition." Most often we will discover that how we receive experiences and communications will produce an image of ourselves. From Cranfield's *Quote/Unquote*:

Our attitude toward the world around us depends upon what we are ourselves, If we are selfish, we will be suspicious of others. If we are of a generous nature, we will be likely to be more trustful. If we are quite honest with ourselves, we won't always be anticipating deceit in others. If we are inclined to be fair, we won't feel we are being cheated. In a sense, looking at the people around you is like looking in a mirror. You see a reflection of yourself.

For months Molly had been planning to attend a show. She traveled many miles and spent a considerable amount of time and money to attend the show. Her horse had been going very well at home, and she was confident that she they would be successful in competition. From the beginning of the trip through the warmup, everything went very well. But when she entered the ring for her first class, her horse stopped several times and was eliminated. She remained optimistic, and attributed her defeat to the very muddy footing. She kept her positive attitude. As she continued through the day, she had a couple of good rounds as the ground dried up, but no ribbons. Naturally she was disappointed. However, instead of becoming depressed, she was proud of herself for continuing the day and improving her performance. Her disappointing performance forced her to review the day. She looked at it from every angle, including through her horse's eyes. Because she started confidently, she figured out that the poor footing and the long trip had made her horse a little sore. Through her reflection, she discovered that she had not been quick enough to evaluate the conditions and support her horse. She gained knowledge and confidence from the experience. It was her way of thinking that tipped the scales in favor of confidence. A person with a negative attitude could have blamed the lack of success at the show on the conditions of the show, complained, and been unhappy. This attitude would not have produced any learning results for the next experience. The negative person would remain at a standstill because of his attitude.

Each of us is responsible for our own attitude. We can choose whether to be up-beat, positive, and open-minded, or discouraged, pessimistic, and negative. Often the decision is unconscious and heavily influenced by our opinion of ourself. It is tempting to blame our environment or co-workers for making us feel bad. Environment and other people DO have an affect on us. When we are aware that our attitude needs an adjustment, we must take a careful look within ourselves, at our environment, and at the people we associate with. It is up to us to do something about the feelings we are projecting.

It is essential to identify and choose a positive physical, cultural, and social environment for your horse activities.

If you feel your attitude becoming negative, you must investigate the reason. The environmental conditions of light, noise, and cleanliness may be incompatible with your needs, but it is more likely that the social or cultural climate may not be meeting your needs. One student's life changed when she finally moved her horse to a new barn. She was being criticized for her desire to learn beyond the confines of her boarding stable. The other boarders' insecurity led them to become jealous of her activities. She tried to ignore the negativism, but after a year found that she was losing interest in going to the barn. Ultimately she decided that it would be better to find another stable where the clientele shared her attitude, even if it meant traveling a greater distance. It was a struggle to make the decision, but once she moved she found a refreshing atmosphere in the new barn. She was able to enjoy her rides and resume her learning, and her positive attitude returned.

Normally, teaching energizes me. One stable, however, drained my energy. It took me quite a while to uncover the problem. Each month when I returned, there had been no progress. Instead, I was offered excuses for not practicing the prior month's assignment; it was too wet, too dry, too hot, car broke down, footing uneven, horse lame, etc. At first I believed these excuses, but later I wondered why most of the riders in this stable made so many excuses and no progress. It was the prevailing attitude of that barn. No matter how much I wanted to remain positive, I could feel my energy drain to zero by the end of the day. When I experience a drain of energy, an unpleasant feeling or negativism, I first look at my attitude, then at my environment, and then at the attitude of those around me. This search will uncover the cause.

When you have unusual problems with your horse, you should perform the same sort of evaluation. In the first place, take an HONEST look at how you feel physically and mentally, then look the same way at your horse. If you find that the problem is physically-induced, fix it if you can. If you cannot fix it immediately, change your program for that day's ride to accommodate the problem. If you find that the problem is mental, use the system of deconstruct, review and reconstruct, and then continue. If the problem is too complex, then either put it 'on hold' or go for a hack. Your horse's reactions are usually a clear reflection of your attitude; for horse lovers, our horse can be our clearest mirror.

For weeks Frank's horse was trying to tell him that something was wrong. Each ride produced resistance and seemingly little progress. Frank began to mope around with a gloomy attitude, while his horse showed more and more resistance during their rides. Finally, because of my compassion for Frank's horse, I had to take the chance of invading Frank's privacy to ask him what was causing his gloomy attitude. He was reluctant to talk to me, but finally admitted that he was discouraged because his training was not progressing. Our discussion revealed that Frank felt that he was not meeting my expectations, and had interpreted my instructions and communications as, "You cannot train your horse, Frank." I had certainly never intended to put him down or discourage him, but his lack of self-confidence and his unwillingness to ask questions had combined to distort his interpretation of my words. Unfortunately Frank was unable to discuss his feelings, thus the discouraging thoughts gradually turned into depression. If Frank's attitude about his instruction program had been more positive, he would have looked at the situation from various angles. This could have led him to ask questions and open the communication between student and instructor.

Frank's misunderstanding is a typical communication problem. Frank felt that he should be able to do whatever I was asking immediately. Because he did not tell me he was frustrated, I did not realize that he was expecting immediate results with his horse. I did not expect instant results; I was expecting gradual improvement. Frank and I had different expectations, and we failed to discuss this very important information with each other. Frank's misunderstanding caused his attitude to deteriorate. No one, instructor, parent, partner or friend should be expected to know how we think or feel. Our privacy should always be respected. It is up to us to express how we think and feel. If something causes pain, confusion, or hurt feelings, it is up to us to ask questions in pursuit of eliminating the problem. It may seem scary or painful to try to understand the cause of a problem, but as we practice communicating our thoughts and feelings with the appropriate people we will discover that it is not as painful as we originally thought. If we do not clear it up, it can manifest itself into a major problem and we may even lose sight of the origin of the depressed or gloomy attitude we are experiencing. Consider the mistakes that you make with your horse. Once you have a conversation with your aids that your horse understands, you move on, leaving the misunderstanding behind. We all have many misunderstandings with our horses, but usually they are resolved and we move on. We can do the same with people.

Frank's misunderstanding had gone on too long for it to be solved by words alone. We must live our positive attitude. Learn to evaluate the results of your actions objectively. Journal-keeping is an excellent tool. Let us return to Frank. Frank had no idea of the effect his attitude had on his horse. Once he began keeping a journal of his daily experiences, he learned that after he began to improve his attitude, he made progress with his horse. His notes provided the proof that improvement was possible, his self-confidence improved, and he began to trust his own abilities. Journal keeping establishes a record of gradual changes in behavior or performance, changes that are often too small to notice daily. The long-term, detailed notes of the journal reveal the pattern. At the end of this chapter is Frank's three month journal. You will find a basic journal for your use at the end of your Workbook. It contains reminder questions from the text of this book.

To avoid Frank's misunderstanding and the many more that we encounter day-to-day, we must begin to train ourselves to have a positive, open-minded attitude about ourselves. There are several methods that we can use to help ourselves create a positive image. One of the most popular is Psychocybernetics. Maxwell Maltz gives a detailed description of his use of imagery, visualization and repetition in his book *Psycho-Cybernetics*. If you use his technique, you can change a negative self-image into a positive one. Jane Savoie describes its use for riders in her book. Both authors expand on the concept of convincing yourself that the problem does not exist. I think that we must go one step further, we must learn to deconstruct what we feel or think and then decide to ACCEPT, REJECT, or REPLACE during reconstruction. Once we have accepted the negative, we can then use psycho-cybernetics to enhance the positive.

What are your attitudes? Questionnaire #7 in your Workbook will help you identify your attitudes. We often do not see our own attitude because it is such an intimate part of our being. It is also a spiritual characteristic that is often dormant. Negative attitudes often conceal our secret fears and weaknesses. Examine any signs of negative attitude in yourself, and try to understand the cause. With understanding and acceptance of what you cannot change, you may be able to

Humility

Humility is an essential ingredient to be in proper balance with our horse and the world.

From the *Living Bible*, Philippians 2, verses three and four: "Don't be selfish: don't live to make a good impression on others. Be humble, thinking of others as better than yourself. Don't just think about your own affairs, but be interested in others, too, and in what they are doing." We can recognize humility by its unselfishness, thoughtfulness, gentleness, unpretentious spirit, and desire to help others. A horse outshines humans in unselfishness, has an unpretentious spirit and a desire to please, and in addition he possesses strength, power, agility, and presence. These attributes should help us recognize humility and strive to be humble.

Humility can affect the way we learn, select professionals, and relate to others. Humility can make the difference between a mediocre and a superior performance. We can ride, perform, and even win without humility. However, humility changes the focus of our ride toward the horse's energy, by allowing us to surrender ourselves to the horse. We then become a partner in the performance that we are directing. We share in his brilliance, we do not produce his brilliance through control.

Our western culture thrives on control. We feel compelled to control ourselves, our families, our profession, our relationships, our environment, and our emotions. We tend to use the same dominant control with our horse. But shouldn't we control our horse's energy? Yes, but through quiet humility, and the control should be mental rather than physical. Because our mind is superior, we can out-think our horse and direct his power and majesty. We can allow him to perform at his best. Just as our self-love motivates us to better ourselves, our love for our horse should prompt us to put his betterment ahead of our needs. Humility has been an age-old problem over the years as expressed by many varied philosophies. To borrow a brief summary from Charles Swindoll in his book, *Laugh Again,*

> *Greece said, "Be wise, know yourself."*
> *Rome said, "Be strong, discipline yourself."*
> *Religion said, "Be good, conform yourself."*
> *Epicureanism says, "Be sensuous, satisfy yourself."*
> *Education says, "Be resourceful, expand yourself."*
> *Psychology says, "Be confident, assert yourself."*
> *Materialism says, "Be possessive, please yourself."*
> *Ascetism says, "Be lowly, suppress yourself."*
> *Humanism says, "Be capable, believe in yourself."*
> *Pride says, "Be superior, promote yourself."*
> *Christ says, "Be unselfish, humble yourself."*

No wonder we have trouble defining our role.

To develop this humble relationship with our horse, we must first understand him, our goal, and our role in the performance. We assume a position much like that of the conductor of an orchestra. He knows the strengths of the individual musicians, and he knows the music. The conductor is the leader, but he himself does not produce the resulting music. However, without him, there would be a lack of harmony. As we ride, we must guide the performance to maximize our strengths and minimize our weaknesses. We know the piece we hope to produce, and we are responsible for its harmonic wholeness.

If our superior mind remains humble, it allows us to direct rather than control the power and majesty of the horse.

Man's ego is often his biggest pitfall. The individual with an inflated ego easily loses sight of his role in the performance or his life. An inflated ego can be a result of the person's position, or it can be a protective mechanism for a person who lacks self-confidence.

Some of America's top equestrians are very good examples of maintaining humility despite their success. The horsepersons who produce countless horses and riders for the top levels of competition have good reason to blow their horn, but instead you will hear them discuss the wonder of the horses. These are horsepersons who have REALLY been successful.

The over-inflated ego, resulting from lack of self-confidence or sound knowledge, is all too common. We all know at least one person who does nothing but talk about his wins, no matter how small. When we hear someone talk about himself or drop names, a warning bell should sound. These habits suggest a falsely inflated ego, which is usually accompanied by shallow or incomplete knowledge. Unfortunately, there are many of these people in the horse world. In the Attitude chapter I suggested a technique for observing the attitude of those around us. The purpose of the observation is not to be critical or judgmental, but to determine whom you should see as a positive role model. It is beneficial for you to see the wrong in these inflated egos; it teaches you to be careful with your own ego. Once you see the deception, you can speculate on the reasons, but you cannot change the condition. I believe that these people, for one reason or another, have not achieved the success that they crave. They are frequently unrealistic in their personal evaluation. Often they are full of hard-luck stories and other excuses. They hang on to small successes and are constantly attempting self-promotion. Your careful listening skills will reveal this self-promotion. Why do these people deceive others? They try to create their wished-for image in the listener's mind. If they can succeed, then they have fulfilled their dream. All of us are capable of creating thoughts, both honest and deceitful. Falsely inflated egos cannot be humble, because they risk exposing their 'real self'. It is possible for a genuinely successful person to have an ego that is out of proportion, but that person will seldom maintain his success over time. Watch for the symptoms in yourself and in others, and beware of persons who are lacking in humility.

How often do you hear something and then ask questions before you believe it? Not often enough. This is a common mistake. When we are impressed, we blindly believe what we are told. We must listen, verify what we hear, and then decide whether we believe it or not. One very clear story comes to my mind. One professional who has been promoted as a distinguished rider and trainer by the media has really done nothing but win one ribbon in one international competition. The sad fact is that this professional has influenced many lives through clinics, articles and other forms of self-promotion. Is he qualified? Of course not, but few know. Very few can even find out. Even if we do want to be knowledgeable consumers in the horse world, we find it difficult because there is no consumer's report! It is hard to know how to verify what we hear or read because there are very few standards for the horse world professionals. Sadly, those who lack humility and spend their time blowing their own horn are often those who influence us the most because they speak so loudly and so frequently. When you are selecting a professional to help you, it is essential that one of your criteria be humility. You will learn the most from someone who neither brags nor tries to sell himself. The self-promoting, horn-blowing, self-impressed person is dangerous—there is a very good chance that he will not have the priorities, knowledge, or attitude that will enable you and your horse to progress.

Another painful complication can be the professional who is less interested in helping you learn, and more interested in taking over your horse to help build his own reputation as a rider/trainer. He will compliment you on your horse or your riding, really making you feel good. Later he will propose the benefit of training with him. It will be very tempting. An example of this is a young woman who was competing in novice level events. She learned by attending clinics. At one clinic, a popular event professional offered to have her move from novice to intermediate in just one year. He told her how talented she was, and that all she needed for success was to train with him. Two months after she moved to his barn, he decided that she was not ready to compete her horse, and said that he should compete the horse for her. Sudddenly she was on the sidelines, while he was having a wonderful time competing and winning on her horse! We must all try to be aware of the self-promotion that exists, both because it influences us and because it can happen to us! One should always stay alert when under the influence of the person who lacks humility. It is essential to remain humble. The best horsepersons are humble.

How to develop and maintain humility.
* *Remember it is the horse who wins!*
* *Enjoy your role in the performance.*
* *Take pride in your role to direct the majesty of the horse.*

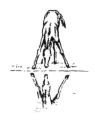

How to stay Humble:
- *Understand and encourage your horse.*
- *Maintain a positive attitude and a clear understanding of the roles of all involved.*
- *Think of your horse first!*

How can you develop humility? The first step you must take is always to give credit to your horse. In all but equitation classes, it is the horse who wins. You make it possible, but he does it. Keep this foremost in your mind, even when your walls are covered with ribbons. The second step is to enjoy the role you play in influencing this performance as rider and conductor. Take pride in your ability to direct the majesty of the horse. If, after a performance, you are able to see your role as the brains behind the performance influencing the horse's power, you have mastered the art of humility.

How is this a tool? If you DEMAND a performance, you will only be able to produce mediocrity. Depending upon the circumstances and conditions of the competition, you may win —but you will not be enhancing your horse's beauty. This is the difference between a quiet rider who understands and encourages his horse to give his all, and a rider who demands, pushes, and physically tries to over-power his horse. A rider who learns humility will have a freer performance, his horse will stay sound longer and, when he wins, he really wins. It is riding on the edge in its purest form.

The second step in remaining humble is to maintain a clear attitude in all the roles involved. Questionnaire #10 and #11 in your Workbook will help you evaluate your role in your performances, as well as the humility of the professionals in your horse life.

Whatever your goal, approaching it with humility will enhance its value and magnify the joy of attaining it. Not only will you better appreciate your horse's role in the accomplishment, but you will also attain a more honest perception of your own contribution. Nothing will be tarnished by pretension.

Develop and maintain your own humility and you will recognize its presence or absence in others.

Expect humility as one of the qualities of the professionals you employ to look after your horses or teach you. Often it is those who have an "ego problem" who try hardest to influence you. Developing your own humility will help you recognize humility, or its absence, in others.

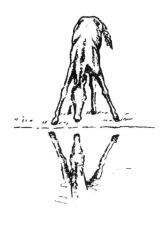

Knowledge

Knowledge is a product of the learning process which acquires and processes information through communication, research, and instruction.

Knowledge, which is a product of the learning process, results from information gathered, experienced, and processed. Information is the data gained through communication, research, and instruction. Horsemen should do most of their processing of information through reflection and critical thinking. The process of gaining knowledge can take minutes or years, depending upon the magnitude of what you are learning. During the learning process, you investigate the information gathered and then synthesize it through critical thinking and reflection. Learning to use all of our learning styles will help us to successfully meet our goals.

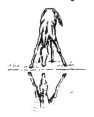

From Beyond the Mirrors;
Whether you are a beginner or an expert, a student or an instructor, seek knowledge continually.

Sources Of Information

The first step in learning is to collect as much information as possible. Each day we are given the opportunity to learn from our horse, instructor, reading, discussion, observation, and participation in activities. The second step is to be open to the possibility of overlap among the various activities in your life. I have discovered that with a learning attitude, I can gain information for better riding from my 'real' life, and my 'real' life can gain valuable information from my horse experiences. When we use our creative mental energy to notice the relationship, we see that all life experiences are closely interwoven. Each component of an experience provides factors for us to evaluate: what we see, smell, hear, taste, and feel. Whether the experience is positive or negative, we can learn from it.

We must learn to collect as much information as possible in both our riding learning and our 'real life' learning. Each experience offers us an opportunity to learn through our mind and our senses.

In horsemanship, our best teacher is our horse. You and your horse are in a partnership. Every partnership requires close interaction between the parties. When you ask your horse a question (e.g., asking him to move, turn, change gait, etc), the nature of his answer will tell you how clear and accurate your question was. Each time we ask our horse to do something, we wait for a response. The response may be what we asked for, or it may be something unexpected. Listening intently with our feel to this response is our greatest way of learning. There is no middleman in this learning. It is one-on-one, thus experiential learning: learning at its best. To make this form of learning work for you, you must become a good listener. While you are mounted, you 'listen' to your horse primarily through your senses. When you have been too aggressive, you will elicit a reaction with the ears, eyes or tail. If you have been too quiet, you may not get a response at all. If you have been unclear, the horse may perform the wrong move. Your horse's answer will tell you how well you have communicated with him.

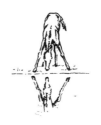

Learning sources:
- ◆ *1. Horse*
- ◆ *2. Instructor*
- ◆ *3. Reading material*
- ◆ *4. Discussion*
- ◆ *5. Observation*
- ◆ *6. Riding experience itself*

Next to the horse, your instructor plays the greatest role in your learning. Your instructor should direct your actions and thoughts with sensitivity, awareness, and understanding to promote learning experiences. Your instructor should see that you gain the necessary theory; and then must encourage you to put the theory into practice. A good instructor's communication is based on what he feels and sees from the student's and the horse's point of view. One of the major tasks of an instructor is to help the student diagnose and remove the road blocks that interfere with learning. This includes helping the student to gain the position and feel that is necessary for effective communication with the horse. The instructor should encourage independence, not dependence. There are times in the learning process when a student may be dependent upon an instructor, but those times should be few. The instructor should ask the rider what his goals are, then develop a program to help him achieve them. Once the goals have been determined, the student should know the route the instructor will take to guide him towards success. It is the instructor's job to help the rider create realistic, attainable goals. The instructor is the producer of the symphony, the rider is a player and conductor, the horse is the instrument. The performance is the symphony itself. By keeping the various roles in perspective, you will avoid disharmony.

Reading is a vital source of information. Reading requires a lot of sorting. There is an endless supply of reading material. The books and magazines often deliver conflicting information. Reading all types of information keeps us well rounded and provides us with a perfect opportunity to practice our critical thinking. Some of the material we read confirms what we DO NOT want to use, some material inspires further thinking, and some material provides the answers to questions that have been 'on hold.' Even if you do not share the opinion of the author, continue reading because there still may be one piece of vital information in the article. However, just because it is in print does not mean it is true! I wrote *Beyond the Mirrors* to inspire other like-minded persons. Although I am by no means an authority, I have found that to many people, the fact that I wrote a book made me an authority. This is wrong, because my opinions are based on my perceptions. If they make sense and apply to your life they may be helpful, but they are not the only way. I want this book to inspire readers to reflect, and to perform a critical review of concepts and ideas. Writing inevitably reflects the author's opinion and experiences, and the article must be evaluated and used as it relates to your life, not taken as the only way!

Information received from your horse, instructor, or reading material is of little value unless you discuss it. Discussion allows you to relate the information to others, to ask questions, and to listen to answers. When you ask your horse for something, you must listen to his answer, and then, through feel and your knowledge, decide whether you should acknowledge his response as correct, or ask again. This is a discussion between you and your horse. If your instructor asks you to do something, you must acknowledge that you understand, or ask a question to make the request clear. This is a discussion between you and your instructor. If you read an article that is controversial or confusing, you should discuss it with a peer or with your instructor so that you can understand it more clearly.

We must know how we want to look, how we want our horse to look, and how we want both our horse and ourself to look together. In other words, we need to hold a picture in our mind; we need to have a visual understanding of our goals. Our best tool for this is observation, and to develop our observations we must practice perceptive, frequent watching. We should spend as much time as possible observing the activity being done correctly, and much less time watching it being done incorrectly. A little time spent watching what NOT TO DO is OK, but this can quickly become counter-productive: observation has a profound effect on learning, and if we spend too much time watching something being done incorrectly, we risk learning it that way. Find someone who is doing what you want to do, and observe carefully. A quote from one of my students:

"I had the instruction and knowledge of what to do and how to do it. I had been practicing the physical feel of the specific movements. However, I had no visual way to watch the knowledge in action [this student lived too far away for regular observation]. When I watched a really good trainer for six days for several hours a day, I put "eyes" to my intellect. I could see and feel what was happening between the trainer and his horses. I began to develop a sense of timing and an understanding of the response of the horse to my aids. I went home and was able to perform much better on my horses. I discovered that after watching I was able to add looking and listening to my knowledge. Each time I rode I tried to feel like the trainer. It really helped!"

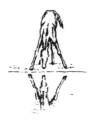

You can learn a lot by watching with a clear mind and positive attitude and relating what you see and feel to your own riding.

As you watch, you must know what you are looking for, and then you must concentrate, relate to both the rider and the horse, and try to feel what you are seeing. Watching with other thoughts on your mind will not help you; neither will trying to pick faults. You must watch, relate, and use your clear mind and positive attitude to help you feel what you see.

Riding itself combined with reflective and critical thinking will help you learn from each ride. Reflective thinking will allow you to review and evaluate each day's ride. Take your ability to reflect even further, and review the details of the ride in relationship to your short-term and intermediate goals. With practice, it will take you only a few minutes to evaluate the experience. This evaluation should not involve detail or an abundance of words, and it should not be done while training. It should relate to your goals and how you performed as both player and conductor, as well as how your horse performed as the instrument. What was the major skill learned or practiced? Remember and review it. All the senses involved in these experiences are vital to your learning. A valuable reflective tool is journal writing. Keeping a journal can help you form the habit of automatic reflective thinking.

Two other, less traditional, learning tools that I have found to be most useful are creating a learning profile and attending a clinic.

I discovered that I gained a lot of confidence in my knowledge by doing a learning profile for my portfolio class. The class required the learning profile for all of my life experiences. This can be a valuable learning tool for riding students. You can help to chart your own progress by keeping a learning profile of your horse-related learning experiences. Questionnaire #12 in your Workbook will help you plot your horse learning experiences.

Attending clinics is also valuable to the learning process. Clinics provide completely different results and methods from your regular instruction programs. Riders often feel that they get dramatic results from a clinic. During a clinic, the clinician must take what he feels is most important and then, in a short time and with great intensity, communicate through you to the horse to get the desired results. Normally, when you attend a clinic you do exactly as you are told. A clinician is usually a good communicator as well as an experienced horseman; you are his instrument to communicate with the horse. Thus you get immediate results. The problem is that you have not had enough time to experiment with the information to be sure it will work without the guidance of the clinician. After the clinic, you must review the day's activities and reflect on them. Then you must experiment and practice, using the new information and ideas. Until you can do it on your own, it is not knowledge. The time you spend in reflection and evaluation is important for other reasons, too. Sometimes the enthusiastic or intimidating attitude of the clinician can cause you to believe that what he is teaching is correct, and what you had been doing before was wrong. This is dangerous, but I have seen it happen. Again, you must evaluate the information you are receiving. Whenever possible, ask your instructor to attend a clinic with you. This way your instructor can learn, as well as discuss with you, any conflicting or confusing information. For years I held regular clinics for my students. At each clinic, I discovered holes in my teaching techniques which I then corrected. I found this an excellent learning tool. I also discovered how valuable it was for my students to be able to discuss clinic results. Each clinic became a very valuable learning experience for all of us!

Investigation

You must always evaluate all sources of information. How do you evaluate them? What criteria can you use to compare them? To become an educated horseman, you should use both intuitive and factual information. Assuming that you are working on your personal balance, one tool you can use is your intuition, which is tacit knowledge. Trust your intuitive feelings related to situations and persons.

Factual information can be verified by any of the national organizations. Please remember that competence is not just a matter of ribbons won. To evaluate someone's competence based on a ribbon or trophy, you must learn about the competition, the qualifying criteria, how many riders competed in the division or class, whether the placing reflected a team or an individual effort. Investigate the number of successes the individual had, as well as the number of students he has coached or trained. You may have to make a considerable effort to find it, but all of this information is available.

If you are researching the credentials of an instructor, investigate his students' results. Observe a lesson at your level. Try a lesson and get a feel for the technique, knowledge, and approach of the instructor. The best-qualified instructor may not offer a teaching style that will correspond with your learning style.

The same criteria are true when you consider purchasing a horse. If you do not have the knowledge and experience yourself, choose a trusted professional to help you find an appropriate horse. You will have to pay for this help, but your money will be spent wisely. Most professionals selling horses have a unique philosophy about honesty. If you do not ask a question that will reveal the problem a horse has, the seller is not obligated to tell you. Therefore, you must know the correct questions to ask!

If you are lucky enough to know other riders in whom you have confidence, you can ask them who their instructor is or where they purchased their horse. My introduction into the Warmblood world started in just that way. Years ago I was searching for a horse for my son, Scott. Every horse we found that was large enough for him and had the potential to event, was vetted unsound. At competitions, I watched to see if there were any horses that met my criteria. At one event I saw a horse that was large and had expressive, elastic movements. I asked the rider where he got the horse. He told me. I then called the seller and went to see his horses. I not only found one horse that I wanted, but a type of horse that was new to most Americans at that time. Warmbloods challenged me to learn again about the bodies and minds of this unfamiliar type of horse. I had gained a major highlight on my learning profile, just because I asked a timely question!

Remember that you are evaluating the results, the technique, the style, and the attitude of the person, horse, or stable you are considering. You will have to invest time and effort if you wish to become a knowledgeable horseperson, but in the long run that investment will save you money and time.

The time-consuming part of learning is the investigation. Once we uncover information, we must follow up by processing it using our critical thinking and reflection skills. We may then practice what we learn. The day-to-day practice, which is the way we investigate the usefulness of the information, automatically employs these learning skills. When you read something that you must investigate further, write it down— or, better still, put it 'on hold', which you will learn how to do later. When you do this, you will notice that various sources of information on the subject will be presented to you. You also will have saved the appropriate questions to be answered later. After you have completed your investigation and discovered new information that feels right, you must be willing to put it into practice.

To evaluate the information that you are experimenting with, you should use the long-term, intermediate and short-term goal techniques. You will need to do this over an appropriate time period, so that you may practice often enough to give the new information an honest chance to work. The long-term goal is the new knowledge itself, the intermediate goal is progress towards attaining results, and the short-term goal is the day-to-day practice. As an example of this, let us look at the process of learning to ride into corners, a must for a dressage rider. Louise had learned to ride first level, but was never taught proper corners. A new instructor told Louise that she could not go any further until she learned to do corners correctly. Louise discovered in her lesson that it is very difficult to coordinate the correct aids and really get into and out of the corners. She learned that her horse was not properly balanced for what she was asking him to do. Her lesson was no fun. It is more fun to continue to do shoulder-in and leg yields. Because Louise had won in shows without riding into her corners, she questioned this new expectation. However, Louise's horse felt much easier to ride after only three lessons with the new instructor, so Louise had to consider whether to listen or to have fun. This is the investigative stage of learning. Louise read about corners and talked to other successful riders. Finally she decided to try it. The instructor told her that once she could successfully perform a movement, she must practice it for at least one week to confirm it. Louise set her long-term goal to ride the corners, and gave herself four weeks to practice before her intermediate evaluation. She then set out to practice corners, her day-to-day goal. She discovered that it took less than a month to ride the corners correctly, and found that correct corners really helped her shoulder-ins and leg-yields.

How We Synthesize Investigated Information

Critical Thinking

According to Stephen Brookfield's book *Developing Critical Thinkers*, there are four parts to the critical thinking process. First, we must identify and challenge our assumptions to examine their accuracy and validity. Secondly, we must be aware of practices, structure, and actions in relation to what they are doing. Third, we must try to imagine and explore alternatives. Fourth and last, we must reflect with skepticism on the issues. No matter what discipline we are studying, we should use critical thinking from the moment we make the decision to learn to ride until we have completed our goal.

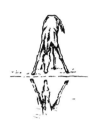

Critical thinking:

♦ 1. *IDENTIFY and CHALLENGE assumptions to examine their accuracy and validity.*

♦ 2. *Be AWARE of practices, structure and actions in relationship to what they are doing.*

♦ 3. *IMAGINE and EXPLORE alternatives.*

♦ 4. *REFLECT with skepticism on the issue.*

Louise made an honest mistake when she began riding, because she did not have enough information to engage in critical thinking. She went to the local instructor to begin riding, and did not do a background check of the quality of the instructor. How could she? She did not know anything about horses and riding. All beginners should try to learn as much as possible before embarking on an activity as involved as horsemanship. We can do part of this by examining the practices and actions of the instructor as they relate to our goals. For example, when Louise began to ride, she knew she wanted to study dressage after she mastered the basics. She could have read as much as possible about dressage, watched qualified dressage trainers, and discussed the fundamentals of dressage with respected, experienced riders. Does the instruction program teach good basics? What level are most of the students? You do not want to be taught by a rider who is so much more advanced than you that the instruction is over your head. Ideally, you would be able to find a stable where there were specialized instructors for the various levels, so that these instructors could teach to your level and move you forward one step at a time. If this perfect stable is not available, try to find an instructor who understands the value of teaching you at your level so that you do not miss any of the FOUNDATION steps that make you able to perform. In the long run, this process will usually require that you change instructors along the way. One instructor is usually most qualified to take you through three to four levels of your discipline.

If Louise had acquired this information, she could have decided how well-prepared her original instructor was to help her achieve her goal. Louise did not become aware of the various levels of competency, because her investigation did not go far enough. She became aware of her mistake while attending a clinic. She discovered that her instructor had left out part of her foundation. When she compared her level to what she needed to learn, she understood that she needed to go back and learn what she had missed. She decided that she also needed a new instructor. When Louise started riding, she did not have enough information to engage her critical thinking steps of imagination and exploration in her learning process. Before any of us can do this, we must have gained a base of information. However, the clinic experience exposed her to new information. When she compared the alternatives she discovered that she had holes in her learning. This new information, together with Louise's increased awareness, allowed her to engage her critical thinking. At this point, her attitude allowed the second step of her critical thinking process to be active.

The first two components of critical thinking are the ones that we begin to use. As our experience expands in each situation, we move on to be able to use the third and fourth components.

Reflecting with skepticism on what is learned can be applied after we have acquired a basic understanding and foundation. Once we have this foundation, each new issue should be looked at with skepticism. Are we getting the results we desire? Does what we are doing make sense? Is what we are doing free from causing harm? These are a few of the questions we must ask. However, we cannot reflect with skepticism until we are certain we understand, without confusion, what we are trying to do. We must also be certain that we have given our body and mind the required opportunity to perform the task successfully. If Louise had been too skeptical in her dealings with her new instructor, she might have decided that she was not getting results quickly enough, and thus moved on to still another instructor. Reflective skepticism must be initiated at the correct time related to what you are learning. It should be an automatic part of all learning. Reflective skepticism will keep you from the sort of unthinking trust that causes you to take action just because you were told to, rather than because you are certain that you need to take that action.

Reflection

From our first moment on the horse, until we achieve our goal, we need to use the reflective process. Boud, Keogh and Walker refer to reflection as "a generic term for intellectual and affective activities in which individuals engage to explore their experiences in order to lead to new understandings and appreciation." Whether we know it or not, we use our beliefs to make decisions, to analyze, perform, discuss, and judge. Reflection is an assessment tool that explains the hows and whys of what we thought or felt, or how we acted. When we reflect, we pause to reassess by examining our actions or thoughts. During our first lesson, we begin to learn position.

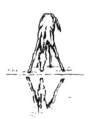

Reflection is an assessment tool that explains the hows and whys of what we thought or felt, or how we acted. When we reflect, we pause to reassess by examining our actions and thoughts.

After our lesson or ride, we reflect on what we learned; between lessons or rides, we reflect again. This form of reflection means that we think back through our experience and the results for both ourself and our horse. Before we begin our next lesson or ride we should be in the habit of reviewing the past lesson or ride. With the help of the horse and/or instructor, we constantly review what we are experiencing, and we constantly evaluate what we must improve or change to continue learning.

This is the learning process. On a broader scale, this process is used to evaluate our intermediate goal. Reflection is the a constant companion of a horseman.

Knowledge is that part of information that we take to be part of us so that we can use it when necessary.

Once there was an article in a magazine about teaching a horse flying changes. The article wrongly stated that if one just taught their horse to change its lead by a touch of the toe on the inside elbow, the horse would forever have good, easy changes. One of my students, who was frustrated trying to learn flying changes, read the article. Instead of believing what she read, she asked why we did not do it that way. As she reflected, she realized why this signal system was not a part of her training program. It was excellent that her critical thinking prompted her to ask for more information to be certain that she what she was learning was correct. This reading experience was a valid part of gaining knowledge, because it triggered questions which led to the affirmation of existing information. Sometimes we learn what not to do!

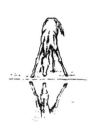

1. Continually seek information.
2. Process all information using reflection and critical thinking. Investigate what is in question—
    Does it make sense?
    Should I investigate this more?
3. Practice what feels right.

How We Learn

We all learn differently. There are three basic Learning Domains; cognitive, psychomotor and affective. For each of us, one of these methods is more dominant than the others. One challenge that riders must learn is to use all three of their learning domains. Studies have shown that the majority of people learn cognitively, by processing information through logical thinking. All of our learning begins this way.

The second most commonly used learning type is psycho-motor or hands-on, physical learning. The third and least common is the affective method, which allows us to learn through emotional or feeling responses. Learning to ride requires the use of all three domains, with the affective domain as the major link between horse and man. All riders must cultivate the affective method.

When we first begin to learn, we use the cognitive learning style. Then we practice our cognitive information using the psychomotor or hands-on method. The symphony is created through the affective style. Most of us unconsciously select a profession that allows us to use the learning style that we find most comfortable or natural. Most of us are cognitive learners. Gifted artists, musicians, and riders are predominately affective learners. To become successful riders, we must train ourselves to use all three learning styles. The methods I explained for balancing your energy will enable you to use all three learning styles.

The Cognitive Domain

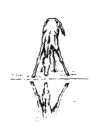

Cognitive Learning Domain: the first step for most riders
- ◆ *1. Introduce*
- ◆ *2. Understand*
- ◆ *3. Apply*
- ◆ *4. Analyze*
- ◆ *5. Synthesize*
- ◆ *6. Judge*

The first lessons for any new activity with horses will use the cognitive learning domain. There are six steps in cognitive learning. The first is the introduction to the fundamentals of the task to be learned. If we start at the very beginning, it will be learning the basic position of our body on the horse. The second step will be to understand how and why this position is to be learned: we are introduced to the effect of position on balance and control. The third step is the application of the principles: the use of what we learned in step one and two. The fourth step of this process is the analysis of what we learned and applied. What were the cause and effect of our actions, and what were the results? How does our position relate to our balance? The fifth step is the synthesis of the information from our analysis. In this step we evaluate what we heard, saw, read and/or experienced in relationship to the results we got and the results we want. The last step is the judgement of the quality based on the criteria that we learned. This judgement is made without the assistance of the outside party, instructor, or trainer; it is the rider's own evaluation. Ideally, we would be able to compare our judgement with that of the instructor or trainer after each lesson. But even if we could practice this, we should not rely on them to tell us their opinion without first making our own evaluation. This process will build up self-confidence. Most people routinely use this learning domain. I have broken down the steps that each person usually goes through without knowing it. Take your cognitive learning process and dissect it; how do you use each step?

The Psychomotor Domain

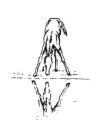

Psychomotor Domain: the second step in learning for riders

- *1. Awareness through senses*
- *2. Set: putting what we learn into action*
- *3. Guided response: practice*
- *4. Mechanism: create habit*
- *5. Complex overt response: putting together groups of habits*
- *6. Adaptation: use for new skills*
- *7. Create new motor actions*

The second learning domain used by the riders should be the Psychomotor Domain. It is the use of this type of learning that allows the new skill learned to become a natural part of our being. This is the practical application of the information we have learned cognitively. We take the first step in this domain by becoming aware of what we want to achieve, and then associating it to the task we are going to perform. While learning to ride, we use our cognitive domain to learn what we must do. Then we must transform this information into a practical awareness by using as many of our senses as possible. Using our earlier example of learning position, we must be aware of our body parts in relationship to the horse's body, and our reflexes in relationship to the horse's, while we learn to control him. Once we feel comfortably in balance on a horse, we know our perception is working. The second step is the set, or preparations for readiness to put what is learned into action. Since learning to ride means learning to communicate with the horse to get him to do what we want, we must be certain we know the steps to achieve this. The third step, guided response, involves our practicing the steps set forth to experience the specific skill being learned. Practicing walking and trotting while maintaining our balance and direction utilizes this step. As we master our position and direct the horse to go where we want him to go, we are demonstrating the first and most fundamental use of this step. The fourth step is mechanism. We remain in this stage until the learned behaviors become habitual. This is one of the most essential steps in building the basic foundation for horsemanship. Mastering this step can take weeks or months, but once we have mastered it, we are ready for the fifth step, the complex overt response. It is during this step that we begin to put together more complex groups of what we have learned. Let us say we have learned the aids to walk and trot, we have learned to maintain our balanced position, and we have learned to sit the trot. Putting these together to do ring figures such as circles, serpentines, or diagonals would be included in this step. The sixth step, adaptation, allows you to adapt the motor skills you have understood and practiced to meet the unanticipated demands of a situation. It is during this step of practical learning that you can test your skills on a different, more challenging horse. The complexities of different horses or different riding conditions will allow you to practice this step. Ideally, you should not ride different horses until you have reached this learning stage. The seventh and final step of this domain is the ability to create new motor actions based on the skills you have been practicing. This means that you are ready to learn something new, so you will move into the affective domain.

Affective Learning Domain

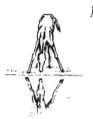

Affective Learning Domain: the third step for most riders
- ◆ *1. Receive information related to its value, belief, attitude*
- ◆ *2. React and respond*
- ◆ *3. Practice consistency and commitment to what we believe*
- ◆ *4. Organize*
- ◆ *5. Characterization, balanced learning*

When we use our affective learning domain, our first step is to receive information in the form of value, belief and attitude. By the time we are ready to put this into effect, we must have a goal in mind as well as a philosophy of the horse's relationship to our life, and a sense that horses and our horse-related activities have become intertwined with the rest of our life. The second step of this domain is to react and respond to information presented as positive or negative because we compare it through our cognitively stored information. By the time we employ this step, we have a reservoir of knowledge with which to compare new information. It was in this step that Louise realized she had not developed a sound foundation. During the third step of this domain, we learn what is related to consistency and commitment to our beliefs, values and attitude. The depth of this step allows us to act clearly and decisively, using our values and experiences. The fourth step, organization, allows us to organize our values, beliefs, attitude, and goals into a system, determine a learning system that is most significant to our goal, and make determinations on the inner aspects as well as the outer aspects. When you decide to compete, you are using this skill. The fifth step is characterization. At this point, our learning is balanced in such a way that we have a become identified with our beliefs. During the time we put into effect the use of this affective learning domain, we are basing our decisions on what we feel; we learn to use our skills in immediate response to an action of our horse. When we become accomplished at this, our horse will identify us with our beliefs. One perfect example is a young horse who is able to talk his lady rider out of insisting that he perform the task asked. He identifies her with passiveness. This young lady's trainer periodically gets on the horse and makes him perform, not through roughness, but through the ability to communicate his aids clearly and definitely through his feel. The horse makes only a token effort to test the trainer, and then performs cooperatively. As soon as the trainer gets on his back, the horse accepts the communication because of his perception of the trainer's identity, and because of the communication he receives. The trainer is identified by the horse as decisive! Most children, but only a few adults, find this their dominant learning domain.

The foundation for our response to our horse is cognitive knowledge. The psychomotor practical patterns train our body and mind to work together. Our aids trigger a response, so we must know when and how to acknowledge the horse's response. If he does not respond, we must be willing to try other aids to get the desired reaction. Only feel can tell us what to do.

We must quickly acknowledge the horse when he is correct and develop a mutual set of values and responses with him. We must be quick to break away from our patterns learned through our psychomotor learning to experiment with what we feel, not what we think. The affective or feeling learning is not useful without the other two, but it is very important: our desired ultimate result, the classical symphony, is only possible through affective learning.

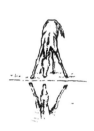

We first learn the facts and theory of what we want to do using the COGNITIVE learning domain. Then we must use the HANDS-ON learning domain to practice until we have the mechanics working. We put these two together with feeling and we begin to use the AFFECTIVE learning domain. It is this final stage that creates the symphony.

As we progress from beginner to advanced rider during our riding career, we will discover that we continue to repeat and intermix these learning domains. Each learning domain requires that we synthesize information using the critical and reflective thinking process. Learning to ride involves many different skills so, depending upon what we are learning, we will be able to use the appropriate leaning domain. Our ability to access what we are learning, be balanced with self and horse, and use all three of the learning domains automatically, will make our learning experience more fulfilling.

All riding requires focusing on what we are doing without extreme concentration. If you are a ball player, your brain is in your hand. A rider's brain should be in the horse (affective learning). A ball player can use his eyes to watch the ball and determine when to hit it. A rider cannot use his eyes, but instead must use his feel to tell the horse what to do. In order to get his focus in the horse, the rider must understand both himself and his horse. He must also be able to give himself up to his horse, to become part of his horse. At this point, the problem becomes one of concentration.

The Workbook contains two additional learning questionnaires. Questionnaire #13 is designed to help you evaluate your most comfortable learning style, and Questionnaire #14 is to help you evaluate your sources of knowledge.

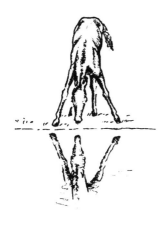

Empathy

Empathy allows you to put yourself into the inner being of your horse or another person where you can understand their motivation, attitudes and actions.

The ability to put yourself in the shoes of your horse is one of your most valuable learning tools. Empathy is a spiritual quality which allows you to feel the attitude, the thoughts, and the sensations of your horse. But sharing the feeling is not enough; understanding the experience, attitude, thought, and sensations complete the deep connection of empathy.

Empathy means sharing both the good and the bad, and so it often lies dormant because of our fear of its painful side. If you intimately share pain or sorrow with another being, you are subjecting yourself to pain. Who intentionally wants to do this? Not many of us. We often put up barriers that will protect us from pain. If we can be brave and open enough to be empathetic, we will open ourselves to joy and ecstasy, but also to pain and sadness. We cannot enjoy the ecstasy without the pain because the same mechanism opens us up to both.

As we release our mental and spiritual blocks, empathy will become a tool we can use. However, even once we have the resources, empathy takes time and practice to learn. Once learned, it will become an automatic way of viewing all situations. Several years ago Tim attended a clinic I taught. When Tim was describing his goals and his problems to me, he told me that he had a bad problem with his horse bucking. Tim explained that his horse had been bucking for at least six months and he had tried everything his instructor had told him, from riding him through it to beating him each time he bucked. I immediately found myself empathizing with the horse. I then watched Tim warm up. I felt that something was preventing the horse from wanting to go forward. Tim came over, and sure enough, his saddle was pinching the horse in the gullet area. I had him add an extra pad and immediately the horse's gaits changed. I explained to Tim that it would take time for the soreness to leave, and that he would need to get his saddle restuffed. At the next clinic Tim told me that he had NO bucking. It was my empathy with the horse that led me to discover quickly what was causing the bucking. Those watching said they could not see anything, how did I know? It was my ability to share the horse's feelings. We are all capable of developing this skill.

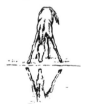

Empathy is the ability to feel and understand the motives, feelings and emotions of another being.

Empathy is a valuable skill, and can be used with both horses and people. I think it is easier to practice first with horses. Take a few minutes to imagine that you are your horse. Perhaps you may want to review the Spiritual Understanding section. Go into his stall. Observe him. What do you think he feels, sees, and hears? Take a few minutes to view the environment from your horse's perspective. Do this exercise as often as you can.

Once you can empathize with your horse in his environment, you can try it while riding. Being able to empathize off the horse will not automatically enable you to empathize on the horse, but it will make it much easier for you to learn. When you are riding you must be able to do this quickly. One rider described it as "riding off the seat of her pants." This is learning by using the affective domain. Empathetic riding is a major tool of the affective learning domain. You must be able to get into the horse, lose yourself through empathy into the horse, and remain there, not allowing anything to distract you. Once you become proficient, empathizing will be automatic, and you will be able to perform while feeling your horse and enjoying your environment. It will allow you to ride a winning performance. To help you learn to empathize with a horse, use Exercise #2 in your Workbook.

Try to become more aware of life from your horse's point of view. The questions in Questionnaire #15 in your Workbook are designed to help you see as if you were a horse.

Once you have mastered this tool for your horse, you should begin to practice it with people. The complex interaction in man's mental and spiritual make-up makes this a more difficult task. If you feel that you can understand and identify with man more easily, begin with man instead of your horse.

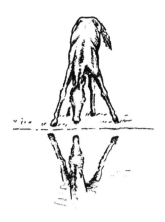

Relaxation

From Beyond the Mirrors

Relaxation is necessary for the rider to attain inner harmony and for the horse to display his natural beauty.

The definition of relaxation includes "the lengthening of inactive muscles or muscle fibers" and "the return or adjustment of a system of equilibrium following displacement or abrupt change." Relaxation should exist on three levels: Physical (suppleness), mental (clarity of mind and emotion) and spiritual (freedom from fear, anger, resentment, jealousy and other negative attitudes). The three are related in both humans and horses. Physical relaxation can be destroyed by confusion or fear, then it is not a simple matter of controlling the length of muscle fibers. In cases when the mind is the cause of tension, stress, fear, or confusion we must try to relax our mind. Even if the cause requires a solution, the starting point is a relaxed mind that can focus. If we hope to achieve physical relaxation, we need to address the methods of promoting mental and spiritual relaxation because they are all so closely connected.

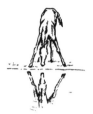

*Relaxation must exist on three levels:
Physical (suppleness), mental (clarity
of mind and emotion) and spiritual (freedom
from fear, anger, resentment jealousy and
other negative attitudes).*

Relaxation has many benefits in terms of both performance and soundness. Communication is more straightforward when we are relaxed. Both observer and horse feel that the rider is lighter and more graceful. Our body will move in harmony with the horse's movements. Our legs will breathe with the horse's sides. Our hands will be the quiet receivers and directors of the forward energy we are sharing. Our body as a whole will be prepared to respond to the horse quickly, quietly, and effectively. This harmony will enable both horse and rider to move forward with power and elasticity, creating a picture of total unity and majesty. The relaxed horse is more elastic, and thus is better able to perform the tasks we ask of him. In fact, the relaxed horse is an amazingly elastic creature, and therefore our goal should be to maintain this elasticity. It involves careful management of his physical body, slowly building up muscle tone. Most horses have an advantage over man, in that they begin with a calm mind. If communications are clear and demands are realistic, they should remain mentally calm. This mental calmness, combined with the proper training of horse and rider, should maintain the horse's elasticity, thus minimizing the wear and tear that cause unsoundness.

Chiropractic medicine, massage, ultrasound, laser therapy, suppling exercises, and heat therapy will help a horse or rider who is physically tight. Some horse therapists insist that once a horse relaxes from the body work they have done, the horse will enable the rider to become relaxed. Without a doubt it is easier for a rider to relax on a horse who is relaxed, but the rider must learn to become supple and relaxed himself so that the horse can stay elastic and relaxed after its treatment. Suppling and relaxation can help both horse and rider. All good therapists and doctors will tell you that most animals need to be treated for tightness only a few times, unless it is a chronic condition. However, an incorrectly ridden or injured horse may need additional treatment. It is the rider's responsibility to maintain the relaxation of the horse. It is more difficult for the rider to maintain a relaxed state, because the rider continues to have situations develop that make it difficult to maintain a relaxed, supple body. It is up to the rider to find an effective method to maintain a well-functioning body.

Each horse, like each rider, is different. Each one may benefit from a different type of treatment. If the treatment works effectively, then it is a rare horse that requires continued treatments. There are only two reasons that a horse might need continued treatment: if he is suffering from a chronic condition, where treatment may keep him comfortable and possibly even in work, or if the rider is not able to stay soft himself. Riders, on the other hand, frequently need repeated treatments because their stiffness is due to mental and spiritual tension.

Emotional turmoil or long-standing spiritual disorders produce disequilibrium in our bodies, leading to physical stiffness. Returning the body to equilibrium is a matter of relaxation. When we feel upset, or experience an uneasy feeling, an upset stomach, a headache, a backache, or another physical symptom, it may be our mental or spiritual self crying out for help. Other cries for help can be nervous habits like nail biting, wiggling our feet, tapping with fingers or feet, messing with hair, smoking cigarettes, or chewing gum. Physical exercises are designed to relax and supple muscles, while meditative therapies provide methods to relax and free the body, mind, and spirit.

"Meditation is any activity that keeps attention pleasantly anchored in the present moment." This definition is from Joan Borysenko. During this unique mental state, you experience less anxiety while you enjoy a sensation of relaxed muscles and heightened awareness of your inner person. There are many theories, but no one knows why this happens. I believe that we lock unpleasant, uncomfortable and unhappy experiences in our unconscious and lose the key. In order to gain access to our inner self, we must find the key to release control. Meditation can be a key that unlocks the control between our conscious and unconscious minds. Some forms of meditation even encourage the individual to ask the two sides of the brain to communicate. If we let the left side of the brain, our logical, analytical, thinking side, give the right side, the creative, intuitive side, permission to interact, more information will be released. This sometimes happens in our sleep when we dream. The study of dreams is useful to some people. Meditation, however, can give us a similar opportunity to become better acquainted with our inner being.

The more of our self we can access consciously, the more control we have over our lives and our goals. The more unresolved experiences we have locked in, the more meditative practice we will need to create the freedom that brings about a useful inner self. Basic meditation will eliminate the tightness in your body and allow feelings and thoughts to flow more easily. However, meditation requires training and practice.

There are many forms of meditation that promote relaxation: Yoga, TM, biofeedback, Martial Arts, Prayer, The Relaxation Response and relaxation therapy are a few. All use deep breathing, going to a quiet place in your mind and becoming one with yourself. Please see the enclosed brief summary of the most common forms of meditation, and choose the one suitable for your life-style and time constraints. Find a qualified course or therapist to help you learn it properly. You will be learning a new skill, just as you have learned to ride. Investigate to make certain that the therapist feels good to you, that he does not have an inflated ego, that he can give you references of people he has treated so you can talk to them. No course or counsellor should promote dependence. You should feel that their goal is to teach you to be free and independent. At all cost, avoid getting involved with a cult.

The form of meditation I use is relaxation therapy, called RSRT after its founder, physical therapist Russell Scoop. If it had not been for Russell, I would not be writing this book today. Before 1981, I did not believe in meditation or stress, but my body had severe physical problems. As part of his physical therapy treatment for me, he used his meditative relaxation treatment. I first recognized the physical tension in my muscles when they relaxed. I had never felt so relaxed, even in my sleep. At first I was frightened because I did not feel in control. I have since learned that I had an exaggerated need for control. Since then, not only have I experienced positive changes in my self-understanding and awareness, but I have witnessed physical and mental improvements in my students who are using RSRT.

I'll give you a short description of Russell's procedure. The therapy involves deep breathing and a feeling trip through your body. He is a facilitator who helps you get into this unique, quiet place. You lie down in a comfortable position. He then asks you to close your eyes and take a few deep breaths. He breathes with you. This is to begin to take you to the quiet place in your mind. He then asks you to listen to him with your total attention as he takes you on a trip through your body, feeling sensations in each joint. After this is completed, he counts from ten to one again while you listen. He reminds you to breathe and relax. Ultimately, you feel the stress leaving your body. Your body will then become either very heavy or very light, depending upon you. Once you are able to do this easily, and your body is relaxed, he asks you to let your mind go wherever it wants to go. You will see, feel, or hear whatever you need to see, feel, or hear. I am certain I could not have learned the techniques alone, but now I can do it alone any time I wish. I use it when I feel physically stressed, when I have an important decision to make, or when I am solving a complex problem. I have also used it to learn more about myself. My students use it for similar reasons, as well as to help their riding.

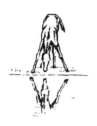

Once you decide to try meditation:
- ◆ *1. Investigate and choose the form that best meets your needs and lifestyle.*
- ◆ *2. Investigate the credentials and credibility of the course and/or the instructors.*
- ◆ *3. Set a goal, commit and practice.*

Exercise #3 in your Workbook will take you step by step through RSRT. Learning the technique with Russell might allow you to learn faster or to relax more deeply, but give yourself time to practice on your own. No matter which form of meditation you learn, you must practice it. Without practice, it will not help you. Meditation is like any other tool, in that maximum benefits come when you use it regularly.

Some of the most common meditative therapies include:

Biofeedback

This method has proved scientifically that relaxing the body and mind has a positive effect on health. By using electronic monitoring, such biological factors as brain waves, blood pressure, heart rate, and skin temperature are monitored. The subject is taught to exert voluntary control to increase his ability to regulate these factors.

Learning this technique requires extensive electronic equipment and the training to use it. It also requires a trained therapist to teach you how to regulate yourself.

Once learned, Biofeedback can be used whenever it is needed.

Martial Arts

The Martial Arts come from the Orient. There are over a hundred different forms, from Tai Chi, a graceful slow movement, to Karate, a powerful method of self-defense. The Martial

Arts train the participant to "make way for harmony of spiritual energy." Through exercises, breathing, and concentration, you must learn to relax in order to be aware of and blend in with every facet of your environment. Harmony with the world, the environment, and yourself are the essence of the Martial Arts.

Martial Arts are all done through exercises and movement.

Any of the Martial Arts must be learned from an instructor. Intensive daily practice is essential.

The Relaxation Response

Through studies of many forms of meditation, Dr. Herbert Benson discovered a simple personal technique to allow the body to relax. His purpose was primarily to improve health. His studies proved that individuals can learn a method of relaxing on their own.

The Relaxation Response is induced by using a quiet place, dwelling on an object and emptying your mind. You can learn this by yourself. It must be practiced daily.

Prayer

Prayer is probably the most widely used form of meditation. The meditative process is dependent upon the individual's religious belief and tradition. The purpose of prayer is to have communication with God, which includes listening to God and thanking Him. During prayer, the individual should empty his mind and allow a direct link with God. If this is done, whatever one needs to hear, feel or see should present itself.

Prayer can be used anytime, anywhere. It requires only the individual. Like all other forms of meditation, it should be used regularly.

RSRT

RSRT has been covered in this chapter. It is done by emptying the mind, breathing, taking a trip through your body, feeling your body parts, and then letting the mind go wherever it wishes. It takes regular practice to learn, it takes ten minutes to an hour to use depending upon the individual and can be done by yourself once learned.

TM

This meditation technique was introduced in the United States in 1959 by Maharishi Mahesh Yogi. It is a simple, natural, effortless process that allows the mind to experience subtler levels of the thinking process until thinking is transcended and the mind comes into direct contact with the source of thought.

TM uses a sitting position and is achieved through breathing, concentration and repeating a specific word (mantra).

TM must be learned through a course and from a trained master. To benefit, you should practice TM twice a day for fifteen to twenty minutes a session.

Yoga

Yoga comes from an Indian philosophy that assumes the existence of God, who is the model for the aspirant to spiritual release. Yoga believes that the achievement of spiritual liberation occurs when the self is freed from the bondage of matter that has resulted because of ignorance and illusion. There are eight stages designed to attempt to reverse ignorance and illusion and free the inner being, so that it can be restored to its original state of purity and consciousness.

Yoga uses various positions and exercises, and you enact the meditation through breathing and concentrating on an object or thought.

Yoga can be learned through courses, instructors, books and TV shows. To benefit, you should practice yoga two times a day for twenty minutes a session.

In addition to these specialized forms of relaxation, there are simple everyday activities that you can use to reduce stress. You must know yourself to know what offers you the greatest tranquility. It could be taking a walk, jogging, aerobics, playing tennis or golf, enjoying a hot bath, or listening to music. These activities are additional sources of refreshment. They should not replace meditation. Choose one or more that will allow you to go to a quiet place in your mind where you are free from thoughts, interferences, or interruptions. You should try to take the time to enjoy one small activity for YOURSELF each day. This is a cleansing time, not a time to watch TV, think through a problem, or recall memories. It is a quiet time for your body to let go of its stress.

Use Questionnaire #16 to track your commitment to your daily refreshing activities and the practice of your meditation technique.

Concentration

Concentration is total attention to the subject at hand, so that your body, mind and spirit are all learning or acting simultaneously and in unison.

A tight mind, one that is concentrating on the TOTAL subject, is a powerful tool in learning to ride. Effective concentration also saves energy. Concentration is your ability to focus on one thing at a time without distractions. In order to be an affective-learning horseman you must be able to focus not only with your mind, but also with your senses, especially your tactile sense. It is relatively easy to focus mentally on FACTS, but it is hard to focus on both a thought and an ever-changing feeling at the same time. For a successful performance, you will need to be able to achieve this dual focus.

Total attention to the subject at hand enables your body, mind, and spirit to unite with the body, mind, and spirit of your horse. This unison can work effectively to produce an enjoyable ride and, later, a symphony. When you focus effectively, all of your energy is directed to the muscles, sensory nerves, motor nerves, and cognitive powers which are feeling the horse and what he is doing. Both your conscious and unconscious minds are focused in unison, allowing your actions to be quicker, sharper and more accurate.

My students have often heard me insist that they stop concentrating so much. Many riders tend to focus on details to such an extent that their detailed THOUGHTS are blocking out most of their ability to feel. Thus they are unable to respond to the horse. Their concentration is singular (mental only), not dual (mental & feeling). You cannot ride a horse with mental awareness alone. Your mind provides just one of the sources of the information that you need. Learn the facts when you are OFF the horse; concentrate on feeling the horse while you are ON the horse.

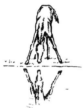

A rider displays good concentration when he is so wrapped up in his horse that he is not distracted by what is going on around him. Such concentration is a joy to behold, and projects a feeling of harmony!

How do we learn to concentrate appropriately? No matter how easily distracted you are, go to your quiet place in yourself, or perhaps you need your mountain top as well! The purpose, your long-term goal, is to learn to concentrate. Your short-term goal is to think of only one thought for one minute! Pick an object that you like. Let us start with an inanimate object, such as a rock. Choosing an object that you like makes it easier; I chose rocks because I like rocks! Concentrate on the rock in your hand for a few moments. Now, empty your mind. Take a few deep breaths, close your eyes, and bring a picture of the rock forward. (If you really have trouble visualizing the rock, you can look at the it again). Now you are visually focused on the rock. Think of how the rock feels in your hand: how heavy it is, how rough it is, how hard it is. How does it smell? How does it taste? What is its temperature? Try to concentrate on what it would be like to be that rock. Do nothing but concentrate on that rock for one minute. Later, you will be able to extend the time. As soon as you are distracted, check the time. Try again by repeating the exercise. It will be necessary to do this many times before you get comfortable with it. To be effective, this exercise must involve all of your senses. Exercise #4 in your Workbook gives you a detailed description of this process. Once you can do this with an inanimate object, try to do it with your horse. Repeat Exercise #2 in your Workbook Resource section, chapter Empathy, using your horse. While you are unmounted, concentrate on all aspects of your horse for one to three minutes. When you start to get a feeling for this, you are learning how to concentrate.

Joe Hyam's *Zen In The Martial Arts* affirms the value of concentration for learning and for not wasting energy.

How many times have I told you both to concentrate all the energy of the body and mind on one specific target or goal at a time. The secret to kime (tightening the mind) is to exclude all extraneous thoughts, thoughts that are not concerned with achieving your immediate goal.

Later Bruce chatted alone with me for a few minutes. "A good martial artist puts his mind on one thing at a time," he said. "He takes each thing as it comes, finishes it, and passes on to the next. Like a Zen master, he is not concerned with the past or the future, only with what he is doing at the moment. Because his mind is tight, he is calm and able to maintain strength in reserve. And then there will be room for only one thought, which will fill his entire being as water fills a pitcher. You wasted an enormous amount of energy because you did not localize and focus your mind. Always remember: in life as well as on the mat an unfocused or 'loose' mind wastes energy.

It has taken me a long time to master kime and I still have a long way to go, but I have found that when my mind is tight, my mental and physical energies are joined and focused. On those days when I have worked with total concentration, I have accomplished more and ended the day less tired than on days when I was easily distracted.

To learn the type of concentration necessary for good horsemanship, employ all that you have learned about your energy. Being able to use empathy will also help you. Practice putting thoughts 'on hold' (see 'On Hold' chapter) so you will not worry that you will forget something. You are going to use these tools to create another useful tool: concentration.

The first step is learning to concentrate on one object. When you can do step #1 in Exercise #4 in a few seconds easily, you are ready for the second step. Now you must try to focus on a few thoughts, most people can do this effortlessly, because memorization is such a common activity in our education. For riders, let us use the aids to canter. With nothing else on your mind, review the canter aids as the second step. When you can review the aids with no effort, add the third step. This step adds feeling to the thoughts. The third step is to feel what you are saying. Can you feel your muscular involvement in the preparation for the canter, and the actual canter depart? Can you feel your body movement in the rhythm? Can you feel your erect and steady position? Can you feel the coordination of your body and aids? Can you really feel it all as you think of it? Practice this until it is easy. Once it is easy and takes only a few minutes, add your horse's feelings to the exercise. Continue with Exercise #4, Steps 3 and Step 4 to further develop your concentration.

It is essential that you have no distractions while learning to concentrate. When you are having a lesson, your instructor is a distraction; this can be a problem at certain stages of learning. You will discover that you are often concentrating on the directions from the instructor, not the horse. This is necessary during the early stages, while you are acquiring the cognitive and psychomotor learning techniques of a new skill. Once you reach the affective stage, which recurs on and off in your learning program, your instructor must talk less and let you experience more. When you have learned the mental and physical requirements of a movement, such as the canter depart, your horse becomes your most influential teacher. While learning from your horse, you are using the AFFECTIVE learning style. Once you have learned the canter depart so that you can feel it, you are ready to start to learn something new. The process will start over again, first with the cognitive (facts), then with the practice (hands-on until you can perform) and finally with the affective (feel). Students often prefer to learn the cognitive skills, because they feel that they are getting faster results. The results, however, depend on your instructor's directions and on your ability to follow those directions, not on the engagement of your affective learning style. You will get results, but they will not be lasting results — they will always require your instructor. When your instructor feels you are ready, you must begin to concentrate on feeling the horse, and your instructor will help you by becoming a quiet observer. Even though the instructor will not interfere, you may be distracted by your own thoughts, such as; "I wonder what my instructor is thinking? This feels wrong, I hate doing this on my own. I will never get it. The poor horse suffering through my mistakes..." Any thoughts you have that are not on the subject are distractions, just as much as listening to the instructor, talking to friends or listening to music. To perform at your best, you must focus on feeling your horse until you need less effort to concentrate, and can feel him naturally.

Concentration or focusing is a vital tool for competitive riders and for riders learning imagery, visualization and 'on-hold'. Effective concentration is a relaxed, empathetic focusing involving all of your being.

Mountain Top

Your 'mountain top' is your personal physical retreat where you are comfortably alone, absorb a sense of tranquility and feel an inner calmness. It should be a place that allows you to be undisturbed.

Your 'mountain top' is a physical location, unique to your needs. This is the place to which you go when you need physical quietness and tranquility to help you find a peaceful place in your mind. In our journey toward self-awareness, we frequently need to retreat and look inward. We need to do this not only to get to know ourselves, but to enable us to make major life decisions. You will discover that you need your mountain top off and on throughout your life. Your mountain top should be a place where you are alone, feel comfortable, tranquil, and calm. It should be a place that allows you to be undisturbed.

How do you decide where your mountain top is? Examine your life. Where did or do you feel the most relaxed? When you are in a stressful situation, what conditions reduce the stress? Perhaps it is on a quiet hack with your horse, in an open field, on the top of a hill, in a forest, along a stream or at the ocean. These suggestions will give you an indication of where to look for your special place. Your mountain top is not a spot where you must go often, but it should be a place you can reach without too much effort. My mountain top is a nearness to water. Close to my home, I had a stream. I could go sit on a rock on the edge of the stream and do some very valuable thinking. For major traumas, however, I found that the pounding of the surf on a rocky ocean front was a powerful source of thinking energy. This book began on the Gulf Coast of Mexico, and was finished on the Clark Fork River in Montana. My mountain top is clearly related to water!

You can often evaluate and solve lesser problems while you are taking a shower, hanging out laundry, driving to work, cleaning stalls or hacking in the country. These are great times to solve simple problems, organize, and then let your mind relax.

Even if your life is free of major crises, you may discover that you would like to get to know yourself better. We never know when we will need our mountain top, and it is good to know it is available when we need it. It may seem strange that a certain environment can have so much influence on our tranquility, but it is true. Finding this place, your mountain top, is another step in getting to know yourself.

Answering the questions on Questionnaire #17 of the Workbook may help you to identify your mountain top, your personal daily relaxing activity, and the value of each of them.

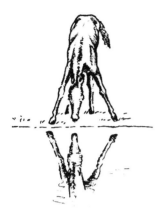

'On Hold'

Learning to put a total experience "on hold" can free you to live in the present more effectively.

M ost of us lead multi-faceted, busy lives, and find it difficult to be really in the 'now'. Being completely in the moment with your horse is essential for the creation of a successful ride. Certain interruptions while riding are to be expected, but you cannot be thinking about other parts of life while you are riding your horse. The one thing that has helped me immensely is putting information 'on hold'.

Being completely in the moment is essential for the creation of a successful ride.

My busy lifestyle had filled my life with stress, and that stress was taking a physical toll on me. When I received my first meditative relaxation therapy, I felt my body relax. It took the experience of feeling my body without stress to convince me that I was stress-controlled. I felt the body-mind connection; however, I refused to reduce my activities. Since I realized I had to alleviate the stress, I developed the 'on hold' solution. First I empty my mind, which I learned in therapy, and then I lock in the information I want to remember. The results were beyond my expectations. Not only could I remember more, but I discovered that I could solve problems with less effort. In addition, I was better able to enjoy each of my activities despite their diversity. It is exciting to learn ways to use our brain more fully; this is another way to use your mind better. For this to work, you only need to know how to empty your mind and how to concentrate. Then you must practice, starting with simple thoughts. Before you can learn 'on hold' you must learn to empty your mind. Start with a form of meditation from the Relaxation chapter.

STEPS;

1. *Empty your mind, retreat to the quiet place in your mind.*
2. *Recall the single issue you must remember.*
3. *Add the sensory memories that accompany it.*
4. *Once your review is complete, lock it 'on hold' and then dismiss it.*
5. *Move on.*

There are four steps in this process. Before you begin, you must make certain you do a quick review of the thought that you place 'on hold'. First, you must empty your mind of all thoughts, go to the quiet place in your mind. Second, you must recall the single issue you must remember. There should be nothing else on your mind, only your review of what you must remember. Third, add to your thoughts the sensory memories that accompany it. Fourth, once your review is complete, lock it 'on hold' and then dismiss it. Once the process is complete you are ready to move on to the next project in your day. This is the most efficient method of doing this. In the beginning it can take you up to a minute, but with practice it will take only a few seconds and eventually you will not even think about it.

While learning to trust this tool, you should practice writing down everything that is on you mind. This will cost you more time, but you may feel safer. Try to include your feelings even though they are hard to put into words. But if you recall the feelings with the facts, you should be able to write the facts and recall both facts and feelings when you are ready. Put the paper aside for review at the end of the day to see what must be carried over for future completion. Keep this list in a safe place and continue updating your list until you have completed all the incomplete thoughts or tasks and have learned to trust the 'on hold' technique. Writing lists will get you into the habit of trusting the process.

Another benefit from this tool is that, like information stored in a computer, all kinds of information can be condensed and stored in your mind for any length of time. It does not matter what aspect of your life you put 'on hold'. Very much like a computer, you can retrieve the information that you store. You must store information without static (interference or negatives). You can avoid or control static and interrupting thoughts, by using a positive attitude and concentration.

Margie, a banker with a family of two children and two dressage horses, found the 'on hold' tool to be very useful. Let us share a typical day with Margie and her use of this tool. Margie gets up at 5:30 a.m. Before she gets out of bed, she reviews her basic schedule for the day, being certain to recall from 'on hold' any special events for today, Monday. Once she has completed this review, she returns it to its place in her memory and gets up, enjoying her quiet time to go to the stable to feed the horses. She notices their health and attitude, and that she is about to run out of grain. She pauses for a moment, empties her mind, reviews the need to buy feed on her way home from work, puts it 'on hold ', and then forgets it and returns to the house. The moon is out, the air crisp, a lovely way to start the day. Once in the house, she organizes breakfast for the children. Just before they all sit down for breakfast, Margie recalls the stored thoughts related to the girls. During breakfast she reminds her youngest that she has dance class after school, and will be picked up at 4:30. They all have a lovely breakfast discussing the expectations for the day, and all take part in the breakfast clean-up and preparation for work and school. While taking her shower, Margie enjoys the fresh clean feeling and decides what to wear to work today. She takes time to enjoy the sun shining into her bedroom window as she dresses. On her way to work, she does a quick review of what she will do after work, what she will prepare for dinner tonight, and what she has to do with her horses. Once she reviews this, she empties her mind, recalls her review and then lets it go. Now is the time to bring forward what she had put 'on hold' on her way home from work yesterday. She recalls her meetings and her goals for the day at work. Once this recall is complete, she returns to the moment and enjoys the remainder of her drive to work. Throughout her day at work, she uses the system when she must remember something or when she has completed something. As she is driving home, she reviews what she has achieved, what she must do the next day and any other infor-mation important to her work. Once this is completed, she lets it go and reviews what she must do with family and horses until bedtime. She remembers that she must go to the feed store. On her way home, she plans her afternoon with the horses and her meal preparation. Once at home, she gets the meat out for dinner, changes her clothes, and heads for the stable. She empties her mind, recalls what she must remember related to the family and lets it go. Now it is time to recall yesterday's ride and what her short-term goal is with her horses. She puts the answering machine on so that she will not be interrupted during her time with the horses.

When tacking up, she notices that her horse is overly sensitive on the right side of his back. She makes a mental note to see if that affects him while mounted. Margie's warmup is complete and she begins to work her horse. She had intended to school her leg-yields today, but her horse told her in the warm up that he was too sore to do this in the limited time she had for training. She decided to work on long and low bending work. As Margie was cooling her first horse out, she emptied her mind and then reviewed how her horse felt, what she did with him today, and what she wanted to do with him tomorrow. She especially noted the degree of soreness he showed. Once the review was complete, she brought forward the next horse's short-term goal and then proceeded the same way with him. As soon as both horses were ridden and fed, she checked everything, reviewed that all was fine, put it 'on hold' and let it go. Now she brought forward her review of the evening, which included dinner, storytelling time and the subject to start the dinner discussion. She noted that she must remember to ask the girls for their report cards because today was the day!

This way of thinking sounds complex, detailed and controlled, but it is not. I over-simplified the method to make it clear. Once you learn to do it, it is like walking. We never tell ourselves to put one foot in front of the other, we just do it. Once 'on hold' becomes a trusted habit, it is an efficient way of using your mind to remember things in detail while giving you more freedom to enjoy the moment. When you first begin to do this, you may need more time to practice, because you are learning something new.

In the chapter on knowledge, I stated that it often takes years to confirm issues that you must investigate. 'On hold' comes into play in this area as well. Let us say that you have a major question related to the complex issue of 'moving forward'. This issue may take years to understand. Your question is in the 'on hold' mode. When you read an article related to the subject, you will automatically bring this question forward, out of 'on hold,' and use the stored information to compare it with, and evaluate what you are reading. You add whatever you feel is valuable from the article and replace the whole subject 'on hold'. Months later you are at a show watching one of the top competitors perform a test. Still trying to get a better understanding of 'moving forward', your unconscious brings the total package forward for your review, comparison and evaluation. You add your visual evaluation to the topic and return the updated information to 'on hold'. This can go on for as long as necessary, until you feel the knowledge is complete. Meanwhile, you will discover that you are using the stored information when appropriate.

Once you are certain that you have completed a thought, question, or task, end the process, take it out of 'on hold'. It takes only a few seconds to review it, acknowledge its completion, and let it go. When Margie finished putting the horse feed in the barn, she had completed this task. She noted it and let it go, so it no longer had to take up valuable memory space. You may do this with everything, whether facts or feelings.

If you are uncomfortable with your lesson results as Frank was in the Attitude chapter, the frustrated feeling can be put 'on hold'. As long as you remember that you are putting it 'on hold' to resolve it as soon as possible, it will work. Often it is not appropriate to deal immediately with a negative feeling or a difficult situation. If Frank had placed his frustration 'on hold,' is he could have been reminded later that he had to deal with the problem. Using 'on hold' would have preserved the frustration problem for later action instead of letting the emotion float around and affect all aspects of Frank's life. Frank's frustration is typical of the way we all feel when we have problems related to our horses or other people. Using 'on hold' and taking action when appropriate would confine its effect and help us remember to resolve it!

There is a danger to watch for while using this process. You must be careful not to lock 'on hold' frustration that is inappropriate. If you are balancing your checkbook but are scheduled to have a lesson in one half hour, and you cannot find the five cent error, you are upset. The half hour you have just spent searching for it has built your frustration to a very high level. If you lock the problem 'on hold' with the frustration, it is likely to have a negative effect on your ride. Instead, you should stop a few minutes early. You must relax for a few minutes, letting go of the anxiety. Once you feel calm, put the facts of the lost five cents that must be found 'on hold', without the anxiety. Otherwise the emotion may spill over to your ride. When emotions become involved, you must learn to program in a time to relax and let the emotion settle down. It takes experience for a stimulating emotion to be put 'on hold'. The time you need to allow between a stimulating emotion and your riding will depend upon the individual. Each person is different. Begin to observe yourself to determine how much let-down time you need; also to determine which meditation works best for your needs. For one student of mine, the five cent imbalance can interfere with her ability to relax while riding. She needs to practice the tool more often. It is different for me. I can put the most upsetting information 'on hold,' go teach a wonderful lesson, and then retreat to a private place for a major crying session. I've had years of practice.

'On hold' is so useful that we may sometimes be tempted to put too much 'on hold'. Especially if you are putting unanswered questions or unresolved problems 'on hold', you must realize that at some point you will need to address and resolve those questions and problems. Putting problems on hold does not eliminate them; it gives you the freedom to organize them, prioritize them, and decide when, where, and in what order you will deal with them.

Does 'on hold' work for everyone? We all have the mental capacity, but it is easier for some. This is a shared activity of all of our senses, memory alone is inadequate. If it is difficult for you, it may take more time to learn, but it is possible.

Please go to Questionnaire #18 and answer the questions. These questions should help you take a look at the separate categories of your life, as well as the situations within those categories that you can review. Remember that the two most important aspects for using this tool are; first, not letting your mind wander during either your concentration or your emptying; and, second, recalling all aspects of the TOTAL experience, feelings and facts. Both are essential.

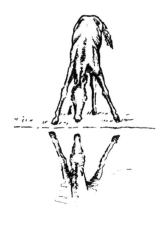

Discipline

Discipline, consistently enforced with fair guidelines, creates improvement in ourselves and our horses.

It is discipline of our self and our horse that leads us to reach our goals successfully. Self-discipline is the training required to produce moral or mental improvement. Discipline for the horse is the systematic training to obtain obedience. Competition requires both mental improvement and systematic training for both horse and rider. One of the most difficult tasks for horsemen is to learn the appropriate combination of discipline for two creatures, horse and man.

How often have you skipped schooling your horse because your friends invited you to a party? How often have you exploded angrily at someone, only to regret it later? How often have you arrived tired at a horse show because you waited until the last minute to get ready? These are all examples which reveal a lack of self-discipline. If you find yourself frequently abandoning what you know you should do in favor of finding a momentary pleasure, or saying things you wish you hadn't, or not being ready for commitments, you may need to inject more self-discipline into your life. The opposite also can be true; you can have so much self-discipline that you function like a machine. People with this level of discipline in their life inhibit their ability to change and be flexible. More often, we see students who fail to meet their riding goals because they are unable to stick with their plans, set priorities, and follow them.

The more precision required in the type of riding you choose, the more self-discipline will be required to excel. Dressage and reining probably require the most precision; pleasure riding, the least. Look at the goals you set for yourself. Did you avoid committing yourself to a goal you really wanted, because you feared you lacked the self-discipline to achieve it? Are you willing to make sacrifices to meet your goals? Do you really want to give up the goal? Or would you rather develop the self-discipline?

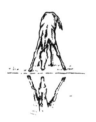

When I feel tempted to stray from the rules I have created for myself, I STOP (for a second), LISTEN (to myself), THINK (about my role in the situation in relationship to my self-imposed rules) and then I ACT.

I like to define self-discipline as training oneself to produce a specific character or pattern of behavior that involves moral or mental improvement. Self-discipline is a matter of training. It is not a gift. If you failed to develop enough self-discipline in its easiest stage, your pre-teen years, it is not too late. The keys are committing yourself to self-improvement and practicing being disciplined. Self-discipline is a mental skill that you can perfect through practice, just as you perfect your physical riding skills through practice.

If you decide that you need to improve your ability to discipline yourself, use what you learned about goal-setting to plan your program. Make sure that you are clear in your mind about your own priorities and your philosophy of life. In exercising self-discipline, you are teaching yourself to make choices rather than allowing yourself to act impulsively. Choosing requires you to know the options, and to be aware of the reasons why you might want to do one thing or another. When you feel that you know yourself well enough, you are ready to commit yourself to practicing self-discipline. I have a simple formula I use to discipline myself. When I feel tempted to stray from the rules I have created for myself, I STOP (for a second), LISTEN (to myself), THINK (about my role in the situation in relation to my self-imposed rules) and then I ACT. This process takes only a few seconds, but it keeps me faithful to my own philosophy and priorities.

To help yourself practice and develop self-discipline;
- *STOP, for a second and breathe*
- *LISTEN, to all sides of whatever upset you*
- *THINK, about your role in the situation*
- *Then ACT*

This system has proved to be most useful during the teenage stage of life; however, it remains a good tool throughout life. Teenagers tend to be impulsive and impatient; they have trouble honoring their life responsibilities. Jane still thanks me for teaching her this formula. No one ever taught Jane self-discipline. She loved her horse, but when she was preparing for the show season she found that her horse was not always cooperative with her time limits and frustration. I often witnessed Jane acting impatiently with Rapid Water, her horse, and also with her family members. Her parents brought her for her weekly lessons, helped her, and supported her competition needs. She treated them even worse than she treated her horse. Finally, I could not handle the abuse any longer, so I talked to Jane. She listened, but she did not take me seriously until a show TD confronted her for her abuse of Rapid Water. After that embarrassment, she asked for help. I taught her the STOP, LISTEN, THINK, and then ACT formula. Even today, as a corporate executive, Jane thanks me for this simple formula. She feels it changed her life.

James E. Loehr, a professional psychologist, athlete, and coach, synthesized the ideas of hundreds of athletes. The book, *Mental Toughness Training for Sports*, emphasizes the need for self-discipline in order to produce consistency in performance. It is consistency that separates the winners from the losers. Over a period of ten years, he interviewed hundreds of top athletes to learn their formulas for athletic excellence. They can be summarized in four steps, the foundation of which is self-discipline.

STEP 1:   *Self-discipline. Everything worthwhile begins at this level. It simply means doing whatever you have to do and making whatever sacrifices are necessary to get the job done the best you know how. It's hard work; it's giving up things you like in order to achieve a higher goal.*

STEP 2:   *Self-control. Self-discipline leads directly to self-control. As you discipline yourself, you experience steady increases in self-control, control of what you do, what you think, and how you react. Without self-control, being the best you can be as an athlete is nothing more than a fantasy.*

STEP 3:   *Self-confidence. Self-control leads directly to self-confidence. What tracks are to a train, self-confidence is to the athlete; without it, he can go nowhere. Self-confidence, that unshatterable belief in yourself, comes from knowing that you are in control.*

STEP 4:   *Self-realization. Self-realization is simply becoming the best you can be, the manifestation of your talent and skill as an athlete. It is the fulfillment and ecstasy of sport. Self-realization follows directly from self-confidence. Once you believe in yourself and feel good about yourself, you are opening the doors to your fullest potential.*

I think that what is most significant in Loehr's description is that excellence is a result of discipline, not raw talent. An enormously talented athlete may win once or twice without self-discipline, but to win consistently he must be mentally tough. Self-help comes from knowing that you have done everything you can with your talent and that of your horse. If you haven't done this, you have let yourself down. If you begin with a carefully-selected goal, you should find it easier to discipline yourself.

Tough Love is the effective discipline I like to use with horses. The ground rules are simple and clear. If the horse breaks the rule, he is quickly and appropriately corrected. Once the correction is made, the discipline is forgotten and life continues in a loving way with no grudges being held. If we react to a broken rule by holding anger or irritation instead of making the appropriate correction and moving on, we can create a lasting problem. While Louise was learning to ride into her corners correctly, she discovered that her horse was not listening to her half-halts. When she used her inside leg, he ran forward instead of stepping into the outside rein. He broke the rule of moving from the leg to her hand and listening to her hand. Louise immediately halted him with more strength than she liked to use. She then insisted that he submit to the rein. After this demonstration of her determination, Louise repeated the corner. Her horse listened perfectly, so she patted him with her inside rein. Now it was up to her to forget the evasion and go on with no irritation or anger. When an act has broken the ground rules, tough love gives us a way to react quickly, correctly, and without holding a grudge.

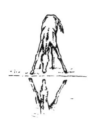

Tough Love:
- ◆ 1. *A few rules*
- ◆ 2. *Clearly define rules*
- ◆ 3. *Make a quick, forcefully appropriate correction for a broken rule*
- ◆ 4. *Once corrected, forget and move forward with love, holding no grudges*

Tough Love should be employed only when we are certain we are not causing confusion. Horses need a consistent training program in both riding and handling. The horse should know the boundaries for his actions. Poorly administered discipline and inconsistent or unclear aids will cause the horse confusion, pain, or fear. These will undermine the horse's trust in the rider or handler. All of us will inevitably make mistakes, and this is OK, as long as we learn to evaluate our role. Listening to the horse's answer to our question will help us to know whether we are expressing ourselves clearly. If we are certain that there is no confusion, we have permission to use Tough Love. To a horse, this is the clearest form of discipline.

For the performance to show harmony between horse and rider, the rider must have learned the guidelines related to the task that is expected by the horse. The task has a direct relationship to the goal of the rider. The rider should know his role in the communication and be certain that his body, balance and aids are communicating accurately. The rider must believe that the horse WANTS to listen and follow the rules if he understands them. These are all responsibilities of the rider, who must practice these beliefs before he disciplines. All of this takes daily practice with our horse, also mental practice while we are off the horse. When you find that disciplining yourself and your horse has become natural and appropriate, you will have mastered discipline. You will know it, because you will need it much less.

To evaluate your self-discipline with your horse and yourself, use Questionnaires #19 and #20 in your Workbook. Chart #3 will help you monitor your mental and physical discipline for a month.

Commitment

*A commitment signifies
our willingness to bind
ourselves, emotionally and
intellectually, to a course of
actions. It is a PERSONAL
DECISION that carries
with it a pledge to
honor responsibility.*

Commitment joins patience in fueling our inner fire. We make two types of commitments; the first to ourselves, and the second to others, including our horse. All commitments must begin with our sincere intention to honor, respect, and fulfill any agreement or decision we make concerning ourselves. Only when we can do this can we make a commitment to others.

Most commitments, especially those we make to ourselves, are unwritten. Some people believe that a contracted agreement has more binding power than a verbal commitment. This is not true. All commitments are bound agreements that we should take seriously, whether they are written or not. When we own a horse or ride, we should have a goal and commit ourselves to that goal. This must include all aspects of the project, from horse care to a regular, well-directed riding program. A commitment signifies our willingness to bind ourselves, emotionally and intellectually, to a course of action. Commitment is a personal decision that carries with it a pledge to honor responsibility. This personal promise creates a basis for you to try harder in difficult times and to continue to strive to fulfill the guarantee.

Dedicating our energy in a binding agreement that leads to our bettering ourselves and helping others should be the foundation of the commitments we make. The decision to make a commitment often carries with it a fear of failure. If you do not make a commitment, you cannot fail. One of the most complex emotions that results from failed obligations is guilt. Let me return to the example from my own life that I shared in the Stages chapter. One of the goals that I failed to achieve, and to which I had committed myself, was to become an "A" Pony Clubber. I felt very guilty because I felt that by failing to achieve the "A" rating I had hurt my parents, who had dedicated their time and money to my horse education for many years. When I married, I quit Pony Club, leaving my goal behind. This was a false guilt, because I made the decision based on the information gathered at that time. I assumed that I had hurt my parents. I could have asked them whether this was true, or I could have chosen to wait to get married until I had completed my goals. Since I had made a conscious choice, I should not have felt guilty; if I did, it was false guilt. On the other hand, if I had continued while feeling I had diluted my time in such a way to make it almost impossible to work toward a test at that level and tried to divide my time among college, riding, and my future family, I would have failed. Failing because I had not fulfilled my commitment in the way I knew to be necessary would and should cause true guilt. If you make a mistake and fail, but tried with sincere dedication, you might feel false guilt; it is much easier to forgive yourself for this. If you were deliberately careless, insincere, selfish, or thoughtless, you will experience true guilt. This guilt will require some serious work over time to forgive and forget.

Dedication to a commitment requires careful advance planning, a consistent set of standards, and regular evaluations. You should never make a promise without considering all the facts carefully. The more involved the commitment, the more thorough the investigation process should be. Deciding to take lessons requires less time-consuming investigation than deciding to purchase your own horse. However, the success of your lessons is directly related to the instructor, the time involved, the stable atmosphere, the horses, the location, and the expenses. If you skimp on the time and effort involved in an investigation, you may destroy or discolor a potentially valuable experience. This would be harmful to you. Your careful investigation and planning will help to eliminate some of the risks that accompany commitments.

Once you make a promise, cheating on it can cause problems with your conscience in the form of a mental or spiritual energy block. If you break a commitment you can feel uncomfortable and can lose confidence in yourself. Our culture and environment have taught us to take commitments very seriously, but often have not trained us in how to make decisions about meaningful and lasting commitments.

Henry loved horses. His dream was to own his own horse. He had saved his money, and when his job allowed him the extra time he bought his first horse. Unfortunately, Henry did not investigate the requirements of long-term ownership. As with other parts of his life, he wanted to give his horse the best of everything. After a few years, Henry realized that his special horse care fund was depleted. If he was to survive financially, he would have to make major cut-backs. Henry bought a lesser quality feed, hired a less expensive farrier, and changed to the cheapest bedding. These changes made Henry feel guilty, a true guilt, because he was taking risks with his horse's health. He was not honoring the commitment he had made to himself about the quality of care to his horse. Henry's guilt slowly destroyed the enjoyment he had derived from going to the stable, but when he did not go to the stable, he felt even more guilty. He thought it was the lack of money that was making him unhappy and less enthusiastic, but it was his guilt. Henry ultimately sold his horse, and suffered a major depression because he had grown fond of the horse and of the horsey life-style. He could have felt guilt because he sold his horse, but it was unnecessary because it was better to sell the horse than not to care for him properly. What could Henry have done? He should have spent more time investigating before he made the commitment to purchase and own a horse.

Becoming a horseowner is a MAJOR COMMITMENT, because a confined horse is a helpless animal who requires daily care. This care costs time, money and energy, three precious items to most of us. Few first-time horse owners are aware of the degree of involvement necessary just to own a horse. Unlike a car or boat, a horse must be taken care of whether it is used or not. Unlike an object, a horse has personal needs that require attention. I encourage all prospective horse owners to spend some time taking care of a friend's horse, or to investigate thoroughly the costs and concerns of boarding. Prospective owners should look after a horse not just for a day or two, but for at least one month. A new responsibility is fun for a few days, but when it is prolonged it may turn into drudgery. This experiment will help you decide if you want to make the commitment and meet the attendant obligations. If you are uncertain about the financial investment, take six months to see how difficult it is to put $500.00 in the bank each month. A horse will cost at least this much, averaged monthly. If the five hundred dollars is not a hardship, you know that you can meet the financial commitment.

Once you own a horse, the magnitude of the time and expense will require self-discipline to honor the commitment. All forms of riding and horse-owning are accompanied by good and bad periods, and our determination to keep the commitment will motivate us through the bad times. Commitment kept

Sue practicing her leg yields with Thunder. It also prompted Joan to seek solutions for her Willy. If Sue and Joan (from Goal Setting) had not made a commitment to their goals, they would not have REACHED THEIR GOALS. It is commitment to the horse and your goal that provides the basis for sticking it out during the frequently-occurring downturns and plateaus.

Commitment cannot guarantee you success, but it will give you a tool that allows success to happen. Owning and riding a horse is a self-imposed responsibility. If you feel that it is difficult for you to honor commitments, try practicing commitment in small ways. If you are a high school student who hates to write papers, commit yourself to have every paper writtenrequired in a marking period written and completed one week in advance. If you have never been responsible for the care of a living creature, try it for at least a month. Some people discover that a commitment to animal care is a positive, fulfilling experience. Others discover that they resent the loss of freedom that accompanies caring for an animal. If you discover that you enjoy being a caretaker, you will have no problem with the time commitment of owning a horse. You must then decide whether you have the time and money that horse ownership demands.

Even after you make the careful decision, your choice is not a certainty. Consequently, many people commit on the surface only. Because of the emotional risks of a commitment, they avoid becoming involved with their total being. Careful investigation can reduce the chances of failure, and careful regular evaluations prevent a mistake from continuing and causing emotional scars. Likewise, committing for a specific time period and dedicating yourself to making every possible effort will help you to make the right decision. If you have made every effort to attain your goal, and failed, you should feel assured that you did not just quit on a whim or because of a bad moment. If you made every effort to fulfill your commitment over a realistic period of time, you should not be afraid to accept failure, change and forgive yourself for the failure. This is what Henry had to do.

It is also important for you not to become rigidly stubborn about fulfilling a goal. Becoming stubbornly focused or wearing blinders while trying to honor a commitment can cause serious road blocks that are just as damaging as the failure to make a commitment. Change is a valid part of our riding life. The goal system of priorities gives the trainer/rider the opportunity to reevaluate at different periods of time. The reevaluation can help one determine if a promise must be changed or not. Commitments can be changed if the circumstances are beyond our ability to change.

If, as you travel the road of life, you discover that you cannot keep any promise to yourself, others, jobs, or goals, you must look deeper. This is a symptom of another problem.

If you honor the responsibility to horse ownership, the commitment to riding will be easy. You will find that your goals will help to motivate you.

Questionnaire #21 will help you look at the commitments of your life, including the natural commitments associated with the various stages and the self-imposed commitments that are part of your life. As you pass from one stage to another, you must redo this chart, because as stages change, commitments change!

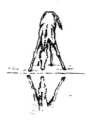

Making a commitment is the foundation for self-discipline that we must use to start, practice and complete the tasks to meet a goal.

Successfully meeting the challenge of a commitment builds self-confidence and can be very fulfilling. Part of goal-setting is making a commitment to meet that goal. The most important discovery will be that we can do whatever we want to do, providing that we are realistic. If you are searching to 'know yourself', you will have a good idea of what is realistic for you. If we take a moment to review Maggie's successful, multi-faceted life, I would assume that she gained confidence each day when she did her review. If she achieved most of the goals that she recalled in the morning, the satisfaction of accomplishment would build self-confidence. Her use of 'on-hold' helped her in yet another aspect of her life: it provided the opportunity to build self-confidence daily! The completion of each task or short-term goal will build self-confidence and trust in ourselves.

Praise

Praise your horse, yourself and others for jobs well done. Praise removes the stress of uncertainty, promotes self-esteem and makes the recipient eager to repeat the job.

Praise is an expression of warm approval and/or admiration. Praise removes uncertainty, and promotes self-esteem and self-confidence. It is much easier to repeat an action that we get complimented for than one that is ignored or punished.

For the horse lover, to praise a horse is easy. A soft pat is an easy way for us to show our approval when he listens to us. A pat can also relax a horse that is tight, nervous, or apprehensive. I will always remember how one of our trainers calmed a nervous, anticipating event horse in the dressage arena. This horse had performed the same dressage test for over a year. His rider was a worrying type, who made the horse very nervous, especially during the transition from trot to canter. Our trainer calmly and tactfully prepared him for the canter. When he did not barge through her aids, she reached forward and calmly stroked him with her inside hand. Instead of bursting through the aids, he relaxed and reached for her outside rein. She also should have felt good about herself, because it was her preparation, sensitive and quick feeling, and tact that allowed the horse to remain calm. The quality of her timely pat was a rewarding experience for both trainer and horse.

A more frequently used form of praise is the softening of our aids when the horse listens to us. Each time we do a correct half halt, the last step consists of an acknowledgement. This acknowledgement is a mild form of praise that is done by softening aids, a soothing voice or a rewarding pat. It is the part of the half-halt that tells the horse that he is doing the correct thing.

Crediting ourselves is not as easy as praising our horse, yet acknowledging our part in a successful half-halt or performance is a vital part of developing our self-confidence and self-esteem. You will have discovered as you read this book that confidence in yourself is essential. Your self-confidence is directly related to your ability to interact effectively with your horse. Taking the time to recognize success and praise yourself is a wonderful way to develop your confidence.

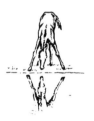

Praising a horse is easy, praising yourself is easily overlooked. Taking the time to praise yourself is a wonderful way to develop your confidence.

Many people find it difficult to accept a compliment, and it is virtually impossible for them to compliment themselves. Review Questionnaire #10 from the Humility chapter, where you defined your role in a performance with your horse. Recognizing your role is the first step. Now take a moment and think back. Did you acknowledge your role by allowing yourself to feel good about it? I hope you complimented both your horse and yourself. If you did not, remember next time that you both have a role in the performance. Allow yourself a few seconds to feel good about it and silently compliment yourself. Keep things in perspective. Remember that you are the conductor and the player, just two parts of the symphony. You must balance praising yourself and your horse.

You can use Chart #4 to map the amount of praise you allow yourself, your horse, and others.

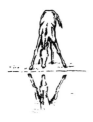

Praise is one of the easiest tools to learn to use. All we need to do is learn to notice positive actions, improvements, and results in our horse, others, and ourself, then acknowledge those actions with empathy.

Patience

*To capture the 'right'
opportunity be patient
with yourself, your horse
and others. Allow yourself
the luxury of mastering
one task at a time.*

From *Beyond the Mirrors*:

"It is a big job for your body to coordinate your mind and
spirit. You were not born on a horse. You do not instinctively
communicate with your legs while your hands remain quiet.
Your natural movements must be tailored to coincide with the
needs of your horse. You have much to learn about how to
influence the horse tactfully and consistently, and it is no easy
job to put your mind into his. Acquiring the appropriate attitudes
and goals for yourself and your horsemanship may take years
of self-analysis and work. Sometimes it is difficult to accept the
need for patience with our own being. In Thoughts to Live By,
Maxwell Maltz suggests you approach your personal development slowly: "Don't make haste or make waste, but sit in the
quiet room of your mind and use your imagination creatively
to relax, to control your fears, anxieties and uncertainties, to find
tranquility through patience."

Patience gives us energy, tolerance, and calmness. We can develop our patience to save us from energy loss through negative emotions as well as allowing us to set aside our needs or desires for the sake of others. Unending patience is required to watch our children make the mistakes which help them to learn. Understanding our horse's need to go for a hack in the country instead of a ring schooling requires patience. Patience gives us the tolerance not to get mad at the beginner who rides in front of the jump just as we are making our approach, and allows us to accept our shortcomings when we take longer to attain a goal than we had originally planned. Patience with ourself, our horse, and others allows us to be calm. This calmness will create an atmosphere that will encourage clearer communications, more efficient use of energy, and more productive results.

To become a patient person takes more than a decision. Patience is a result of knowing, understanding, and accepting all that we can discover about ourselves. It should not be confused with passive acceptance. A person who exists without opinions appears to be patient, but in reality is living on the outside of life. Patience is our capacity for calm endurance. It is knowing and being able to wait for the right time to take action.

Patience is our capacity for calm endurance. It is knowing and being able to wait for the right time to take action.

As with many other tools, we must first believe in the value of, and need for, patience. Then we can try to become calmly accepting. Most successful equestrians will emphasize the need for patience. Suenig, the master, in his book *Horsemanship* expressed it this way:

"Anyone who loves his horse will be patient, and patience, inexhaustible patience—especially when psychological and physical defects are present—is necessary to make the horse understand what we want of it. Patience is equally necessary in order not to grow immoderately demanding, which always happens when we do not reward an initial compliance by immediate cessation of demand, but try to enjoy a victory until the horse becomes cross or confused."

How do you develop patience? Go to a quiet place in your mind and relax. Use one of the techniques described in the Relaxation chapter. Examine your fears, anxieties, and uncertainties, which contribute to a lack of patience. Your search through these feelings may reveal physical, mental or spiritual causes of impatience. Often it is a good idea to make a list of situations that could trigger your fears, anxieties, or uncertainties. The questions on Questionnaire #22 are designed to help you understand what interferes with your patience. To eliminate impatience, you must first discover and examine its cause. Once you know the cause, work to fix it by changing what you can change and accepting what you cannot change. This will improve your patience.

You may discover that when you are worried about a lesson your stomach gets queasy and you try too hard, becoming impatient and too rough with your aids. Your queasy stomach is a sign that something is bothering you and causing you to become impatient. Upon examination, you realize that you are worried that you have not made enough progress between your lessons and that your instructor will not be pleased. Your anxiety makes you try too hard and be too rough during the lesson. You realize that ultimately it is your lack of self-confidence that is causing your impatience. Why are you lacking confidence? What do you need to do to become confident? Perhaps you need to discuss these feelings with your instructor prior to your lesson.

I'm certain that other instructors share my lesson-starting procedure. I ask my students if they have had any particular problems or successes between lessons. This open question gives them the opportunity to discuss any concerns. In this case, it would be appropriate to discuss your perceived lack of progress. You might learn that you are expecting too much, or too little, or that you are on the right track. Your self-confidence will improve and your instructor will be able to provide a suitable plan for you and your horse. Your instructor may find that he is going too fast or too slow for you.

This type of self-examination will help you to become more patient. Whatever helps you to know and accept yourself and to balance this knowledge with your goals is OK. Sharing your problems with an intuitive instructor will enable the instructor to ask you questions that will help develop your understanding, confidence, and patience.

When you feel that you are becoming impatient, learn to recognize your symptoms. The symptoms are the indications that will lead you to the real problem itself. When you find the real problem, change what you can change or accept what you cannot change. Either way, you will be better able to use your patience to find tranquility.

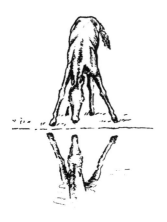

Forgiveness

We must be able to forgive ourselves, our horses and others for unacceptable behavior or actions and then forget and move on.

Mistakes are part of life. We say things we do not really mean, and later wish we hadn't said them. We do things out of haste that we later come to regret. A communication that is misinterpreted leaves us with unpleasant feelings. Our horse repeatedly shies in the same corner and we grow irritated and rough. The stable manager orders the wrong bridle. Any of these acts can create uncomfortable, negative thoughts or feelings that discolor our attitude and use up valuable energy. What can we do? We can forgive our horse, ourself, or the other person. Forgiveness is a gift to ourself.

Forgiveness is a gift we can give to ourselves, other persons and our horses.

Without developing this gift we will never really be happy, be at peace with ourselves, or have balanced energy. Holding onto negative thoughts or acts hurts not only us but hurts all who contact us, including our horse. The energy in an unforgiving mind is blocked by anger, fear, guilt, disappointment, or poor judgement. Retaining any of these thoughts or feelings initiates a negative process. The negative feelings slowly accumulate, undermining other parts of our being until they start to stiffen us physically. At some point in the process, they affect your relationship with your horse. Since your horse is a sensitive creature who feels your energy, he may react, even if it is not in an overtly obnoxious way. Lack of forgiveness will create havoc in your life if you do not learn to give and to accept forgiveness.

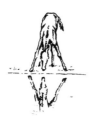

Horses are much more forgiving than people. To learn to forgive, start by observing how often a horse forgives!

I think our horses can be excellent teachers of forgiveness. We constantly give them wrong messages. No matter how many false messages we give them, they forgive us and listen to the next message and try over and over to give us what we want until the message is clear. Horses are much more forgiving than people. To learn how to forgive, start by observing your horse. Go to Questionnaire # 23 in your Workbook, and list three times that you know your horse forgave you. Now take this one step further. Go to that quiet place in your mind and imagine how your horse saw the situation. What enabled him to forgive?

Horses seem to forgive easily, because they do not feel guilt. Guilt is a result of our mental and spiritual intermingling. If we make a mistake we should not feel guilty but often we do. Why? Expectations are placed on us by our society, our environment, and ourselves. These expectations have been collected and stored in our unconscious. To a horse, a mistake or misunderstanding is directly related to the action or reaction of the moment. To humans, the mistake is encompassed by a wide variety of complications and factors. We should accept our mistakes in the same way that a horse accepts us. We should forgive ourselves and free ourselves from false guilt as quickly as a horse forgives us.

Paul wanted to do a canter depart at 'C'. When he asked Snow Flake to canter she just trotted faster. Paul reorganized and then tried again. This time she trotted even faster. Paul tried again and again until he had passed 'C' at least four times. I could stand it no longer. I stopped Paul and explained to him that he could not keep repeating the same thing, but that he needed to examine what he was doing that caused Snow Flake to trot faster instead of cantering. Paul was learning how to choose his aids based on what he felt, instead of what I told him. He went out to the rail and started again. This time he was holding too hard and Snow Flake slowed down. Poor Paul could not figure out what he was doing wrong. Four more times around the ring, then I asked him and the confused Snow Flake to stop and review. Paul was totally frustrated with himself. Since frustration leads nowhere, I explained to him what to do. He complied and Snow Flake happily cantered off. Snow Flake had immediately forgiven Paul's twenty minutes of confused communication. By the end of the lesson and many correct canter departs later, Paul still had not forgiven himself. I asked him to look at the situation through Snow Flake's eyes. She had a calm acceptance of what Paul was trying to do. She just was not getting a clear message. Once she got it, she did what she was asked. Part of the reason is that Snow Flake lives in the moment. She does not rehash the past as we do. While our ability to recall and evaluate is a valuable learning tool, it also can be detrimental if we do not learn to forgive. If we can learn something positive from our mistake we must do so, and let the negative feelings of frustration, disappointment, or confusion go, and move on. This is what the horse does. Later, Paul realized that he was being too hard on himself. He understood that he had to go through this learning experience, he had to try the depart, using the aids he had learned cognitively, and he had to learn to accept his mistakes. If he did not, his worry would interfere with his progress.

Practicing forgiveness is essential. Learning forgiveness is so fundamental that you should go to your mountain top with Questionnaire #24, a pencil and a piece of paper. Review your past and recall all situations and people that you have not forgiven for any reason. Do not deny them. Remember that an unresolved thought or feeling remains in some level of your being until you specifically let it go. A situation that was particularly painful may make you very sad. You may need to spend a long time in recall. Don't worry, because once you bring the information forward and release it, it will be truly gone. You should never need to repeat this deep review. Once you have made your list, ask yourself what you are still upset about and what you can do about it. If you can do something, do it. If not, accept the fact, forgive whatever needs to be forgiven and let it go. Forgiving means quietly, deeply, totally doing nothing, thinking nothing, carrying no judgement. When you forgive completely, you liberate your energy so that you can be happy and live freely.

Another form of guilt that we can carry is true guilt. This form of guilt is a result of our wrongdoing, the result of us doing harm to ourselves or others. The rule of living our life for betterment and not harming others is a difficult rule to follow. We do not always know what is betterment. What we felt was a good or harmless decision at one time may later have proven to be a bad decision that did cause harm. When we recognize the harm, we must have the courage to take action. The action includes resolving the problem with the party involved, forgiving yourself or the other party, and then letting it go.

The story of Ann and her misleading instructor is an excellent example of the releasing power of forgiveness. Ann had taken lessons from Mr. X for several years. Mr. X suggested that she should buy a new horse, which she did. Several months later, he suggested to Ann that he should be the one to show the new horse, and she agreed. After two years, Ann asked when she could ride her horse. He told her that it would be years, if ever, before she could ride her horse. She was shocked and hurt because she had followed his advice to buy this horse as her ideal teacher. She had put her trust in her instructor, invested a lot of money, and lost two years. She decided to leave the barn with her horse. After that, Ann never talked about Mr. X, nor did she talk about the experience. She made progress with her horse and obviously was enjoying her learning experience. When I asked Ann how she could be so calm and accepting about what had happened, she explained, "I had to forgive him or I would never have been calm and peaceful enough to ride. I learned from the experience that I will be a more careful consumer. Once I investigate a situation, I will again trust. However, I will never trust Mr. X and, if asked, I will tell anyone my experience. If not asked, I will not mention it. Mr. X must have a difficult time living with himself. I really feel sorry for anyone who is driven to such deceitful and selfish behavior. I will not do more than say hello to Mr. X again, and that will be out of politeness. It would be stupid for me to subject myself to the same abuse again. Then I would not have learned anything." As it happens, Mr. X continually derided Ann behind her back, trying to blame the failure on her. It never seemed to bother her, even when they were at the same show. Ann was an example to me about the value of forgiveness.

A situation like the one Ann experienced calls for forgiveness. Forgiveness seldom returns the situation back to its previous state; the experience itself will create a change. This change can be directed positively. Each party in a situation will change, based on his own outlook. Ann became a wiser consumer, and Mr. X had more complications to deal with in his inner self.

Test yourself with Questionnaire #24. If you are not holding any bad feelings about a person, horse, or situation, you are ready to move on. If you do, you must deal with those bad feelings you still hold. Once you let go of them, you will be more aware of the need for forgiveness. When the need arises, stop and follow the same procedure as you did on your mountain top. Do not let much time pass while you hold on to an unforgiving state of mind. Look at your horse. If he did not forgive you, where would you be? Put yourself into his shoes and look at the bothersome situation. It is not easy to be forgiving, but once you experience the peace and tranquility of living without that energy block, you will try to make forgiveness an automatic function.

Imagery & Visualization

Strive to include total sensory perception into these powerful tools.

Even though the dictionary treats imagery and visualization as synonyms, I feel they represent two different techniques and I want to give them a clearer definition. I believe we use imagery when we want to reproduce in our mind a picture of what someone else is doing or has done. We use visualization to form a mental picture in our mind of something that we have done or want to do. Both are complete with feelings and the influence of all of our senses.

Both imagery and visualization are stored in our unconscious mind in the form of sight and sound, like a video tape but with the added dimensions of feel and smell. They are learning tools that can be used for different purposes as our riding advances. When you are a beginner, imagery is a vital tool to understand the elements of position and the feel for the movement and rhythm of the different gaits. If you are an intermediate, you will probably be refining your position, learning to feel more quickly, and understanding the basic use of the aids. As you advance you will observe specific movements that you are learning. In the Knowledge chapter, I discussed learning through observation. Imagery is the tool to use for proper observation. Watching what you want to imitate will help you to reproduce it. As you get better acquainted with the use of this tool, you will discover that you can zoom in on areas that are most appropriate for what you are learning. If you have learned imagery correctly, all of your senses will contribute to the dimensions of the experience that you viewed.

The first thing that you must do to employ imagery is to empty your mind. If you are worried that you might forget something, you can put it 'on hold'. Then you must empathize with the horse and rider that you are watching. First look at the total picture, defining and absorbing what you feel. Then carefully observe the specific action that you are trying to learn, and absorb first the feeling and then the look. If your concentration is complete, there will be no distractions, and your other senses will also register the experience. As you watch, here are some descriptive words that can help you: soft/hard, following/against, comfortable/uncomfortable, quiet/busy, and balanced/unbalanced. Try to imagine how the horse feels under your seat, under your legs and in your hands. How do you imagine that both horse and man feel inside themselves? Words that can direct you are: straight, relaxed, willingness to go forward, light/heavy, even or irregular rhythm, and lazy or impulsive. While you are watching the performance, you should not allow yourself to be distracted by anyone or anything. There should be no conversation. As soon as you stop watching, you should go to a quiet place in your mind and review what you just experienced. Lock it 'on hold' before you embark on the next experience of the day. If you cannot use 'on hold,' take a few minutes to write your reflections and try to feel and picture them as you write. Whether you are using imagery or visualization, all distractions must be evaluated, put into perspective, and dealt with appropriately. If you are watching a lesson, it is very likely that stable friends will be watching as well. They can be distracting, unless you politely tell them that you want to watch quietly and then move away to your own area so that you cannot hear them talk. If you master the art of concentration well enough, you will be able to block out their presence and conversation. That is a highly developed use of concentration! You are then in the quiet place in your mind where you must be to use any of these tools.

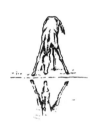

IMAGERY and VISUALIZATION steps:
- ♦ *1. Put 'on hold' anything on your mind.*
- ♦ *2. Empty your mind.*
- ♦ *3. Go to quiet place in your mind.*
- ♦ *4. Observe while concentrating; allow no distractions.*
- ♦ *5. Put your observations including sight, sound, feel and any others experienced 'on hold' by reviewing in your mind.*
- ♦ *6. Move on with the day . . .*

Do not use this procedure if the performance is bad: you can lock in the bad as well as the good. If you watch and evaluate a bad performance, do so with your conscious mental energy only. Using imagery involves the other levels of your mind, and therefore has a more lasting and pro-found effect.

You will be surprised to find out how much of what you have absorbed while watching will filter into your actual riding. In most cases, you will not be consciously aware of its use. It enhances other practical learning techniques and trains various levels of your conscious that are involved in affective learning. Exercise #5 in your Workbook will give you some practical guides for imagery.

Visualization has several uses. If your riding requires learning a pattern, visualization will enable you to learn the pattern with your total self, so that while you are riding the pattern, your mental energy can be completely available for riding the horse. Visualization is also a vital tool if you have a poor image of yourself and you need to change that image. If you are unable to ride regularly, daily time spent practicing in your mind can maintain what you have learned. Visualization can be a vital asset in helping a rider to deal with competitive stress. Practicing visualization has been especially helpful for riders starting at middle age.

Uses of Visualization:

♦ *1. Proper learning of a pattern for jumping, dressage, roping and other forms of riding*
♦ *2. Improving self image*
♦ *3. Managing competition stress or other stress*
♦ *4. Practicing in your mind when you cannot ride or need extra practice*
♦ *5. Coordination problems*

Use the same learning procedure for visualization as for imagery. Put floating thoughts 'on hold', go to a quiet place in your mind, concentrate on the subject, review it, put it 'on hold' and move on.

For learning a pattern through visualization, first go over the route with the proper gaits, in relationship to the area where it will be performed. Once you can follow this route without having to think about it, add all communications or half halts that you think will be necessary. In dressage, this will be before and after each corner, figure or transition. Once you can do this and feel your body enacting the half-halts just as if you were on the horse, with your eyes closed and without much thought, you are ready to add the last step. The last step of this phase is to include the necessary half-halts that relate to what you know about your horse. If your horse shies by the judge's box at every show, you should program slight bending past the judge's box into your minute around the arena. You are not just thinking, you are feeling and seeing the entire experience. You must do this as often as necessary, until you can reproduce an instant replay. In the replay, visualize the route with all the feelings as you know them, related to your horse. Once you have reviewed this often enough, put it 'on hold' and move on.

If you are using visualization to improve your self-confidence, you should see yourself looking your best and performing the best ride you can recall. Often during our learning journey, we experience performances that have mixed feelings of good and bad. One day we may feel a magnificent balanced trot, two weeks later a really forward transition to trot, and at some other time we may experience a balanced, relaxed canter. When you practice your visualization, bring the best trot you felt into ALL the trot work, the best transition you felt into ALL the transitions and the best canter you felt into ALL the canter work. To know which are best, you will need your instructor to help you recognize what is correct and give you time to feel it and place it 'on hold'. While cooling your horse out, you will want to recall and confirm the correctness of your movements. These feelings should be included in your daily mental training to help create a POSITIVE image. The same is true about yourself. Go back to the Love chapter. You must do whatever you can to love yourself, to give yourself a positive image of yourself. During visualization, view yourself as you REALISTICALLY want to look. Be careful about imitating someone else. It is important not to deceive your conscious mind, because, in the long run, deception causes imbalance. Imitate only what is realistic for you. For example, to help riders who frequently look down, I suggest that they imitate Carol Lavell, who never looks down. This is safe, because we all can look up! You must accept who you are, but you can visualize yourself at your best.

If you do have a poor image of yourself, go back to your comparisons with the ideal in the physical understanding chapter. If negative experiences such as failure, discouragement, or anxiety plague your life, spend some time thinking about how it would be to feel differently. In the Forgiveness chapter, we examined viewing situations from all perspectives. Reread that section related to any defeating feelings. During visualization, practice the same situation, replacing the negative viewpoint with your new positive viewpoint resulting from your conversation with your thinking mind. The combination of that chapter and your positive attitude will help you change what you can change or accept what you cannot change.

James Loehr's *Mental Toughness Training for Sports* states: "Visualization is one of the most powerful mental training strategies available to performing athletes." Jack Nicklaus attributes much of his competitive success to his dedicated practice of visualization. Using visualization competitively is much like learning a pattern. You mentally rehearse your performance as though you are actually performing it. You want to use the MOST positive recall from every aspect of yourself and your horse. Whenever possible, for instance if your discipline of choice is dressage or roping, practice it before a competition. For eventing and show jumping allow enough time at the competition, once the courses are posted, to practice your visualization. Know yourself. If you are easily distracted, you may need to get away from all the competition distractions. You may need to get up early before the activities begin, or wear a Walkman to abolish external sounds. Be creative in finding ways to get to the quiet spot in your mind, FREE FROM DISTRACTIONS. Then practice the visualization as frequently as YOU NEED to do it, until the performance can be zoomed through complete with all the feelings that create the PERFECT performance.

For anyone who rides irregularly, practicing daily through the use of visualization is a valuable tool. Spend your cooling out time free from distractions, reviewing the positive aspects of your performance and putting it 'on hold' to recall for your next ride. On days when you cannot ride, recall this performance, complete with all the senses, and review it during visualization. If you spend just a few minutes once or twice a day doing this, you will discover that it will partially replace a few missed riding sessions. Naturally, you must have the physical practice too. The most important recall is the feel, but seeing the ride in the mirror or on video can be a good starting point. Between rides, you can mentally re-ride parts of your last ride.

I have also found visualization valuable for those experiencing coordination problems. Once they have mastered the movement, I ask them to do it again, concentrating on the feel only. Do this exercise several times while it is quiet. I only acknowledge it if it is correct. After they have completed the movement, I ask them to walk and review it, because that confirms the movement and experience in their memory. This is a useful mental tool even without visualization. A two minute review may save you hours in the saddle or hundreds of dollars in lessons!

As with imagery, this use of visualization ends with a review of what was experienced. The review should encompass as many of your senses as are involved in the experience. Without the quick review, it will be difficult for you to retain the image. The review step completes the cycle for your recall.

To make imagery and visualization part of your vocabulary of life skills, practice Exercise #6 in your Workbook.

Journey

Introduction

The more significant and challenging your journey, the more obstacles, setbacks, changes of direction or surprises you will face. You can be better prepared for the trip if you are willing to develop your resources. Coping, whether in life or with your horses involves AWARENESS, ACCEPTANCE, DECISION MAKING, and COMMUNICATING. The interaction with your world involves CONFRONTATION, RESPONSIBILITY and TRUST. How well you learn to cope, accept yourself, and deal with life's road blocks, will affect the quality of your travel and the amount of time it takes to reach your goal. Progress is never steady, so realistic EXPECTATIONS are critical to your APPRECIATION and enjoyment of the trip.

This section is designed to share the many ways that your resources can help you have a more fulfilling journey.

Decision Making

Decisions put our thoughts into action. Horses give us the opportunity to gain confidence in our ability to make dependable decisions.

We make thousands of decisions in our journey with horses. Our ability to make decisions will have a major impact on the length of time our journey takes, the success we experience during our trip, and on the end result; will we achieve our goal or not? Our decisions put our thoughts into action. Some decisions affect only the specific moment of our performance, while others affect the road toward our goals.

In the three major areas involving goals, long-term, intermediate and short-term, we must use different procedures to make our decisions. To determine our long-term goal, we must collect information, evaluate our motivation, our stage in life and the outside influences, and then retreat to give considerable, devoted thought to all the information. To establish our intermediate goal, we need to evaluate the results of our daily work in relationship to our long-term goal. For us to decide to make changes, or continue the same day-to-day program, we must have a clear perception and recall of our work. Our day-to-day decisions have the greatest impact on us, because the results of these decisions often affect our daily mood and feelings. These decisions are difficult to make in a different way. They must be made immediately, based on feel.

All decisions must have a solid foundation based on the desire for improvement. It is essential that your first requirement for any decision is to know that you do not want to cause harm. The second requirement for all decisions is to gather information that gives you the facts or theory necessary to make an educated decision. The third requirement is to have a positive attitude: you must want to make the best possible decision, and you must believe that you can make that decision. If you do not yet meet all three of these requirements, you must spend some time thinking about your opinion or views and establish a philosophy. Without this foundation, all your decisions may prove frustrating and inconsistent.

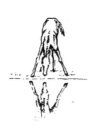

Foundation for all decisions:
- *1. Have a desire for betterment, not to cause harm.*
- *2. Gather the necessary information to become informed.*
- *3. Have a positive attitude: believe that you want and can make a decision.*

Deciding on our long-term goal is the first decision a horseperson must make after establishing a basic foundation. The long-term goal is the underlying concept on which we base all other decisions. These decisions require very careful consideration. One whole section of this book was devoted to establishing goals, because of the effect our goal or purpose has on each of our decisions. Our mountain top is most useful in this case. Once we have gathered all the information we need about our motivation, stage in life, and outside influences, we should retreat to our mountain top with a clear mind to concentrate on all this information to make our long-term goal decision. The charts and questionnaires in your Workbook may help you understand yourself better and see yourself more clearly. Once you make the major decision of your long-term goal, you should wait a day or so, then review it to reconsider how you still feel about it. If you still feel good about it, finalize the decision.

Steps For Making Long-Term Goals:
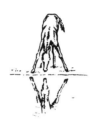
- ◆ *1. Gather information about yourself*
- ◆ *2. Go to your mountain top*
- ◆ *3. Concentrate on all the aspects of your various possible decisions*
- ◆ *4. Make the decision*
- ◆ *5. Wait a day or two, and then reconsider*
- ◆ *6. If you still feel OK, activate the decision*

Joan entered a state of existence with Willy once her instructor had told her that he was not capable of meeting her long-term goal of showing amateur/owner. After the clinician gave her hope, she was forced to reconsider her long term goal seriously. She retreated to a soft bed of fragrant pine needles in a small opening in the woods, where the sunlight filtered thorough the pine branches, her mountain top, to decide on what to do. She took with her the information from the clinician, from her current instructor, and an open mind. She then concentrated on whether to sell Willy and stay with the current instructor, or keep Willy and find a new instructor. She spent a considerable amount of time evaluating her motivation, her family situation, her love for Willy and her commitment to her instructor of five years. It was not easy, because she was uncertain if her emotional attachment to Willy was overriding her logic and commitment to her instructor. She decided that her love for Willy was the most important ingredient to her, and that she should break the bond with her instructor, find a new instructor who had the same approach as the clinician, and reinstate her old goal, amateur/owner. It is clear to see how easy it would be to avoid such a decision, especially when it forced Joan to break the connection with her instructor of five years.

The next type of decision is to determine the criteria for your intermediate goal, the necessary steps toward achieving your long-term goal. Again, you must gather information about what both you and your horse will need to learn and achieve. You can gather some of the necessary information by reading, but most of it will come from a trusted professional instructor or trainer. It is this person's job to know you and your horse and make the necessary suggestions that will build the quality foundation for your successful journey. You should have many active discussions with your instructor or trainer while you are in the process of collecting information, because these decisions affect the direction of your day-to-day riding as well as your ability to attain your goal. In addition to the factual information, it is good to have a mental picture of what you are trying to do, as well as a realistic idea of how much time it will take to learn new concepts properly and establish them as permanent parts of your vocabulary.

Joan's second important decision was not easy, because she first had to find a new local instructor. Using the criteria described in the Knowledge chapter, she found Cynthia. After taking a couple of lessons with Cynthia, Joan arranged for a consulting lesson, to discuss the steps she needed to take to show Willy amateur/owner. During the transition, Joan herself discovered several flaws. Willy needed to become more supple, and she needed to learn to feel more quickly. Joan also realized that she did not have a clear mental image of what she needed to do. Cynthia rode Willy a few times, and explained to Joan what she was doing and why. Together Joan and Cynthia watched some properly supple and balanced horse/rider combinations, and they discussed the steps that Joan and Willy would need to take to become competitive in the amateur/owner division. This gave Joan a clear picture of what she needed to learn. Cynthia also suggested that Joan had to learn some form of relaxation therapy to speed up her ability to feel and relax. Joan researched relaxation therapies, and she decided to study Tai Chi. Once Joan had the clear picture of what she wanted to do, and found professionals who could help her do it, she was able to make a commitment that put her intermediate goals into action. Her aim was to evaluate her progress every three months, with Cynthia's help. She would compare Cynthia's evaluations, her own feelings, Willy's progress and her videos to determine if she was making the desired progress toward her long-term goal.

Steps For Making Intermediate Goals:

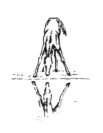

- ◆ *1. Get a clear picture of what both you and your horse need*
- ◆ *2. Discuss the necessary steps with a trusted professional*
- ◆ *3. Decide on a time period for evaluation*
- ◆ *4. When evaluation time comes, use:*
  a. Instructor/trainer's opinion
  b. Your opinion
  c. Video reviews
- ◆ *5. If you are progressing as expected, continue, if not, change*
- ◆ *6. To change, reevaluate your process using above criteria*

The next type of resolutions we must make are difficult in a different way. They are our day-to-day decisions. Most of them must be immediate and spontaneous, because they affect our performance. While riding, these decisions are based on feel, using the practical knowledge that we have practiced until we can use it naturally. Some riders ride without learning the practical information, while others have a wealth of practical information that remains practical only, not affective. The riders without the practical knowledge tend to act inappropriately, too quickly, or both. Riders who have the practical knowledge tend to think too long and make their decision too late, and are therefore ineffective. To make the necessary day-to-day decisions, we must learn the theory, one step at a time, practice it until it becomes second nature to us, and then apply it to the horse affectively, through feel. A rider who rides 'off the seat of his pants' is a rider who has the feel to apply the theory in response to the horse. We all want to learn to ride 'off the seat of our pants'. This, combined with a good seat, is what makes a rider look like part of his horse, the basic goal for ALL HORSEPERSONS.

Daily practice with our horse is our best teacher. The forgiving nature of our horse gives us permission to make the necessary decisions to get the performance we have clearly pictured in our mind. Each day's ride should begin with a review of our intermediate goal, a review of yesterday's ride, and a clear view of what we want to achieve in the day's ride. All else in our life should be 'on hold', so that the horse can receive the benefit of our unobstructed concentration. Because we have been attentive to our horse from the beginning of our preparation through our warmup, we have gathered additional information that will help us determine whether we can follow our initial plan, or whether we need to make a change. Once we make this decision, we are ready to begin the day's ride. As we begin our ride, we must practice what is necessary to progress in our training. If you are in the practical stage of learning, you must practice the steps needed to create the correct habit. If you are in the affective stage of learning, you must practice responding to your horse immediately. By practicing acknowledgment of yourself and your horse, you will build confidence in your ability to make decisions and in your general knowledge. Your willingness to listen to the response of your horse, regardless of the stage of learning, and your commitment to praising what is good and changing what does not work, will build your own confidence and the confidence of your horse.

Steps For Making Short-Term Goals:

- ◆ *1. Have a clear picture of today's goal.*
- ◆ *2. Recall and review your immediate goal, yesterday's ride, today's expectations, and your horse's response during the preparation for this ride and during the warmup.*

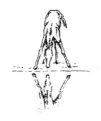

- ◆ *3. Decide whether you can progress as planned or whether you must change the plan.*
- ◆ *4. Decide what you are going to do.*
- ◆ *5. Activate the decision through your aids.*
- ◆ *6. Acknowledge the response.*
- ◆ *7. Recognize if horse is responding correctly or not.*
- ◆ *8. Correct and move on.*

Joan made many wrong decisions while she embarked on her new training program with Willy. She discovered that he quickly forgave her when she was wrong, and quickly listened to her when she was right. Joan's two main goals were to teach Willy to bend and to teach herself to respond to him promptly. She realized that she had to be patient, both with herself and with her horse. Because she knew what she wanted to achieve, she would catch herself when she became too demanding, asking more than either of them was able to do. Cynthia helped her understand the need to go slowly while suppling and strengthening Willy's muscles. Gradually Joan learned to ask more clearly and appropriately, and she felt both of them improving. This improvement gave her more confidence in her decisions. She discovered that the more certain she became, the more quickly her training program progressed.

From beginner to advanced training, in our real life or our horse life, decision making is a constant process in our journey. Our ability to recognize the need to make a decision, as well as our ability to make it, activate it, and acknowledge the response, requires the use of many of our resources. As our journey progresses, our decisions become more natural, more precise, and more quickly activated and evaluated.

No matter what type of decision you must make, each decision will involve the proper foundation, the most possible information about your goal, self, and horse, the ability to recognize the cycle of the decision, and the willingness to forgive and try something else if the response is not correct. You must be willing to be patient with yourself when you make mistakes. But most of all, you must not be afraid to make mistakes. Almost all mistakes can be corrected. With each decision we make, we take the risk of making a mistake. Mistakes can lead to feelings of guilt, both true and false guilt. We almost never make a bad decision deliberately; a bad decision is usually a result of the circumstances that existed at the time the decision was made. However, we can make a bad decision, and we can lose our self-confidence as a result. Many people avoid making decisions because they can seldom be certain of the outcome. They decide that it is easier to do nothing than run the risk of making a mistake. But without risk, there is no gain, so we must all have the courage to learn to make decisions.

I have made many bad decisions because I tend to be too reactive and not think enough. Horses taught me that I could change this pattern, and that I could also learn to forgive myself. I learned that when I made a mistake, I had to take action once I realized it was the wrong decision. By taking action, I could avoid feelings of guilt. I tend to be very determined, so when I communicate to a horse, he gets the message clearly, whether it is correct or not. If it is not correct he will not listen, if I immediately change the aids and try something else, he responds to that action. I can make many mistakes and he keeps trying. Could I do the same with people? Not exactly. But I can initiate this action: when I realize that I have miscommunicated or created a misunderstanding, I will apologize as soon as possible.

I have learned to empathize with the other person in the same way I empathize with a horse. I am less spontaneous with humans than with horses, so I am not able to be in the 'now' with people as I am with horses. When I am left with a 'funny' feeling inside, I have learned to review my day. During my review, I usually discover where the uncomfortable feelings came from. I then know who to apologize to. I have had to apologize so many times that, in addition to learning how to empathize, I have also learned to slow down and think. In this way, I avoid these inner feelings of guilt or discomfort. While I still experience these feelings from time to time, they are reduced because I listen to my inner self in relationship to a decision I had made, and make another decision to remedy my error! It is harmless, and very freeing. But these are not the high-risk, costly mistakes.

The costly decisions are those that we do not recognize as bad decisions until the consequences produce devastating results. If we act in haste, or carelessly, or make a decision without evaluating the consequences, we may cause a catastrophe. A case like this can cause true guilt, which is a major test for forgiveness. If we are driving too fast and kill an innocent animal, we have made a very costly decision that will cause true guilt. What can we do? We must face our mistake and accept our emotions, and then we must make another decision. This should be not to drive so carelessly again. Then we must allow time to heal our feelings, we must keep to our intention of becoming less careless, and we must forgive ourselves. This is the only way we can go on with our life without destroying other areas of our life. We cannot bring the animal back to life, so we must fully experience the guilty, sad, angry feelings, and then we must move on. Each time the emotions reappear, we must look at them, and remind ourself that we are letting them go, and that we are not going to drive fast again. Eventually our attitude can help us relieve the true guilt that we feel. However, if we deny our wrongdoing or our emotions, we will not be able to move forward. We will be creating one of the road blocks discussed in the Energy chapter.

Luckily, we do not make too many costly decisions in our life, but we do make many, many mistakes. We can and should learn from our mistakes. We do this by evaluating the decision, deciding what we can and should do differently, and then implementing our new decision. You can learn to make effective decisions by gaining knowledge, activating the knowledge through decisions, acknowledging the good decisions with praise, forgiving and changing the bad or ineffective ones, and moving on toward all levels of your goals. With time and practice, you will find that effective decision making has become a habit.

EFFECTIVE DECISIONS ARE
FOR EVERYONE.

- ♦ *1. Seek and collect knowledge*
- ♦ *2. Activate the knowledge through a decision*
- ♦ *3. Acknowledge a good decision with praise*
- ♦ *4. Forgive and change a bad or ineffective decision*
- ♦ *5. Move on with confidence*

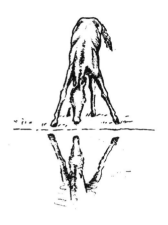

Awareness

Awareness allows us to conquer our road blocks and capture the joy of riding and life.

Will we recognize the road blocks and the highs that we encounter during our journey? Not if we are unaware. Awareness is the barometer of our sensitivity, it allows us to experience the 'now'. It sets the stage for our performance. If we are sensitive to our self, our horse, and our environment, we will be able to take action when necessary, use our knowledge to make decisions, and enjoy our experience. Average awareness will allow us to enjoy our activity, but we may not get the most out of it. The more awareness we have, the more tools we will have to conquer the road blocks and capture the joys of life.

The most difficult aspects of horse and man, and those requiring the most awareness on our part, are the spiritual aspects; love, energy, and attitude. The more aware we are of the spiritual aspects of life, the more enriching our life experiences will be. The spiritual aspects of life add depth to our experiences and give us a broader view of life's situations.

Most of us go through life only aware on the surface, because we have not learned to be observant, or because we are afraid of the pain that can accompany awareness. The door to awareness opened for me with RSRT, the meditative form of relaxation described in the Relaxation chapter. It took the power of a meditative experience to open my closed mind. When I began on this part of my journey, I had no idea that my level of awareness was not high. I had no desire to participate in something weird like meditation. It was only out of respect for the therapist that I tried to listen and follow his directions, but I did not inwardly believe in it. Only my logical mind was participating. Despite my limited involvement, I had a physically relaxing experience. What would have happened if I had started with a more willing attitude? I felt the physical relaxation first. The mental exercise produced a physical experience, and this new awareness put me on a path to discover more about the inner aspects of my life. As I became more aware of my physical body through a mental exercise, I began to discover my spiritual being. This process did not happen overnight; it took years of investigation, research, and patience. For those of you who wish to become more aware, I will share what I feel could have speeded up my journey. However, you must all remember that each of us learns at a different rate, in a different order, and from a different set of circumstances. I hope that you will find some of the suggestions helpful. There are variations in what works best for each individual.

I am convinced that the first most important step on this journey is an open, positive attitude. If I had been willing to trust this therapist and believe in the value of relaxation, I feel certain that it would have taken only three sessions instead of ten to have the experience. Over the years, I have discovered that attitude plays a major role in the outcome of all situations. Our attitude affects our thoughts, our feelings, and our inner being. We can try to fool ourselves and the world with positive words, but if we do not have a positive attitude to back up those words, the words themselves will carry little meaning. If we decide to do something, we owe it to our decision to have a truly positive attitude in regard to all aspects of the decision.

Empathy with horses was the next most important step in my journey towards awareness. It was easy for me to share feelings with a horse, so I began to observe them more closely. I tried to imagine which senses a horse would use most easily and most frequently. Watching them alone and watching them with their riders or handlers helped me learn to be more aware. I discovered that I had missed a lot even with the creatures I most loved. Gradually I was able to transfer this empathy over to people, although I still do not understand human behavior as well as I understand the behavior of horses. However, I have become much more alert to all aspects of both horse and man by practicing empathy with a horse.

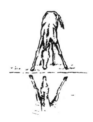

Watching horses closely, both alone and with their riders, will help you learn to become more aware.

Energy is the third resource that can enhance awareness. When my trip began, I did not have a clear view of energy, but I did have an idea of its existence. As I studied I became more aware of its role and of its meaning to life's balance, in which energy plays a major role. Since 1974, I had been aware of the aspects of psychological balance which were necessary for the emotional, intellectual, and educational life of healthy, functional, young people. These mental characteristics had been my first introduction to the concept of balance within our being. Once I was introduced to this, I returned to my beloved horses for a better understanding. Their energy always flows freely, allowing them to act quickly. Horses are able to sense when we are afraid, confident, loving, or hostile. How can they feel this in us? They must feel our energy fields. Dennis Reis, creator of the Universal Horsemanship, describes the energy field as a 'body bubble' or 'personal space'. New age terminology calls it an 'aura'. Whatever this field may be called, it is the energy-filled area that surrounds our body or the horse's body. This allows the being, whether horse or man, to remain awake and react to a stimulus before it actually touches the body. Horses naturally use this energy field, but it is often blocked in people. However, we can all learn to become aware, unblock, and even expand our energy field. If they can feel us, we should be able to feel them and each other. I believe that our energy is easily blocked through lack of communication, miscommunications, misinterpretations, misperceptions, or through denying ourselves the total emotional experience. Our mind creates these blocks, while a horse's mind does not. There is no easy answer to getting in touch with our energy and eliminating the blocks, but if you feel that you need some help, go back to the Energy chapter. Energy plays a vital role in our awareness. If we have created blocks in our inner being, there will be limits on our ability to be aware of all that is around us. If you feel confronted with unpleasant or difficult feelings, try to uncover the cause.

I have left the resource of love until last, but for many it can be the first. I have always loved horses, but my love of horses alone was not enough to create the awareness that I needed to enrich my life. However, once I began my journey, I discovered that I was lucky, because I understood love from my unconditional love of horses. The loving interaction I recognized and experienced with horses helped me to understand the need to love myself and others. Even though I understood the need, I discovered this to be a difficult process to undertake. Even with all the books I read, and even though I had the dedication to develop it, I found that the processes of learning to know and love myself and others were slow and difficult. I think that horse lovers are at an advantage, because they can try to learn self love and acceptance from their love of horses. Once we begin to love and accept ourselves as we are, we are ready to share our love with life, thus having a loving effect on those around us. Being aware of love and its relationship in our life helps to fill each experience with peace, joy, and enthusiasm. Sharing time with persons who love life is an enlightening experience.

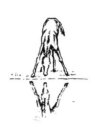

The resources that enhance awareness along our journey:
- ◆ *1. Meditation*
- ◆ *2. Positive Attitude*
- ◆ *3. Empathy*
- ◆ *4. Free flowing energy*
- ◆ *5. Love of self, horse and life*

Unaware riders cannot feel what their horses are doing. I made a startling discovery: most people do not know how items feel in their hands! In trying to help riders understand how to maintain a constant contact with the mouth of the horse via the reins, I began to ask them if they knew the difference between the weight of a can of soup and a dinner fork. Not one was aware of the difference. I stopped asking the question, and began to suggest that they should become aware of the difference in this feeling, because what they feel in their hands has a direct relationship to their communication with their horse.

The first recognition for beginning riders is the relationship of their balance and their skills. First we learn position in relationship to the seat we are studying. Next we must be aware of our body and the horse's body. This allows us to develop the necessary balance for a safe, harmonious seat. We cannot balance properly if we do not know the route we want to be on. We must be alert to where we are going, as well as where we want to go. We must evaluate what effect the weather and the footing will have on each ride. The first awareness we learn is to be aware of the physical aspects of riding. Those aspects continue to play a major role throughout our lifetime of learning with horses.

A horse is reactive, responding immediately to external stimuli. We can be either reactive or analytical [which is part of the cognitive learning process]. To ride, we must become reactive enough to respond to the horse immediately, without thought. Correct reactiveness is learned through the cognitive learning process, practiced during the practical learning process and becomes useful during the affective learning process. We must first teach ourselves the correct habits, and then we must trust ourself to act, using the habits we have developed. The more aware we are of this process, the more likely we are to gain the necessary responsive feelings. Joan learned that she was inappropriately reactive with Willy, causing him to lose his balance on the turns between jumps. She was turning him with her hands only, instead of preparing him for the turn with all of her rebalancing aids. Once she became aware of her error, she spent two weeks practicing nothing but correct preparation for turns. The two weeks she focused on creating this new habit ultimately prepared Joan to ride a course with Willy without increasing speed. She was elated to discover that she had improved her awareness and responsiveness to Willy so much that he no longer needed to speed up to regain his balance. Now they are both reactive related to turning!

Instructors must be patient while exposing students to awareness, one of the most significant jobs the instructor undertakes. It takes a long time for riders to become aware of what their horse is doing under them. Repetition is essential to the rider. It may take years for the rider to become aware of something that their instructor has been frequently repeating. Often I have students come to their lesson and tell that they had a startling revelation. They learned during their practice that if they keep their leg on their horse, the horse will perform better. This revelation comes after two years of hearing me repeating, in as many ways as I know, that they must keep their leg softly on their horse. However, they could not do it. Why, after two years, do they think that it is something new? For two years they have heard the words and understood the theory, but they were not ready for the realization. However, the repeated explanations gave them the information to use when they were ready for their discovery. The constant repetition prepared them for the affective learning experience once they were ready.

It is the instructor's responsibility to be patient and to repeat information in a variety of ways. This encourages the student to experience the awareness that will incorporate the affective learning experience of feel. There is no predetermined period of time for this; it will happen when the student is ready.

The desire to become aware is your first commitment to this phase of your journey. As you become more aware, you will discover more about yourself and life, thus making your journey more enriching. If you feel that you are bound by stress, tension, frustration, fear, guilt, or jealousy, seek a comfortable source of help. Do not remain stubborn and feel that you can do it alone. Often even a small amount of outside help will open the doors to new experiences that will change your life for the better.

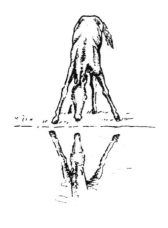

Expectations

*When creating expectations
we must remember
to consider both
partners' thoughts,
moods and feelings.*

One key to a successful journey is to have REALISTIC expectations. These are based on a clear, honest look at all levels of our goals. Expectations can be our road map, or our desired results. Their role in our journey can be good or bad, depending upon the amount of time we have dedicated to setting our goals, how well we can evaluate the circumstances that we encounter along our journey, and how well we know ourselves. Expectations can help us monitor our progress by giving us a set of criteria to guide us.

Realistic expectations go hand in hand with realistic goals. We have spent many chapters on developing appropriate goals. If you have selected suitable goals for yourself, then it is easier to have reasonable expectations. However, even the best planned goals can suffer from false expectations, those that are too high or too low for the event or situation.

How often do you go to a clinic to show the clinician how well your horse is going? How often are you prepared to share the problems that you have faced during your training? More likely you present yourself and your horse as a problem-free duo, and you think that you are attending the clinic only to take the next big step ahead. Here is the scenario. You were looking forward to the upcoming clinic, your horse had done well at home, and you expected to start jumping higher fences. On the way to the clinic, you came upon a long delay from a traffic jam, you became worried because you were going to be late, you did not get your horse properly prepared, and then to top it off, your horse was upset by the strong winds. Instead of reevaluating the conditions and changing your expectations for the day, you ignored the circumstances of the day and presented yourself to the clinician with your original high hopes. Your first mistake was not to change your expectations when the circumstances began to change. The second mistake was not to share with the instructor your experiences since leaving home: the traffic jam and the influence of the wind. Had you been smart enough to change your expectations, you might not have become so depressed when the instructor had to spend all his training time on basic relaxation for you and your horse. Your expectations were too high. As you rode around, you became increasingly frustrated because you kept thinking about the clinician's opinion of you and your horse, the audience's comments, and the foolishness of spending money on what you already knew. You forgot to realize that the instructor was not familiar with your normal performance. As the instructor's time wore on, your irritation grew, making you feel worse. You did not think to evaluate and create a different approach, to accept the consequences of the situation, and to adapt to the conditions. Perhaps you would have relaxed inwardly, and the results would have been different.

On the other hand, you could have attended the clinic with no expectations other than surviving the clinic (yes, there are those who feel this way!). You had no questions, you were satisfied if your horse gets from one side of the fence to the other.

You would not have been likely to gain anything from the clinic, because you were too busy being satisfied with no expectations or goals. Your expectations were too low.

Each day's ride should have some expectations, because the absence of expectations is an indication of no goal planning. Much time and effort can be wasted with no evaluation tools.

Expectations begin when you plan your long term goal. Is it appropriate or not? Joan thought her long-term goal with Willy was safe, but it was shattered when her instructor told her that she needed to buy another, more talented horse. Were Joan's long-term goals and resulting expectations too high? Joan thought that she had made her decision based on good information. When she heard the statement that her horse was not good enough, Joan looked more closely at her expectations. She had not been meeting her goals, but she thought that her failure was a result of her not being ready, not the fault of her horse. Later she discovered that the problem lay with the instructor who had skipped part of the foundation, and not with Willy's inability. How could she have known? Perhaps she needed to ask more questions and investigate further. Her instructor's doubt caused her to question her expectations. Perhaps the timing was a necessary part of the experience. During this time, Joan did not sell Willy, instead she attended clinics where she was exposed to a greater awareness and more information. She shared her doubts and concerns with the clinician. Joan's love for Willy created a bond that allowed her to take her time. When her goal was questioned, she changed her expectations and decided that she would simply enjoy riding Willy, and dedicate more time and energy to her family. When the clinician offered her hope, it was an unexpected bright spot in her journey. It also presented the necessity of another awkward decision: whom should she believe? As you know, she retreated to her mountain top and made the decision. Joan had overcome a road block when she confronted the issue and decided to return to her original long-term goal. She did not have any assurances that it would be successful—we never do—but all the information made sense and reinforced her positive attitude.

Once goals are set, we must understand what is necessary for us to reach those goals. Both horse and rider will be expected to learn new skills, refine old skills, or eliminate bad habits. Each horse is different in body and mind. Since both must be trained, you must know what will be necessary to prepare this horse for your long-term goal. If you feel that you do not have a plan, or do not feel confident with the one you think you should have, discuss this with your instructor. Your instructor's duties include teaching, reassuring and building up your confidence.

With the help of her new instructor, Cynthia, Joan made new intermediate and short-term goals. These forced Joan to create an entirely new set of expectations. She had to supple Willy during her daily rides instead of doing so much jumping. She also discovered that on some days Willy responded as she expected, while on other days he did not. Why? Joan expected every day to be the same, instead of considering the relationship of the previous day's ride, the weather, the footing, the time of the day, and how she felt. With Cynthia's help, Joan learned the difference between expecting too much and accepting Willy's feelings and moods. During one of their discussions, Joan told Cynthia that she felt very uncomfortable when Willy resisted. She felt that she was causing him to resist, therefore she did not feel it was fair to correct him. Cynthia taught Joan a simple diagnostic technique that she could use whenever she felt this confusion. First Joan should do a quick trip through her body, feeling the relaxation in each joint, making certain that the stress of her life was not being transmitted to Willy. If she discovers tightness in her body, Joan learned to walk and do some physical and mental exercises to relieve the tightness. If she does not feel any tightness, she should continue. The second part of the test is to examine what she is asking Willy. Perhaps she is asking for too much bend to the left, instead of asking for three inches, ask only for two inches. This may be less than he gave yesterday, but perhaps yesterday his body was overstressed and he is still feeling a little sore. He will not resist just for the sake of resistance. If Willy responds to the lesser bend, then she has made the first affirmative diagnosis. Now she knows that she must reduce her expectations of the day or run the risk of creating more soreness or more evasions that could cause physical or mental tightness.

Day-to-day expectations can lead to frustration or subsequent loss of self-confidence, or to pleasure and subsequent confidence-building. It depends upon your ability to be consistent and to remember to evaluate the conditions of each day. The factors that you should consider each day include: the results of yesterday's ride, your horse's attitude while you were tacking up, the sensitivity of his body to your grooming, the weather conditions, the environment, and how you feel. None of us deliberately have inappropriate expectations, but often we are carelessly unaware of all the factors that affect ourselves and our horse. Because our partnership includes two living creatures with thoughts, moods, and feelings, we have the responsibility to take all of these into consideration when setting appropriate expectations. Setting, changing and evaluating our day-to-day goals is experiential learning at its best. We are learning to be aware of our horse, our self, and our environment, and listen to what we see, hear, feel, and sense. If we notice a change from the 'normal,' we must consider the role of the change in our expectations for the day. Failure to do so can result in a frustrating day with our horse. Remembering to do so can provide a rewarding experience. While riding, notice your horse's stiffness, tightness, or confusion. If what you are doing is not producing the expected outcome, be aware of it and try something else. When you get the desired result from something that has been causing you difficulty, pause for a moment, reward the horse and yourself, and place the entire experience 'on hold.' This will store it for the next time you need it. Each successful item you put 'on hold' will build your experiential learning knowledge. These items are the lessons taught to you by your horse.

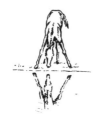

To plan appropriate daily expectations, consider:

- ◆ *1. Yesterday's ride*
- ◆ *2. The plan for today's ride*
- ◆ *3. Your horse's response to grooming and tacking up*
- ◆ *4. Your horse's warmup*
- ◆ *5. Environment conditions*
- ◆ *6. Weather conditions*
- ◆ *7. How you feel*

Don't be afraid to change your plan if one of the above factors indicates a need for change.

Joan's intermediate goal was to jump three feet quietly without running or refusing. This set the stage for her day-to-day goals with Willy, which involved constant revisions. I teach my students the following technique to help them learn how to create successful day-to-day goals. First, I expect them to store 'on hold' each day's ride, including the good, the bad, and the expected plan for the next ride. On the way to the barn, the rider recalls this information. While the rider is tacking up, the horse should be observed and any deviation from normal should be noted. Warmup is a time for the rider to evaluate the condition of his own and the horse's body. While loosening up on a long rein, the rider should always take a quick trip through his body, and feel each joint and body part. It is during this exercise that the rider can decide if and how the day's stress is affecting his control panel. This trip through the body should only take one or two times around the ring. After this is done, it is time to evaluate the horse's straightness, rhythm and relaxation. Is he going faster in one direction than the other, is he leaning, is he worried? How does this warmup compare with yesterday's? How does he feel compared with the end of yesterday's ride? This information tells the rider if he can continue with his original expectations as planned, or if they must be changed to meet the conditions of the day. The more observant and flexible you are, the better your training program will progress.

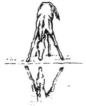

The more observant and flexible you are, the better your training program will progress.

Our expectations should come from knowing ourself, our horse, and our goals. Instead, they often come from our peers, our instructor, the media, or our dreams. Sometimes it is not outside expectations but our discolored attitude that sets our expectations. Children have the greatest expectations put on them by their environment. Parents and teachers must be careful during the different stages, because while certain expectations are good, too many can lead to problems. Clean, simple, and fair expectations can be made only when you know, understand, and accept yourself as you are, not as you wish you were.

As you travel the journey of life with an open-minded, positive attitude about getting to know and understand yourself, you will discover that you can better accept the real you. This automatically helps you to create realistic expectations. You also will discover that most people do not put demands on you, you only think that they do. You may discover that if they do inflict their expectations on you, you must acknowledge that you know yourself better than anyone else knows you. No one has any right to inflict their expectations on another without their agreement. Our role in the partnership gives us the responsibility of creating expectations for our horse. This fact is all the more reason we must learn to 'know ourselves'. Because the horse has been taken from his natural environment and put under our control, we must be fair, honest, realistic, and flexible in what we ask. If Joan had continued to ask Willy to jump high fences before he was ready, she would have been inflicting her will unfairly. In addition to causing him confusion and fear, she could have hurt him. There can be dangerous consequences if we inflict poorly planned expectations on a horse; these are errors we must try to avoid.

Creating and achieving successful expectations builds confidence and helps us to accept ourselves. Learning to accept ourselves is one of the longest journeys in life. Expectations help us to determine when and what we must change. Horses are a great help to those of us who love them, because we can learn by observing their acceptance of themselves, of us, and of our demands.

Communication

*Communication is an art
that is learned through
effective use of body,
mind and spirit.*

Decision making, awareness, and expectations are of no value unless you can communicate with your horse. Conversation with horses is through body language and energy fields, rather than through the words that dominate human interchange. Since body language and energy fields play a major role in our horse interaction, we must learn the art of a new type of communication. In order for our body to be a relaxed and supple communicator, it must be in balance with our mind. Only then can it offer us the highly refined interaction necessary for the quick, effective conversation we need with horses.

Our philosophy sets the tone for all forms of communications. The more we can believe in a positive attitude, unconditional love, and free flowing energy, the more likely it is that our interactions will have a positive outcome. By now, I hope that you have spent some time determining your personal philosophy and purpose in life. This paves the way for the most effective communication.

Our philosophy sets the tone for all of our communications.

Whether communicating with horse or man, all interactions have a three-part cycle. These three steps are clear and concise; question, answer and acknowledgement. For humans; "How are you?" "I am fine." "That's good to hear." Complete. For the horse; close your legs, then close your hands (question), horse stops (answer), you soften (acknowledgement). Each of these is a complete part of the communication cycle. How often have you left communications incomplete? An incomplete cycle leaves the way open for confusion. While learning to ride corners, Louise learned the importance of all three steps for Snowdrift. If she forgot to release her legs after he responded, he would speed up or pin his ears back. If she forgot to release her hand, he would get harder and harder against her hand. If she held in her seat, he got more and more resistant. All these evasions were a result of Snowdrift's efforts to do what he thought Louise was asking. It took several months to uncover all the different confusions that she was creating because she did not follow the simple communication formula.

All communication should have three clear, concise steps: question, answer, and acknowledgement.

Every aspect of our life is influenced by communication. Intimate disclosures, ones that require us to express what we really feel, are frightening. They frighten us because we are not certain if what we are feeling is acceptable or correct. Our feelings may not match what we THINK is expected. Riding requires intimate communication. I think it is easier to learn this type of conversation with a horse because a horse is non-threatening, responds without preconceived notions, and is non-judgmental. Intimate communications do not begin until we have learned the fundamental skills. Position, control, and relaxation must become second nature to us, before we can begin to concentrate on communication. The first part of your riding journey encompasses learning position and basic control. While learning these skills you begin by using your hands, legs, and seat to control your horses safely. Initially, your communication is limited to stop, go and turn. Ultimately, however, control is through feel, so a rider must be comfortable, confident, and relaxed on the horse. A stiff rider inhibits his horse's ability to respond, and is deaf to the responses of the horse. As a rider gains experience, these basic raw skills will become more refined, creating a solid foundation for more intimate communication.

Position, basic control, and relaxation must become second nature to us before we can begin to concentrate on communication.

The relaxation required for basic control is not difficult. This level of relaxation means that you are comfortable and balanced in your position. Once you decide to specialize, your communication skills will be developed to meet the requirements of the discipline of your choice. No matter which horse sport you pursue, relaxation is a prerequisite that allows balance, both with yourself and your horse. Becoming more deeply relaxed allows the muscles to supple, the energy to flow, and the body to move more freely. If you do not feel you are getting the results you want with your horse, you should first look at your ability to relax both mentally and physically. To review methods of relaxation, return to the Relaxation chapter. The relaxation of your body allows your thoughts to travel most efficiently from your brain to your hands, seat, and legs.

Non-verbal communication results when a relaxed body allows thoughts to travel from body extremities to the brain and back to the aids freely. If a rider does not feel he is getting the desired results, he should first look at his ability to relax.

Learning to communicate with your horse is similar to learning a foreign language. Although you cannot communicate in a language until you have learned the fundamentals of grammar, vocabulary and syntax, you need to hear the language spoken many times to get a feel for its cadence and flow. Likewise, in riding you need to learn how to use your hands and legs effectively to give the aids. You also need to learn the feel of the horse when he is straight, balanced, and rhythmical. Relaxation enhances your ability to empathize with the horse, and strengthens your ability to feel what you are seeing. This makes the language easier to learn!

Assuming we have taken great care to learn how to communicate with our aids, to practice our balanced seat and to relax our body, now we must make the commitment to take the risks involved with asking our horse to do exactly what we want and expecting him to listen. The risk of failed communication always exists, but we must bravely declare our will despite the possible problems. No risk, no gain. Your horse will quickly let you know if he understands you or not. If not, you can try again and again, as often as necessary, until he shows you that he understands through a correct response. This risk-taking with a horse is much safer than it is with people.

Miscommunication with a horse is immediately recognizable, because we do not get the result we expect. When this happens, we should pause for a moment and try again. If too many retries are necessary, we should walk and review what is happening. Somehow we are not getting the message through to our horse.

Misunderstood communications, whether with horse or man, are the root of most problems. Each of us has an obligation to try to avoid failures in communication. The first step is to believe that we do not want to cause harm or discomfort to another being. The second step is to be observant of the response to our communication: we must notice the reactions of our partner. If we notice any reaction other than the one we intended, we must change the way we phrase our question until we are certain that the other party understands what our statement or question means. We can never ASSUME that the other party understands our meaning, we must always closely observe his reaction. This we do automatically while on our horse. Horses demand an immediate response or they do not know what to do. People do not. Even the simplest exchange between two people can result in a misunderstanding. If the receiver is preoccupied, upset, tired, or angry, his attitude may make him receive your words wrong. Your clue is that your simple statement got a bad reaction. To leave the conversation with a clear positive outcome, you must invest more time with this person. This calls for a priority judgement. Do you have the time now, or should you come back to this when you have more time? Time constraints frequently influence our communications. It is important to remember that, whether you are dealing with a horse or a human, unsatisfactory communications that remain unresolved do not go away. They will contribute to the mental road blocks we discussed in the Energy chapter. The longer they remain, the more negative energy they accumulate. What began as a simple misunderstanding can become a resentment, grudge, hostility, or even aggression. Therefore, it is important to resolve ill feelings as soon as possible.

Riders should learn to interact verbally with their instructors. Students are too often afraid to express their concerns, confusions, frustrations, or fears openly with their instructor. They are afraid that the instructor EXPECTS them to know. If feelings, problems, confusions, and concerns are shared, solutions may be discovered more easily and the problem solved more quickly. Most instructors do not take on the role of mind or spirit reader, nor should they. They make decisions based on what they see. Many hours of frustration could be avoided if students developed the confidence to express themselves to their instructor. Ideally, students should try to achieve a complete communication cycle with their instructor. The student asks a question, the instructor answers, and the student then acknowledges the answer. Effective communication is the essence of teaching, and it is also fundamental to the process of learning.

Confrontation

*We must not be afraid
to confront or to be
confronted in our journey.
Confrontation can lead to
preventing road blocks.*

Having the courage, confidence, and knowledge to confront a problem will help your journey move on with a minimum of road blocks, frustrations, failures, and conflicts. Confrontation does not eliminate problems, but the action of confrontation helps you to solve a problem, not let the problem control you. If problems, misunderstandings, or conflicts remain unattended, they can gain the power to snuff out your flame; if you deal with them, they will create a clean burning fire.

Steps in Confrontation:
- *1. Know that something needs to be changed.*
- *2. Confront it with a loving, caring and calm attitude.*
- *3. Through energetic and patient communication find a solution.*
- *4. Once solved, forgive and move on without grudges.*

The first step in confrontation is knowing that something needs to change. The second step is confronting it with a loving, caring, calm attitude. The third step is the search for a solution; this involves energy and patience. The last step involves letting the situation go as soon as it is resolved, without grudges and in a forgiving way. This is more easily said than done.

Tough Love, as described in the Discipline chapter, is a good example of effective confrontation. It is most commonly associated with teenagers. Tough Love was the only way I could help difficult teenagers. I used it to enforce the house rules. This is the way it worked. Each teenager signed a contract to follow the house rules. If a teenager broke a rule, the agreed-on consequence was that he would then spend a certain amount of time alone in his bedroom. If a teenager broke a rule and refused to go to his room, I took him to his room. Once he had 'served his time' in his room, the situation was released as though it had never happened, and we returned to our loving, caring relationship. It worked, and it was the only solution that worked. I cared too much about those teenagers to let them break the rules. I understood the importance of learning to follow rules to honor the contract that they signed. Following tough love with these young people involved risk. They could have hit me, or their parents could have pulled them out of the program. Neither of these things happened. Instead, most of them have since told me that I was the first person who showed them that I cared enough to confront them so severely. They are all glad that I did. The results gave me the confidence to use Tough Love, not only with teenagers, but with horses as well.

The house rules for the teenagers were simple and reasonable. The rules with your horse must be the same. Louise realized that she had to gain the knowledge needed to set rules. She needed to have the commitment and discipline to enforce these rules consistently. Louise's first rule during this leg of her journey was to ride deep through the corners. If Snowdrift broke this rule by going off route, she must immediately get him back on route. The action that she took was confrontation with her aids. If she asked him to go to the outside and he did not listen to her soft leg and hand, she would use a stronger leg and/or hand. Once Snowdrift was back on track, Louise would reinstate her reference feel, letting go of any tension, and ride him as though nothing had ever happened. If Louise had kept tension in her aids or irritation in her mind, she would have been holding a type of grudge. This grudge would have caused further confusion, and the confusion would have shown up as resistance in Snowdrift.

If any type of action or grudge is held after a correction, there is a potential danger for another road block in our energy or in our horse's energy. Lasting anger, guilt, fear, or confusion can gradually undermine our balance, and this, in turn, can affect our confidence, our clear thinking, and our actions.

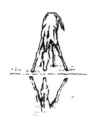

Tough Love:
- ◆ *1. A few clear, simple rules consistently followed.*
- ◆ *2. Clear definition of limits expected with rules.*
- ◆ *3. Appropriate confrontation immediately following broken rule.*
- ◆ *4. Once confrontation is over, forgive, forget and move on lovingly, with no grudges.*

Half-halts and corrections made using Tough Love are the most effective. Soon after you have learned the three basics; position, control and relaxation, you are ready to practice Tough Love in your communication. Your first confrontation should always be with the ideal softness, expecting an immediate response from your horse. If you do not get the response, you must intensify the aid to whatever degree is needed for the horse to understand clearly. Once the horse listens, quickly and completely acknowledge his answer by returning to the reference feel. Then ride as though there had been no confrontation.

Our confrontations must be governed by love, energy and a positive attitude. Louise loved Snowdrift and understood his confusion from her years of riding him without asking for corners. This knowledge allowed her to be patient. She had gained enough confidence from her knowledge to know that her expectations were fair. When Snowdrift did not respond to her aids, she felt confident in the need to confront him. This enabled her to use Tough Love. While learning, she made many misjudgments: sometimes she was too strong, sometimes too weak. Each time she made a mistake, Snowdrift's response gave her more information. Over the months of practice, she confirmed much about her riding by listening and responding to Snowdrift's response to the rules about corners.

Confronting a horse can sometimes present a frightening risk. If you make a horse angry, you are putting yourself in danger, because he is stronger and more agile than you. Major confrontations should be avoided if you do not feel you can deal with the reactions. On the other hand, you cannot let him get away with unacceptable behavior, therefore the best action is to avoid major conflict through careful planning. Careful planning always takes into consideration awareness and realistic evaluations of both your own and your horse's capabilities. One major mistake taught Louise a lot. When she first started riding into the corners, she became very aggressive, trying to get straightness, rhythm, and roundness all at once. In the process, her aids became very restrictive, making Snowdrift feel locked in a vise. In his confusion, he stopped and refused to go forward. Louise continued to kick and hold, until finally Snowdrift started to move backwards. By the time he met the next wall, Louise realized that she was miscommunicating, and she released her grip. Then she reevaluated her expectations. She was lucky. Some horses would have reared or leaped to escape their inability to know how to respond. This was a quick lesson for Louise, because she asked for more than she was ready to get.

Far more frightening for Louise was confronting her first instructor to end her lessons. Louise did not know how the instructor would react, but she was certain the instructor would not be happy after their eight-year relationship. Louise retreated to her mountain top to make this important decision, to confront or to ignore. While there, she evaluated her options: doing nothing, or trying to explain the change. She decided to confront the situation so that she could feel she was not leaving room for mistaken thoughts and feelings. Louise invited her instructor to lunch and thanked her for the many years of devotion but explained that she felt she needed a new and fresh approach. Unfortunately, but not unexpectedly, the woman took it wrong and tried to destroy Louise's confidence through guilt. Louise had spent enough time with her new instructor to feel secure, and her security did not allow the attack to have a lasting effect. She listened, let it go, and after she let go of the negative emotions, felt good that she had completed the communication cycle despite the difficult confrontation.

It is a little easier to confront an ongoing situation that you are not planning to end. I was lucky with Frank (from the Attitude chapter). I took a risk when I discussed his depressed attitude. He stubbornly denied his depression. However, he could have denied my point of view and gotten so threatened and angry that he quit lessons with me. Like most people who have an inner conflict, Frank did not see or understand the cause of his negative attitude. Secretly, Frank had expected his horse to progress much faster than he admitted. The seeming lack of progress was upsetting him. While he was suffering, his gloom was interfering with his horse's training. Frank's depression caused him to be too slow to correct his horse. His communications became ineffective. If Frank had been able to confront his disappointment, he could have had a better understanding of what his horse needed. Accepting this understanding should have eliminated his depression. If he found that the explanation received by his instructor was inadequate, he could have sought more information. At all costs, he should have confronted his mood. Sometimes I take the risk with students, family, staff, and close friends. It is difficult to decide whether to ignore or confront an issue that may help the person attain his expressed goal. The risk may have unpleasant results. I hope that those I confront can feel my loving, caring attitude that prevents me from ignoring something that can really affect their life. I try to recognize when the student gives me permission to confront. Sometimes I have taken the risk and lost a student. But many times I have really helped the student face and eliminate some road blocks. Before I confront, I feel confident that continuing without dealing with the issue will prevent the results expected by the person. If the person was able to trust my intentions, he would know that there was no harm intended, and understand that the confrontation was for his benefit.

Confrontation involves knowing what you want and what is fair. You must then consistently expect it. If there is a detour, take the risk and confront the block. Take the time you need to be certain that the person or the horse understands your positive intent. Once the confrontation is completed, forgive, forget, and move on.

Responsibility

Responsibility plays a major role in successful horse involvement.

Once we decide to become a horse owner, we place ourselves in a position that requires many responsibilities. We must act responsibly toward our horse, ourselves, our instructor/trainer, and the professionals that we employ. Our horse is totally dependent upon us for his feed, his care, and his general well-being. We owe ourselves dedication toward achieving our goal. The ultimate results of our success are directly related to our responsibility toward learning. The instructor we choose can teach us, but it is our responsibility to learn. A responsible student chooses a responsible instructor and then practices what is taught. Professionals are necessary to care for the horses. They expect to be paid for their services, and they expect us to follow their advice.

Most important is the care of the horse. The more we learn, the more we discover what we do not know. Horses are sensitive animals with a unique set of personal requirements. First, we must learn that it is our responsibility to keep them healthy, both mentally and physically. Second, we need to put what we learn into practice. Horse care is not a once-a-week activity, but rather an activity that requires a minimum of two times EVERY DAY OF THE YEAR. If we want to take a night off or go on holiday, we must find someone who is responsible enough to look after our animal. Looking after a horse is not as simple as looking after a tank of fish, a dog, or a cat. It takes a considerable amount of preparation and money to enable someone to take care of a horse. The sensitivity of a horse makes his physical needs a PRIMARY responsibility that we cannot take lightly.

I think that we also have a responsibility to our horse to learn to ride him as well as possible. If we do not work on our seat and aids, we can cause him discomfort. According to my philosophy, in order not to cause another harm or discomfort, we must learn how to ride, how to condition and how to communicate effectively with a horse. No matter what motivates us, it is our responsibility to learn as much as we can. If recreational riding is our goal, then learning can stop when we have gained the basic knowledge and skills necessary for both horse and rider to enjoy the trail. If it is competitive riding we are going to pursue, our learning responsibility will take much longer. Whatever our goal, it is our responsibility to our horse not to expect him to perform without us gaining the necessary knowledge and skills.

For us to reach our goals successfully, it is important that we have a dedicated attitude to learning, commitment, discipline, and patience. Once we commit to horse ownership or involvement, we must be faithful to learning, to the time requirements, and to our purpose. It takes discipline to follow the day-to-day schedule that horse ownership and activities require. Progress toward goals is never a steady climb; on a chart, it would look like a series of ups, downs and plateaus. We need an inordinate amount of patience to sustain ourselves during the 'downs' and the plateaus. We are the primary responsible providers.

How can we remain responsible when so many things can interfere and tempt us? Well-planned goals can play a major role. Joan regularly rode Willy four times a week, had a lesson one of those days, and turned him out in the field three days a week. In addition to her horse goals, she had to divide her time carefully among family, work, and social engagements. During one particular week, she had obligations every day of the week. She knew it was her duty to herself, Willy, and her instructor to keep Willy on his training program. She called her instructor and arranged to pay her to maintain the program for her. While this cost her money, it was her only way to fulfill her responsibility. It would have been unfair to all involved to ignore Willy's training program. Once we take on a major responsibility, we often find it necessary to trade off in either time or money. We must be aware of this before we make the commitment, because with commitment comes responsibility.

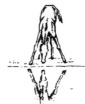

With commitment comes responsibility.

As I write this book, I continue to wonder where truth should come into consideration. I have chosen to include it in this section, because I think truth is a personal responsibility. Many horsepersons are quite honest with themselves as to why they are involved with horses, but some are not. Whether the lack of honesty is deliberate or not, there can be a lingering dishonesty that prevents the person from achieving his goals. In keeping with my positive attitude, I would like to assume that what causes people to be dishonest with themselves is merely a lack of ability to know themselves. Instead of knowing and understanding their motivation, they are influenced by family, friends, society, ideas, or a search for identity. I have often witnessed riders trying to achieve something in such a strange way that the only conclusion I could draw was that they were searching for something, but they were not certain what that something was. Often it is loneliness for social interaction. If the individual could identify it as such, it would be fine, because then their goals could be appropriate. However, these individuals usually come out under the mask of a competitive rider. One extreme example that I will always remember was Cindy. Cindy had comfortable financial support, and came from a family who expected her to achieve in whatever she undertook. Although she was a star athlete in her school years, she never liked competition. Instead, she loved the outdoors and animals. Cindy thought that if she bought a nice horse, nice equipment, and associated with the prestigious people in the nearby dressage stable, she would fulfill her needs to interact with people and fulfill her family's desire for her to be competitive. Every day she would come to the stable and dress her beautiful horse to match her beautiful wardrobe. She spent years on daily lessons, trying to learn to sit the trot correctly. Her fellow boarders heard every excuse imaginable for her lack of progress. While she loved her horse and the outdoors, she rarely was able to enjoy either one because of the pressure she placed on herself to do something that she had no real desire to do. Her dishonesty with herself was preventing her from even moving up to first level. As her friends progressed, Cindy stayed at the same level. Her personal imbalance preventing her from progressing. As Cindy's friends moved on, Cindy moved to another barn and another group of people. I hope that someday Cindy gives herself permission to be honest with herself and enjoy her horse as she wishes!

Last but not least of our responsibilities to ourselves is to learn to know and accept ourselves. This may be the biggest undertaking of all. As you have been reading this book, you have been exposed to many reasons and suggestions on how to get to know and accept yourself. All of them require time to learn and time to practice. None of them are achieved just because we want them or are aware of them. However, it is getting in touch with our inner self that will ultimately give us the rewarding experience of achieving our goals, as well as providing us with a more peaceful and satisfying day-to-day life. Each reader should decide what area of personal development he most needs to learn, and then be responsible enough to commit to learning and practicing it!

As students, we hire our instructor/trainer. Once we have done this, we have created a partnership in learning with that person. Whenever we receive instruction, we are exposing ourself to more obligations. Our horse must be clean, we must be on time, we should have practiced what was suggested for us to learn in the previous lesson, we must be willing to communicate honestly with the instructor, we must be amenable to do what the instructor asks during the lesson, and we must be able to pay the person. We have many responsibilities in this partnership. In return, our instructors should give us their undivided attention, share their expertise and help us to learn what we must learn to reach our goals. We owe it to our instructors to share what we do not understand, ask questions to be clear in mind, and work together to create a better partnership with our horse. Instructors should not be expected to create miracles, but they should help you produce the results you are working toward. If you stop making progress, if you feel they are loosing interest in you and your horse, or if you feel they are not teaching you something that you should know, you owe it to them and to yourself to discuss it. They should be the first person to know that you are not satisfied with your riding life. Evaluate what they offer in the conversation and go on from there. Again, never leave the conversation until you are certain that they understand you and you understand them. You may not agree, but there is no need for an unpleasant conversation.

In addition to your instructor/trainer, there are other professionals that you pay: dentist, farrier, feed supplier, and veterinarian are the most common. Before you consult these people, be a responsible researcher and investigate them before you hire them. Once you select them, you owe it to them to respect their professional knowledge.

If we meet our obligations as horse owners, caretakers, and students, we will act responsibly toward our horse, our instructor, and the other professionals whose expertise we require. We will also act responsibly toward ourselves and toward our learning. By fulfilling these obligations and responsibilities, we will also improve the quality of our own life, and make steady progress on the path that leads to our goals.

Trust

*Trust is a product of
love and consistency
that are clear and reliable.*

Trust is built by reliable, consistent, decisive, and loving actions over a period of time. For a lasting relationship, trust must be present between horse and man, between man and horse professionals, and between professionals and horses. True trust allows us to relax in the partnership. Relaxation in relationships helps set the stage for closer, more efficient and effective interaction, and thus for better results as well.

Both horse and man begin life trusting their parents. It is our parents' love that gives us the security to start life. Our caretakers introduce us to a secure, trusting relationship with each other. It does not take long for the conditions of our environment to have an effect on our ability to have faith in other people. The instinct of all creatures is to find their place in the social order. With both horse and man, this process of socialization begins very early. Soon after we interact with our siblings, or in nursery school, we are exposed to painful situations that damage our ability to trust. Horses' environments play the same role in their lives; however, they are able to accept the pecking order of other horses. Unless they have been abused, horses trust their position in life.

Abuse in humans can come about simply by an incompatible set of circumstances in the life of a person. When even the mildest form of abuse occurs, the child can begin to lose trust, which causes some loss of confidence. As the child passes through the stages of life, trust can be rebuilt or demolished, again depending upon the character of the person and the turns of the road in their life.

Even if children or horses grow up in the perfect loving environment, they are still subject to complications that can cause them to distrust others. What can we do if we lose our trust? If you really want to trust a person who has broken trust with you, several things must happen. First, you must forgive the person for his actions. Second, enough time must pass to give that person the opportunity to prove his credibility to you through his actions. A shying horse and a teenager who breaks the rules are much the same. It is hard to trust either one, and yet we must. A clever rider learns to feel if the horse is going to shy, and bends the horse away from the object before the shying allows the horse to leave his route. We know that if we do not trust the horse after the correction, the horse will become tight and more resistant. However, we cannot allow ourself to be unprepared; we must be aware that the shying may recur. We must be prepared for the possibility of a shy without actually anticipating one; in other words, we must be alert to what may happen, but at the same time we must remain mentally and physically relaxed, comfortable with the assumption that there will be no shying. If we allow ourselves to be unprepared, the horse will be able to shy through our aids and then even the first correction will have been wasted. I call this guarded trust. After days and maybe weeks of using guarded trust with a shying horse, the relationship can turn into true trust. In the case of the teenager who broke the rules, it will take him a longer time to prove to me that he can be trusted. He may stay in the guarded trust stage for six months to a year. This is because the clever-minded teenager will be able to follow the guarded trust deceitfully for two weeks, but not for a year!

Many everyday activities include trust that is out of our control. We have learned to trust what the system has given us permission to trust. We trust the car we drive to be safe, the food we eat to be free of harm, the qualified pilot to fly the plane safely, and our vet to have the knowledge to treat our horses. We base this trust on the guidelines of pre-tested standards. We must create the standards that we expect in our instruction, in our relationships, and in our horses. The criteria are not standardized, so we can create what we feel is appropriate for us. In all our horse-related relationships, and with our instructor, we should make every effort to verify the information we are given. As with all other information, it must be checked for corresponding actions, proof, or results.

Occasionally we bump into a dishonest horse, and we know it because his actions demonstrate his dishonesty. I believe that a horse is not capable of intentional deceit. What we see is what we get. Therefore it is easier to trust a horse than a person. What can we do to trust man, whether an instructor or a friend? First we must start with a trusting attitude. This attitude must have a positive outlook unless proven wrong. With our positive and careful approach, we should investigate. Once Joan had gathered the facts, evaluated her lessons and watched others being taught several times, she knew she was ready to become more involved. However, Joan remained observant to be certain that she was making the expected progress, which was realistically determined between Joan and Cynthia. If a rider does not trust the instructor, each resistance could prompt a question instead of a confident decisive action. In order for Joan to put her whole self behind the action, she had to trust the information and the source. Gradually, as students meet their expectations and goals, their trust grows.

While all relationships should begin with a trusting attitude, people should be careful not to submit to blind trust until you have had a long-term relationship.

A formula for trust:
- *1. Learn as much as possible about the subject involved.*
- *2. Verify the information by investigating with your mind, intuition and facts.*
- *3. Begin with trust, but remain aware. Is the relationship meeting your standard criteria?*
- *4. If yes, the relationship is likely to produce lasting and satisfying results.*
- *5. If no, ask more questions, look at yourself, your expectations, the situation, the information, and the source—reevaluate.*
- *6. When trust has been broken, give yourself time to recover from the devastating effect it has on your life.*

Horses will do almost anything for humans they trust. Their trust is conditioned by the love and compassion they feel from the human, as well as the regular care given to them by humans. I will always remember the quarter horse who went blind from ophthalmia. Two years later, he was competing in dressage at shows. He loaded into the trailer, went away with his owner to have lessons, and competed successfully at recognized shows. There was true trust between this horse and his owner.

Trust is a product of love and consistency that are clear and reliable. There is no miracle way to develop trust during your journey, but I feel that the first place to look for a trusting experience is with your horse. If you can learn to accept the ingredients of a trusting relationship with your horse, it may help you with the people in your life. Usually we select the horses in our life carefully; try to apply the same careful selection policy to the humans in your horse life. There is more likelihood of a trusting relationship to develop if you have carefully investigated the background of the professionals you hire. If something damages your trust, forgive, give it time, and observe to see if the subsequent actions can rebuild your confidence and ultimate trust in the person or horse.

Appreciation

*Each moment of each day
provides a new opportunity
to appreciate joy and beauty.*

A ppreciation of our gifts, of the nature around us, of the people and the horses in our lives, and of our life experiences is not a requirement of life, but it can make our journey much more rewarding and satisfying. It can help us experience positive results and day-to-day joy while we work toward our goal.

Your body, mind, and spirit each contribute to your ability to participate in, and appreciate life. Throughout this book, you have been working toward creating better balance that will help you become more aware of each of your contributing parts. Better balance will help you appreciate the beauty of watching an eagle soar over the river, listening to the pounding rain on the barn roof, experiencing the challenge of solving a complex problem, watching your horse roll in the mud with great pleasure, or enjoying the comfort of knowing that you can help a person through a tragic experience.

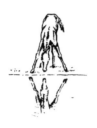

*Each time we feel like complaining,
wishing we had more, wishing we were
someone else, or griping that life is unfair,
we should STOP and REVIEW these
thoughts, VIEW them from all angles,
and see the good in each situation. This will
help us experience the delight and awe in
all of our activities and experiences.*

Your ability to love and accept yourself helps you appreciate the highs in your life and cope with the lows. Love combined with a positive attitude helps you see the good in an event or a person. You will see the bad, but you will be able to put it into the proper perspective and not take it personally.

Often we must remind ourselves to remain appreciative. A good exercise that I practice is to make an agreement with myself each morning before I get out of bed, to see the best in all things that day. Each time I enter the stable, especially at feeding time, my empathy for a horse is a second reminder of the importance of treasuring the moment. I allow myself to be reminded of the importance of enjoying each aspect of life.

Borrowed from *Beyond the Mirrors,*

"Horses offer many opportunities for appreciation. On a very basic level, you can enjoy watching your horse enjoy himself. You should be able to feel your horse's peacefulness and comfort as you watch him sleeping in the spring sunshine. Horses offer companionship, give you a chance to retreat to your 'mountain top,' and give you a sense of physical exhilaration. When you perform together, whether it is in your ring at home, on a ride through the countryside, or in a show, you should feel good each time he does something especially well. These moments may be rare—no one can perform perfectly 100% of the time and, anyway, your sense of appreciation would be dulled by a uni-

*formly and continuously excellent performance. When that
moment of excellence occurs, you can be ready to recognize it,
reward it, and enjoy it for what it is."*

Learning to appreciate the small pleasures associated with
the interaction of the people in your life, the ever-changing
beauty of nature, and the joy of your involvement with horses
can help to brighten every day.

Acceptance

Accept what you cannot change and change what you can change.

Early in our journey, we begin to accept who we are. Each successfully completed experience should build our confidence, which should further develop our self-acceptance. The most difficult part of this aspect of our journey is knowing when to accept what we cannot change, and how to change what we can. If we try to change something that cannot possibly change, it can lead to defeat and scar our self-confidence. On the other hand, we must try to change what we can change or we will not fulfill our capabilities. As we advance through the stages of our life, our experiential learning progresses; as we seek to balance ourselves through a positive philosophy, knowing when to accept becomes more clearly defined and more easily enforced.

Joan accepted her plight with Willy while she was trying to decide whether to keep him or sell him. She did not get angry or upset; she understood that the road was not going to be smooth. If she had not accepted the situation, she might have given up riding or given up Willy. One of her mountain top considerations was whether she preferred to accept Willy's limitations and work with him, or not. She decided that, rather than change horses, she would accept him with his physical limitations, and try to help him become more supple. Once Joan made the choice, she committed herself to learning everything she could to help Willy be able to jump so that she could meet her long-term goal.

Notice that change is a key part of acceptance. The ability to change is an important part of our uniqueness. Each experience, each personal encounter, as well as what we hear and see, changes us. We are not the same person from one day to the next. Each time we come across a road block, we should review it and see if it can spark an improvement in our life.

If we accept the circumstances of life and learn to evaluate them, we discover that experiences combined with a positive attitude and a philosophy of betterment can turn many experiences into positive assets. The relaxation that I learned in my personal life became an asset to my professional life. Willy's forgiveness of Joan's errors taught her how to develop patience and forgiveness with her family. The interchange of experiences through open-minded evaluation followed by acceptance or change has a powerful influence on all areas of our life.

Accepting the circumstances of our life and learning to evaluate them will help us gain confidence. Experiences combined with a positive attitude and a philosophy for betterment can turn many experiences into positive assets.

People are often afraid of change, because change represents the unknown. This fear could have contributed to Joan's unwillingness to sell Willy, which was one factor that she had to review on her mountain top. One of the factors that helped

Joan's acceptance of her situation was her love for Willy. She recognized the role he played in her life. If her competition career was more important to her than her love for Willy, perhaps she would have made a different decision. In all the journeys I have shared, some form of change was always necessary. Most riders were able to make that change, some with more discomfort than others. As time passes and our experiences are dealt with positively, such changes have less impact on our life.

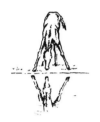

Requirements of Acceptance:
- *1. View all situations from as many sides as possible.*
- *2. Understand the type of barrier presented, deal with the emotion. Cry or feel the pain if you experience pain or sadness, anger, guilt, frustration or confusion. Confront to find a solution as soon as you are emotionally calm.*
- *3. Dissect the situation*
- *4. Find a solution and ACCEPT or CHANGE*

Pain, frustration, and crises in our complex day-to-day life can easily mask the joy and beauty that are also part of each experience. Problems are a significant part of life. How do we deal with them so that they do not dull our delight in life? All situations should be viewed from two sides, both the bad and good, or from our point of view and another's point of view. First we must allow ourselves to experience the pain or sadness with our total being. A good cry is sometimes essential. If the emotion is anger, guilt, frustration, or confusion, we must calm down so that we can see through the emotion. Once we have reached a calmer state, we can determine whether the situation is something we must accept; then our calmness will help us to begin to accept it. If it is something that requires a change, then we will have to do something about it, and sooner rather than later. Once we have allowed ourselves to experience or confront our emotion, we must become calm about the situation so that we can inspect it carefully and decide how much time we will need to accept or change it. This method will keep the experience as short-lasting as possible with the minimum of side effects. Our mental evaluations help us find the solution, whether it is acceptance or change.

There are some factors that we can change that can make it easier for us to accept our lives and ourselves. These factors are, at least to some extent, under our control. They include our environment, our schedules, and our social activities.

Recognizing our assets and liabilities is the most difficult acceptance during our life's journey. When Louise realized and agreed that her body stiffness was interfering with her coordination, she realized that she needed help. She sought a relaxation therapy that ultimately helped her. She also had to recognize that the results would take time, and that she had to be willing to practice regularly for several months or even a year to make the changes she wanted to make. She had to commit to this new information with a positive energy. Many students are not like Joan and Louise; they are unwilling to acknowledge their need for help from other areas, or to allow themselves enough time to relearn or learn a new skill. They continue to think that riding is a cognitive and physical skill only.

The quality of our journey can be improved if we change what we can change and accept what we cannot change. What we cannot change is part of the uniqueness in us. Your horse accepts you with your uniqueness. He does not judge that you are too fat, too thin, too tall or too short. If you can accept yourself as your horse accepts you, you will discover that your weakness can become an advantage. Along with my controlling life-style, I was embarrassed beyond imagination by letting anyone see physical weakness. As a child I broke my foot, and no matter what my parents did, I refused to go out in public for one solid month. I wallowed in self-pity and watched TV for a month. Later, in my early adult years, I began to suffer from worsening eyesight. At the time I did not have an accepting attitude, but to be functional I had to wear very strange looking glasses. Each time someone would make a remark, I felt that I was being stabbed in the deepest core of my being with a knife. There was nothing I could do; I had to wear the ugly glasses to see. While I could not put up with my weakness, I did accept the fact that I could not change my eyesight. I had accepted the situation conditionally. This is wrong. I should have accepted it as me. Who knows how much I could have gained had I been more accepting? As it turned out, during those years I developed a keener sense of hearing and a more compassionate attitude. Without acceptance, it is easy to get caught up in resentments, self-pity, and anger. These resentments can begin to govern your life, and the discoloration can prevent you from enjoying the beauty and the awe that are part of every situation.

We should not accept a painful or negative situation without challenging it. Each time a road block is presented, you must investigate it thoroughly, understand it, do what you can do to change it, and then accept what you cannot change. This is much easier said than done. However, the result is well worth the tough path to it.

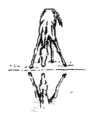

We should not accept a painful or negative situation without challenging it. Each time a road block is presented, we must investigate it thoroughly, understand it, do what we can to change it and then accept what we cannot change.

Almost every one of us has some type of problem to deal with. Often people feel alone or unacceptable because of their problem. The increasing number of support groups is an indication of one type of attempt to help people cope with problems. Support from other people who have similar problems has proven to be valuable to many. Our uniqueness makes us feel alone with our conflict or problem. Society does not encourage intimate communication. The difficulty of trusting others with our deep-rooted problems or concerns contributes to our loneliness. Loneliness delays our search for acceptance. It really helps to have someone, a spouse, parent, close friend, psychologist, or a horse to give us understanding and support. While we often feel that we should not require support for our small day-to-day problems, we often do. During my lonely times, I always had my horses. When I was young the horses were enough, but as I grew older I needed solutions for the problems. Journal-writing became a valuable tool. It helped me to express my feelings, thus allowing me to release some anxiety. Sharing and expressing our ideas and feelings, whether with a person or by means of pen and paper, can help to relieve the pressure and loneliness of a problem. It also can help us find solutions. We are unique human beings. Our horses are unique creatures. Each individual horse and each individual human has some irregularity to deal with. Understanding this somehow helps us accept ourselves, our horses and our life. The more clearly we can understand ourselves and our horses, the more thoroughly we can look at our environment. The more realistic our goals, the more we can accept the joy and beauty that surrounds us.

Discovery

Introduction

You may ask yourself, why do I devote so much time and money to horses? What are my goals? I hope that your journey through this book has helped you to answer those questions more easily. You may have discovered a more definite direction with horses. Perhaps you have come closer to some answers to questions about life, such as: Who am I? What is my role in life? What is important to me about my relationships in life? What makes me happy? These are difficult, very personal issues. While exploring the roads on your journey, you may have come to a clearer understanding of yourself. Almost every person would agree that happiness is the most desired yet least attainable aspect of life. Happiness is a result of inner harmony or balance. The balance that creates inner harmony also contributes to the success we experience in our life. It takes experiences to create the inner harmony. This leads to happiness, so again the interaction of ourselves and our experiences will lead us towards happiness. Once we discover, accept, or change our strengths and weaknesses, the interaction of body, mind, and spirit, the role of positive attitude and thought, and the value of the 'now', we will be able to discover the relationship between goals and harmony, a uniqueness of man. This discovery will help us relate better to ourselves, horses, man, and the world.

Being a horse lover gives us a definite advantage over many people. From the moment we enter the stable to feed in the morning until we go to sleep at night, we have an ongoing opportunity to see ourselves in relation to our horse, to get reinforcement about ourselves from our horse's response, and to be confronted with constant challenges that require actions. There are many opportunities that help us see our role in life, change, grow, and move towards inner harmony.

I hope that the questionnaires, charts and examples help you to uncover more of your hidden gifts, talents, and beauties; help you to release some of your road blocks, and help you to have more hours of joy in life with your horses and all your other partners. Before beginning the Discovery section, I would like to share a story by Pamela Lowe, "Everyday Angels." It is a beautiful story of what Pamela discovered in her journey. This has been reprinted with permission from *Karmakaze*, Issue #9.

One of the very special angels that entered my life was not a human, nor was she a supernatural being. She was a retired race horse named Lynda's Ruby. I met Lynda at a time when my whole system of self identification was crumbling around me. We had just made a major life change, leaving the corporate world behind for peace and serenity. Our teenage daughter made her feelings quite clear about our change of life style. I was being bombarded daily with messages of failure. Needless to say, my health began to fail. Daily I prayed for some relief, some sign that I was making the right moves in life. One night while meditating, my inner voice told me to make a list of all the things I wanted to do in life, but put off because of my sense of duty to family. At the top of my list was learn how to ride a horse.

I had always wanted to have and ride horses, but circumstances never were right for me to pursue this dream. So acting on my inner guidance, I did not think, but visited a local horse ranch that offered riding lessons. After about three weeks of lessons, Lynda entered my life. I had been having trouble finding a horse I was comfortable on. The day I walked into the pasture and met Lynda, I knew I had found my horse. We had so much in common. Lynda had been rescued from a one-way ride to the glue factory because she could no longer race and didn't breed too well. I was being "put out to pasture" by my children. Lynda had bad feet, I had bad knees. We were a perfect match.

Whenever the pressures would get to be too much at home, I would head for the stables to visit Lynda. When my daughter was emancipated and left our home, it was Lynda who provided the hugs I needed. The doctors would draw blood, do brain scans, and shake their heads. Lynda would offer comfort without judgement. All she asked of me was a carrot treat and a few gentle strokes.

Unfortunately, as my health improved, Lynda's declined. Her feet, never really good, began to cause her problems. Riding her was now impossible. Still I held out that there would be something we could do that would give me back the freedom and release of pressure I had when we were riding. Finally the word came that Lynda would never be ridden again. The news was devastating to me. I felt, once again, God was removing a loved one from me.

In desperation, I drove to the future sight of Shangrila Farm. I walked the land and thought about all the wonderful times I had spent with Lynda. I sat under the oak tree and allowed my emotions to flow outward. I released all the pain and grief of the past year. And then suddenly I felt a presence next to me. I was surrounded by the angels of nature and for the first time I really looked at the land I was standing on. I began to see that everything in our lives is a pattern of cycles. Death, rebirth, growth. It was time for Lynda to move on and do her work elsewhere. It was time for me to move on and grow. I no longer needed my crutch angel. My daughter had a new life, my health was finally stabilized and we were preparing to start building our Shangrila. It was time for a new phase, more growth. My angel of healing was leaving to heal others and I must move on. I rose from under the oak tree and followed the nature angels into the meadow. Wild flowers had started to bloom. I was surrounded by signs of new life. Slowly, I began to move with the angels. Together we danced of celebration, of life and of growth.

Lynda has a wonderful new life. She was retired to a farm that allows animals to live out their lives naturally. She is pampered and loved by all who visit her. In her own quiet way, she is still being an angel, still healing those who need a little bit of unselfish love.

The message she left with me was one of hope. I find myself looking at the world with less critical eyes. I know in my heart that each person I meet, each living thing I come in contact with, is a potential angel. How can you react with anger over trivial things when in your heart you know you may be insulting one of God's silent messengers? And how much better for this world if we all strived to be a little more angelic in our dealings? A smile and a kind word cost little and gives much. Who knows, perhaps our small acts of kindness may be perceived as angelic messages to those whose lives we briefly touch. What better vocation in life than trying to be an everyday angel? Perhaps if we all tried to do our best to be silent angels, peace on our planet would not be a dream but a reality.

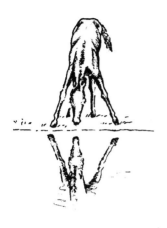

Strengths & Weaknesses

Understanding and accepting the unique you, leads toward harmony and happiness.

E ach creature, whether horse or man, is a unique being made up of its own set of characteristics and experiences. These characteristics make up our strong and weak points. As you read this book, you should have discovered what makes you unique: your personal strengths and weaknesses. Our strengths are the attributes that we can use to promote both our life's requirements and what we choose to undertake. Our weaknesses are those characteristics that contribute to our road blocks, frustrations, and disappointments.

Questionnaire #1 in the Discovery section of your Workbook asks you to list the strengths and weaknesses that you have identified since you began reading this book. Do you know and use your strengths? Do you accept your strengths? Have you identified your weaknesses? Have you tried to change your weaknesses? If you cannot change your weaknesses, have you been able to accept them as part of yourself? Strong and weak points are real parts of each one of us. It is important not to be afraid to look closely at them. However, you must be careful not to be too impressed by the good points, allowing your ego to get out of balance, or to be too discouraged by your weak points, allowing yourself to become depressed or overwhelmed.

Once you have identified these points, you must try to conquer or accept them one at a time. Like a horse, we can only learn one thing at a time. Often with personal issues it takes us longer to accept or change something because we have already learned to deny or cover it up, allowing it to remain hidden. Like all bad habits, we must first let go of the old habit and then replace it with a new understanding.

Your strengths help you to balance your weaknesses. Perhaps you discover that one of your strengths is sensitivity. You can easily empathize with your horse. However, one of your weaknesses is being slow to react and respond to what you feel. Can you change your slowness? The answer will be determined by what causes your slowness. Is it a lack of knowledge, confidence, or experience, or is it the natural way you think? You must make this determination by reflecting on all the aspects of your discovery. If you uncover a lack of knowledge, confidence, or experience, then you must create a program for yourself to correct this weakness. If you find that it is your natural way of thinking, you must accept your mind as it is and adjust your goals to take advantage of your sensitivity. Training thoroughbreds may be a goal that will satisfy your love of horses and capitalize on your strengths.

On the other hand, your strength may help you to cover up your weakness. Let us take the same combination of slowness and sensitivity. Instead of confronting your issue of slowness, you pretend it does not exist. It is wrong to constantly make excuses, allow yourself to get upset and not try to improve or change your slowness. As time passes and your experience and knowledge increase, your demands increase. However, you are still too slow. Naturally your horse will become confused, and you begin to dominate and punish him with unfair late harshness. The horse suffers from your weakness. This is wrong.

There is seldom a perfect horse. We accept a horse with his imperfections, so we should be able to accept ourselves. It is permissible to examine a horse before he is purchased. During the pre-purchase exam, he is carefully evaluated by a professional who will end up with a list of what is good and what is bad. Once we have this information, we can use it to make a decision, to accept or reject purchasing the horse. How often do we examine ourselves? Many people avoid self-examination because they are afraid of what they may see. If we examine ourselves with a positive attitude and the intention to change what we can change and accept what we cannot change, we have taken a valuable step in our journey towards self-knowledge. Joan choose to accept Willy's problems and work with them. To work successfully with Willy, Joan discovered some of her own failings and set out to improve them. Identifying our personal characteristics and then taking an honest look at them is our first step towards achieving balance.

The second step is working on our weaknesses. We seldom see immediate results from the actions we take, so we must be patient and continue to try. This is another use of goals: we can set a goal to overcome a weakness. In time, we will discover that we can learn to use these qualities to find happiness or we will become happy and have no idea why.

First discovering, then acknowledging and finally changing or accepting our characteristics are all parts of the process of learning to love ourselves. A major part of understanding yourself is learning to love and accept the unique you. This understanding leads you toward inner harmony and happiness.

Interaction of Body, Mind and Spirit

Balancing the interplay between our body, mind and spirit and our horse's body, mind and spirit can lead us to ecstacy....

Our body, mind, and spirit play a major game of interaction with each other. I hope you have realized that one without the others is very limiting. Our body can only do what a clear mind has asked it to do. Our mind is much clearer if we understand that it is a complex and finely tuned instrument. If we allow our spirit to remain dormant, we are denying ourselves one of our greatest assets. Our spirit allows us to empathize, feel, and experience the deepest form of love, compassion. All three contribute to our ability to meet our goals and to know ourselves.

Questionnaire #2 in the Discovery section of your Workbook will ask you questions to uncover what you have learned about the interaction of your body, mind and spirit.

A horse's body, mind, and spirit are much more balanced than ours. Why? He has fewer obstacles to overcome, his makeup is simpler than ours, and he is free of responsibilities. His focus is on the simple needs of life. If we observe our horse, we can see his contentment, which is an indication of inner harmony.

How can we learn contentment? We can learn to dissect the simple tasks of life and allow our horse to be a role model. Once we can do this, we can transfer what we learn to the individual areas of our complex life. It is the balance of the horse that enables him to perform the tasks we ask with a minimum of resistance. His inner harmony allows him to be spontaneous, responsive, and accepting, many of the factors that draw us to horses. By careful observation we can gain valuable insight into the importance of balancing ourselves and allowing ourselves to reduce each task to the simplest form. This will give our unique complex gifts freedom to act naturally.

Being able to do the physical tasks required in riding will provide us basic control of the horse. Knowing all the facts related to what we want to do will provide us with a vast vocabulary for discussion. When we allow our spirit to unite with the horse, we can better feel what the horse is doing and the relationship of our body to the horse's body. While we can ride safely for pleasure and exercise without involving our mind or spirit, imagine the pleasure and satisfaction we can add to the experience by enjoying it with all parts of our being.

You may have discovered that you ride too much with your mind, that you do not use your mind at all, or that you 'ride off the seat of your pants.' The discovery of what you do use, and the understanding of what you want to learn to use, will provide you with valuable insights that will help you attain inner peace and meet your goals.

If you go to your mountain top and review your horse activities, what activity makes you feel best? What part of that activity do you enjoy most? Questionnaire #3 in your Workbook will allow you to answer this question in detail. This will help you recognize the factors that influence your inner balance.

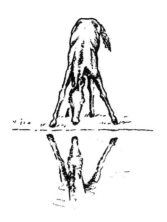

Role of Positive Attitude and Thought

Positive thoughts,
backed by a positive attitude,
create positive results.

Positive thoughts, backed by a positive attitude, create positive results. Do you have a positive attitude? To have a positive attitude, our spirit must be flowing freely and we must not be afraid of our innermost feelings. Are you a positive thinker? Do you recognize the power of attitude and thought? Questionnaire #4 in your Workbook will help you examine how positive or negative you are.

For weeks Pete and Lori had planned a trail ride along the river. Their busy work schedules prevented them from enjoying the regular trail rides that they loved. Sunday's ride was going to be a highlight of their week. Pete constantly worried that the weather might be bad and ruin his day on the trail. Poor Pete lost many hours worrying about his weekend. Sunday came and it was overcast, with showers predicted. They decided to ride despite the forecast. As they drove to their starting point, Pete was upset and irritated. Lori tried to convince him that the weather was to their advantage because there would be no bugs, fewer riders, and a cooler temperature. Lori enjoyed her horse and the gentle patter of the rain on the leaves. She noticed new depths in the colors. She was refreshed and energized by her ride, while Pete felt he wasted a day. Pete went home tired and irritable. They had experienced the same day and the same set of circumstances, but one rider had ridden with a positive attitude and the other with a negative attitude.

What if they had planned to attend a competition instead of a trail ride? What effect would Pete and Lori have had on their horses' ability to perform? I doubt if Pete's horse would have been able to produce an award-winning performance while Pete worried and complained. Lori, on the other hand, had an attitude that would have helped her horse perform to his potential.

Your thoughts and attitude affect everything that you do. Almost all situations have two sides, negative and positive. I hope that this book has helped you to see all situations from both sides. This will enable you to view one subject many ways, and it will help you to think positively, producing positive results.

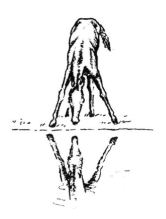

Value Of The Moment —'Now'

Do you know what each moment offers you?

W e can live life without being in the 'now', but we cannot successfully or safely ride or handle a horse without being in the moment. Almost all our resources have been giving us tools that will help us to experience our current situation, whatever it may be, to the maximum.

Safety is one of our first concerns. If only part of us is in the present, we are very likely to find ourself in the path of a fall, kick, or bite. Horses can be quick, requiring the rider or handler to react instantly. A split-second delay can lead to a crushed toe or a broken bone.

Split-second decisions are necessary to control our horse. There is no time to think a thought through, we must react instantly. Such reactions can only be achieved through training, and through being truly relaxed with the horse. This requires that we be in the moment. These split-second decisions and reactions give us the power to communicate clearly with the horse. Our clear aids prevent confusion, and allow the horse to respond to our requests. Clear communications provide the pathway for meeting our goals.

Direct your mind to the moment and immerse it in each activity. Can you empty your mind and then focus on the moment? This will enable you to react in the 'now'. First we must know what we want, and then we must allow our entire being to become involved in the experience. The result will be compatible interaction with the horse.

Can we be too much in the 'now'? Yes, we can react quickly but inappropriately, if we lack a proper foundation and have not learned to have correct instant reactions. Appropriate spontaneous reactions are typical of a balanced person who is likely to have the foundation to make the correct responses and reactions. Rudeness to horse or human is often the result of a reactive person who is in the 'now' but who has missed the fundamental development of the balance of mind and spirit.

To examine your preparation and ability to react correctly to the situation at hand, go to Questionnaire #5 in the Discovery section of your Workbook. Answering the questions will provide you with an idea of what you have discovered about the 'now' and yourself.

Goals' Relationship To Harmony

Achieving goals leads to confidence which allows us to better unite with our horse though growth and harmony.

Goals play a major role in growth and harmony. Achieving goals creates confidence. Confidence in who we are, and in what we do, allows us to trust our values. Which comes first, attaining our goals or achieving inner harmony? Some goals can be attained without inner harmony, while other goals need harmony to be achieved. It depends upon the goal.

Goals must be realistic. Realistic goals set the stage for success, while unrealistic goals can cause failure. Initially, goals should be kept simple and easy to fulfill. It would not be a good idea for a beginning rider to decide that he wants to go to the Olympics. After a many years of experience, perhaps this could become a realistic long-term goal, but initially it could undermine his progress. As we become more and more accomplished, our goals can become more sophisticated. They are goals that we are likely to achieve with hard work, dedication, and support. It is attaining these goals that gives us confidence, which creates harmonious moments. Eventually the harmonic moments become more and more frequent. We then begin to feel inner harmony.

Once we have complex goals, we need to be in tune with ourselves and our horse to produce the symphony. It is the symphony that will allow us to accomplish the performance that can lead us to the Olympics, or whatever goal we create for ourselves.

Think about it: a horse shows his balance in harmonious actions, but he has no goals. His harmony is based on fulfilling his survival requirements. For us to experience harmony, we can try to reduce our lives to the simple forms of a horse's life, and then inject these forms into the complex requirements set forth by ourselves and society. Goals are a simple way to organize life's complexities and challenges. Perhaps if we retreat to a mountain top with no societal requirements or human interaction, we might attain this harmony, but that is not the life that we were destined to live. We are meant to have a role in the world of people and society. Therefore we must reduce our goals to the simplest forms that we can, and work to achieve them one by one. The more reduced they are, the more confidence we will achieve by meeting them.

Our uniqueness of being human places an added responsibility on us. We can gain confidence by creating, working toward and meeting the goals we establish in all of the areas of our lives.

Questionnaire #6 in the Discovery section of your Workbook will help you discover the role your goals have played in your life.

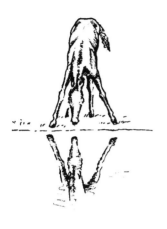

Our Uniqueness

Who we are dictates our role in life. This role changes as we make move forward on our journey. How well we know ourselves influences how well we can get our horses to perform for us.

Your interaction with your horse, your family, your friends and the community all have a direct relationship to who you are. How do you relate to those involved in your life? I hope that you have discovered some of who you are, and how you relate to yourself, your horse, and others. Questionnaire #7 in the Discovery section of your Workbook should give you a good idea of what you discovered.

Conclusion

Conclusion

There are no right or wrong discoveries. They are all personal. Making discoveries is a never-ending process. As you travel the journey of life, you should continue to make more discoveries. The more we learn, the more we realize that we have still more to learn. Discoveries are part of the foundation of our growth.

Do not be discouraged as you discover that life has many more challenges than you ever knew. Sit down, decide what is the most important issue for you at the moment. Once you know the issue spend as much time as you have to learn, reflect, and act on what you discover, one issue at a time. Think of your horse: he can learn only one thing at a time, but once he learns it, it remains with him and becomes a spontaneous response.

As I proofread *In Search of Your Image*, I was reminded of how much I am still searching for my image. As I wrote this manuscript I thought that I was sharing a well-rounded picture through text and examples. However, I discovered all the examples and combinations of experiences that I did not mention. I felt myself wanting to go back and rewrite. I had to have a serious conversation with myself, I could never keep this information up-to-date because I was constantly having new experiences and constantly changing. The conclusion of my discussion was to accept what I had shared and hope that each reader will find at least one small discovery about themselves from the material that I have shared.

Both the book and the Workbook have been designed as a self study course. This self study is never ending, but it should begin wherever you feel the MOST COMFORTABLE. While I recommend that you read it cover to cover to get a feel for the information, you DO NOT need to work from the front of the book to the back. As you read you may have identified with something that you would like to understand better, that confused you or that inspired you. Start there and move in any direction that you wish, one subject at a time. It will offer you many more discoveries this way. It takes years to become a good rider, it also takes years to really begin to 'know' yourself.

When you begin your self study and find an area of interest, browse through a book store and read more on the subject. I have included some books in my Bibliography as suggested reading, they may make a good starting point.

Ask questions of yourself and as you seek the answers, information to answer the questions will present itself in some way to you if you are open and ready. You will uncover what you need to know.

It is important to remember that there is no right or wrong philosophy, you are unique, your philosophy will be unique. However, I do think that we will all agree that we want to include the concept of trying not to harm another being. You probably would not have gotten this far in this book if you did not agree with this point.

Your Workbook has been designed in such a way that you may wish to buy another Workbook next year and repeat the excercises, keep photos and your learning profile. You will accummulate a very interesting personal history. I have invaluable journal notes since 1983, I wish they were in a workbook format.

While you experience the challenges encountered as you make your journey through life, you may discover that you can meet these challenges and at the same time experience joy, success, inner harmony, better performances, more peace, and improved health. Your symphony is performing in harmony with yourself, your horse and life.

I wish you an enjoyable journey!

Jill Keiser Hassler

DEFINITIONS

The subject matter is controversial and can be difficult to understand. In order for the reader to have a clear perception of my meaning, I am including the definitions behind the words I use. Please do not read this book without having a clear understanding of my definitions. Definitions vary depending upon the dictionary used, so please use the following explanations.

Characteristic

Quality making person, horse or thing what it is.

Mental	Spiritual
Knowledge (man & horse)	Love (man & horse)
Commitment (man)	Energy (man & horse)
Discipline (man)	Empathy (man)
Patience (man & horse)	Humility (man)
Forgiveness (man & horse)	Attitude (man & horse)
Praise (man)	
Imagery (man)	
Decision Making (man & horse)	
Expectations (man & horse)	
Confrontation (man & horse)	
Responsibility (man)	
Trust (man & horse)	

Balance-Equilibrium

A stable state characterized by cancellation of all forces by equal or opposing forces. A harmonious or satisfying arrangement or proportion of parts or elements. A finely tuned state of existence in which the body, mind and spirit of man and horse are in harmony with each other.

Brain

The portion of the central nervous system in the cranium that is responsible for the interpretation of sensory impulses, the coordination and control of bodily activities, and the exercise of emotion and thought.

Conscious

Having an awareness of one's own existence, sensations, and thoughts, and of the environment.

Emotion

Any strong feelings, such as joy, sorrow, reverence, hate or love, which arise subjectively rather then through a conscious mental effort.

Empathy

Ability to understand emotionallly and spiritually: projection of one's total self into another being in order to better understand the other being.

Feel

To perceive through touch, to experience emotion, to be aware of.

Humility

Modest view of self-importance.

Instinct

Inborn impulse; natural tendency, ability, aptitude, or talent; behavior as characteristic of species.

Mental

Performed by the mind.

Mind

The totality of conscious and unconscious processes of the brain and the central nervous system that directs the mental and physical behavior of a sentient organism.

Spirit

That which is believed to be the vital principle or animating force within living beings.

Soul

The animating and vital principle in man, credited with the faculties of thought, action, and emotion, and conceived as forming an immaterial entity distinguished from but temporally coexistent with his body.

Unconscious

The part of our mind that records information without our awareness.

BIBLIOGRAPHY

AHSA Rulebook, American Horse Show Association, 1991.

Benson, MD, Herbert, *The Relaxation Response*, Avon Books, 1976.****

Bloomfield, Harold H. and Kory, Robert, Happiness, *The TM Program Psychiatry and Enlightenment*, Dawn Press/Simon and Schuster, 1976.

Borysenko, Joan, *Minding the Body, Mending the Mind*, Bantam, 1988.****

Buscaglia, Leo, *Living, Loving and Learning*, Ballantine Books, 1983.****

Buscaglia, Leo, *Personhood*, Ballantine Books, 1982.****

Carr, Rachel, *The Yoga Way to Release Tension*, Coward, McCann and Geoghegan, Inc. 1974.

Chopra, Deepak, *Quantum Healing*, Bantam Books, 1990.

Gawain, Shakti, *Creative Visualization*, New World Library, 1978.

Grazier, Jack, *The Power Beyond*, MacMillan, 1989.****

Hastings, Arthur, *With the Tongues of Men and Angels*, Holt, Rinehart and Winston, Inc. 1991.****

Hyams, Joe, *Zen in the Martial Arts*, Bantam Books, 1979.****

Karwoski, T.F., & Stagner, Ross, *Psychology*, McGraw-Hill Book, Inc., 1952.

Kauz, Herman, *The Martial Spirit*, The Overlook Press, 1977.****

Loehr, James E., *Mental Toughness Training for Sports*, The Stephen Greene Press, 1986.****

Lofthus, Myrna, *A Spiritual Approach To Astrology*, CRCS Publications, 1983.

Maltz, Maxwell, *Psycho-Cybernetics*, Prentice-Hall, 1960.****

Nadel, Laurie, *Sixth Sense, The Whole Brain Book of Intuition, Hunches, Gut Feelings and Their Place in Your Everyday Life*, Prentice Hall Press, 1990.****

Ornstein, Robert, *Psychology, The Study of Human Experience*, Harcourt Brace Jovanovich, 1988.

Osborn, Carol, *Inner Excellence*, New World Library, 1992.

Peck, M. Scott, *People of the Lie*, Simon and Schuster, 1983.

Peck, M. Scott, *The Road Less Traveled*, Simon and Schuster, 1978.

Savoie, Jane, *That Winning Feeling!*, Trafalgar Square Publishing, 1992.

Suenig, Waldemar, *Horsemanship*, Doubleday & Co., 1956.

Sheehy, Gail, *Passages*, Bantam Books, 1977.

Smally and Trent, *The Two Sides of Love*, Focus on the Family Publishing, 1990.

Smythe, R.H., *The Mind of the Horse*, The Stephen Greene Press, 1965.

Swift, Sally, *Centered Riding*, St. Martin's/Marek, 1985.

Swindoll, Charles R., *Laugh Again*, World Publishing, 1992.

Time-Life Books, *The Trained Mind*, Rebus, Inc., 1988.

Wynmalen, Henry, *Dressage*, A.S. Barnes and Co., 1971.****

SUGGESTED READING

All the above books that have **** are suggested reading. The following books may also prove interesting.

Belasik, Paul, *Riding Towards the Light*

Blake, Henry, *Think Harmony with Horses*

Wanless, Mary, *The Natural Rider*

Wanless, Mary, *Ride With Your Mind, An Illustrated Masterclass In Right Brain Riding*